THIRD EDITION

SCENIC DRIVING
TEXAS

LAURENCE PARENT

WITH BILLI LONDON-GRAY

travel

Guilford, Connecticut

To buy books in quantity for corporate use or incentives, call **(800) 962-0973** or e-mail **premiums@GlobePequot.com**.

All photos by Laurence Parent.

Editor: Amy Lyons
Project Editor: Heather Santiago
Layout: Joanna Beyer
Maps: Tim Kissel © Globe Pequot Press

ISSN 1551-2959
ISBN 978-0-7627-4889-1

Printed in the United States of America
10 9 8 7 6 5 4 3 2 1

CONTENTS

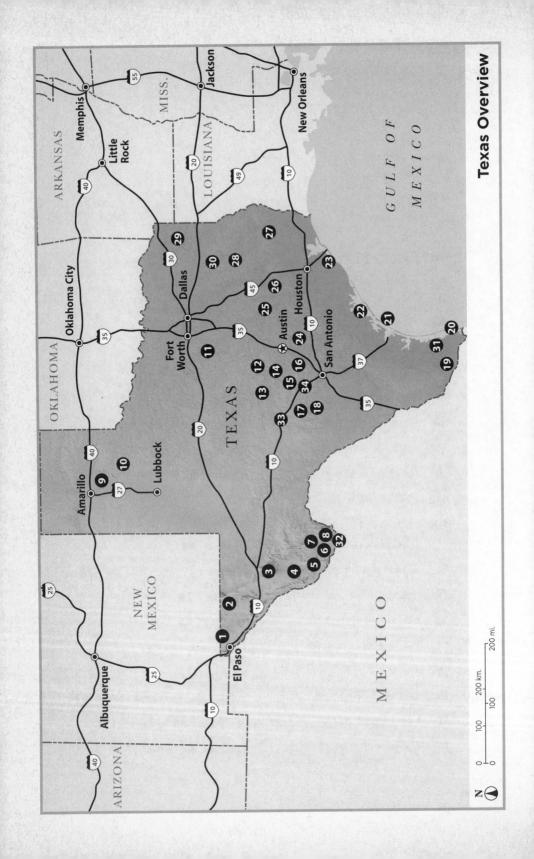

Texas Overview

ABOUT THE AUTHOR

Laurence Parent is a freelance photographer and writer specializing in landscape, travel, architecture, and nature subjects. He has written and/or photographed 39 books, including 7 FalconGuides. His latest book is *Death in Big Bend*, which chronicles fatalities and rescues at Big Bend National Park. He also photographs and writes for numerous magazines, including *Texas Monthly, Texas Highways, Texas Parks & Wildlife, Arizona Highways*, and *Backpacker*. He lives with his family in Wimberley, Texas.

ACKNOWLEDGMENTS

Special thanks go to Billi London-Gray for doing much of the editing and fact checking in the revision.

Several people helped considerably in producing this book. Thanks go to my wife, Patricia, for helping me on a number of drives, plus enduring my long absences on others. Lynn Herrmann, Lora Hufton, James and Patsy Caperton, and Elizabeth Comer all helped with drives, posed in photos, or put me up for the night during the course of this book. Larry Henderson helped bail my wife and me out of some car trouble. Many people with the Texas Parks and Wildlife Department and the National Park Service, too many to list, helped in many ways, both big and small.

Featured Route	
Featured Route (unpaved)	
Interstate Highway	10
US Highway	27
State or County Highway	58
Local Road	FM 555
Local Road (unpaved)	FM 555
Railroad	
Trail	

Visitor, Interpretive Center	?	Small State Park, Wilderness or Natural Area		
Headquarters		Point of Interest		
Campground	Λ	Primitive Campsite	▲	
Building or Structure	■	Amphitheater		
Historic Site		Airport	✈	
Museum	🏛	Wildlife Management Area		
Mission		Pass	) (	
		Mine		

Mountain, Peak, or Butte	▲ *Pummel Peak* 6,620'
River, Creek, or Drainage	
Reservoir or Lake	
State Line	TEXAS
National Park, National Forest, Large State Park, or other Federal Area	
Wilderness Area	

Map Legend

INTRODUCTION

Texas has possibly the greatest variety of culture, terrain, and climate of any state in the Union. For thousands of years, various Indian groups hunted, farmed, and fought with each other across the vast breadth of the state. After Europeans arrived, an array of governments claimed dominion over Texas, starting with Spain and followed by France, Mexico, the Republic of Texas, the Confederacy, and the United States. Possibly the most influential period was Texas's years as an independent republic. Texas is the only state in the country that fought its own war of independence and ruled itself for 10 years. The experience instilled a certain sense of pride and independence in citizens that is still apparent today. Unlike other states, where a single flag pole flies the American flag above the state flag, Texans often have two poles of equal height, one for the American flag, the other for the Texas flag.

The Landscape

The state is so large that it crosses multiple, very different ecosystems. Texas forms a bridge between East and West, from the Deep South on the Louisiana border to the Old West in El Paso. Follow I-10 for the 834 miles from El Paso to Orange, and you pass from the arid mountains and basins of the Chihuahuan Desert to the lush, fetid bayous of the Big Thicket. The change from north to south is no less extreme. On a given winter day, residents of Brownsville may be sweating in the citrus groves of the Rio Grande Valley while Amarillo shivers under 2-foot drifts of snow.

People unfamiliar with the state often believe that Texas is little more than flat desert, grazed by underfed cows and littered with oil wells. But Texas's tremendous size and wide elevation range create a surprising variety of climates, vegetation, and terrain. East Texas receives 50 or more inches of rain annually and is covered with a mosaic of lakes, rivers, and forests. Bald cypresses and water tupelos line the swampy bayous, while dense pine and hardwood forests blanket the uplands. Spanish moss festoons live oaks and fragrant magnolia blossoms perfume the air; alligators bask and swim in the marshes.

A visit to West Texas will dispel any notion that Texas is flat. Texas may not have the high elevations common in some western states, but the highest point, Guadalupe Peak, still reaches a respectable 8,749 feet. Its steep slopes and sheer cliffs tower a vertical mile above the salt flats at its base. Numerous other mountain ranges pepper West Texas, with many peaks reaching 7,000 and a few reaching 8,000 feet.

The misty peaks of the Davis Mountains rise above Davis Mountains State Park.

Live oaks and junipers cloak the rolling terrain of the Hill Country, in the center of the state. Crystal-clear streams tumble down canyons cut through the limestone plateau. Secret places lie hidden in the folds of the hills: the fiery red maples of the deep canyons of the Sabinal River, the labyrinthine Caverns of Sonora, the pink granite dome of Enchanted Rock.

The Panhandle also guards its secrets. The Canadian River breaks the endless flat plains into a series of bluffs and gullies. The Prairie Dog Town Fork of the Red River cuts an 800-foot-deep gash known as Palo Duro Canyon. Gnarled junipers cling to the red and ocher slopes of the canyon. Hidden side canyons and eroded pinnacles belie the stark treeless plains above.

Weather

Elevation, the presence of the Gulf of Mexico, and the sheer size of the state largely control climate in Texas. The gulf provides a moisture source and a moderating influence on temperature in the coastal areas of the state. Overall, Texas is a warm state because of its southern latitude and low elevation. But the Panhandle, reaching far to the north, and the mountains of West Texas get at least a few snowstorms every winter.

Texas weather is famous for its unpredictability. No mountains block the flow of cold fronts from Canada in winter, so occasional northers interrupt the warm weather and bring surprisingly cold temperatures even to the southern part of the state. The northers sweep in suddenly, dropping the mercury 30 or 40 degrees overnight. Historical temperature extremes in Texas run an incredible range, from minus 23 degrees to 120 degrees Fahrenheit.

Cold fronts barrel south and collide with warm, moist Gulf air and create tornados and severe thunderstorms, particularly in spring. Fall can bring hurricanes to the coast. The September 1900 hurricane that hit Galveston Island claimed more than 6,000 lives, making it the deadliest natural disaster in American history. Fortunately, Texas weather is rarely extreme enough to hinder outdoor activities. All of the drives in this guide can be done year-round, although some seasons will be more pleasant than others.

An Invitation to Explore

Except for West Texas, most of the state is fairly heavily populated and developed. Because of Texas's status as an independent republic before it joined the United States, little land remains in public hands. Thus the only really large tracts of public land are the two national parks and one state park in West Texas, and the four national forests in East Texas. Big Bend and Guadalupe Mountains National Parks are the premier wild areas of the state that are open to the public. Happily, Texas has been adding new state parks, many with beautiful scenery such as Big Bend Ranch State Park.

Although the drives in this guide may keep you busy for a long time, many other beautiful routes await exploration. In fact, a side road may entice you away from the route described. Don't be afraid to try that little county road; it might lead you to the prettiest spot you've ever seen or the best chicken-fried steak you've ever eaten.

USING THIS GUIDE

Scenic Driving Texas describes 34 drives scattered widely across the state of Texas. The map at the start of this book indicates their locations. With a current state highway map or GPS device and the directions given in the descriptions, you should have no trouble locating the start of each drive in this guide. Using the guidebook's maps in conjunction with the written directions should make following any of the drives easy. Not all of the roads within a given drive may be shown on standard highway maps.

A more detailed map book of the state, such as the widely available *The Roads of Texas* (see Suggested Reading in the back of the book), will help in planning side excursions or alterations of the described route. Other useful maps would be the detailed maps of the national parks and forests through which some of these drives pass. They show additional information that could not be squeezed onto the maps in this guide, including hiking trails and small side roads. The park and forest maps are usually available at park or forest headquarters and at many outdoor shops in the larger cities.

How to Get There from Here

Texas has two levels of state highways in addition to the federal highways. The busier, more important roads are designated as Texas highways and use the abbreviation "TX" in this guide. The smaller, less busy tier of paved state highways is designated as the Farm-to-Market and Ranch-to-Market road system. In this guide I use the common abbreviations FM and RM for these roads. The signs marking either a farm or ranch road look almost identical.

Unless the drive described is a loop, the length specified is the one-way distance. Distances were measured using a car odometer. Realize that different cars will vary slightly in their measurements. Even the same car will read slightly differently with different tires or driving uphill on a dirt road versus downhill on a dirt road. GPS devices also may provide slightly different distance measurements than this guide. Be sure to keep an eye open for the specific signs, junctions, and landmarks mentioned in the directions, not just the mileage. The drives can easily be followed in reverse from how they are described.

Recommended Seasons

The travel season specified for a drive is the optimum or ideal season. Since snow does not stay on the ground for extended periods of time in Texas, all of the roads in this guide can be driven any time of year. A few snows usually fall every year in the mountains and Panhandle, but they usually melt off within a day or two.

Summers are typically hot, so spring and fall tend to be the best times for the drives. Of the two, spring is more likely to have rain in the central and eastern parts of the state, but it's also the best time for wildflowers. Most rains fall in West Texas from July through September, but these are short-lived and bring cooler temperatures. To escape the heat in summer, take the drives in the West Texas mountains, or pick one with a lake or river for swimming. Otherwise just turn on the air conditioner and enjoy the drive anyway.

Precautions on the Road

Almost all of the drives in this guide follow paved roads, and all but one are generally passable with an ordinary passenger car. A few narrow or winding routes, as noted, may be difficult for large recreational vehicles or trailers.

Remember, these drives have all the traffic hazards of any road anywhere. Use normal caution and drive defensively, particularly on some of the narrow, winding routes described here. The terrain these highways pass through is beautiful, but be sure to keep a close eye on the road. Watch out for blind curves and water crossings. Never drive into a flooded stream crossing. Most storms are short-lived and the water will quickly recede. Pull well off the road if you stop to sightsee. Watch out for deer and other animals on the road, especially at night. The author had an unfortunate and expensive experience with a deer. A few of these roads pass through open range, so also be aware of livestock.

Go Prepared

Before setting out be sure that your car is in good condition. Top off your tank, especially before driving some of the more remote highways in the western part of the state. Check weather forecasts. Snow and ice storms are rare but can be particularly hazardous because most Texans are not used to driving in them.

Carry some extra food and water with you in case you have trouble on the road. Many of the drives pass through small towns and villages. Each write-up notes the availability of food, gas, and lodging, but realize the status can change with time. Don't count on finding gas stations and restaurants open late at night in small towns.

A road winds through the thick forests of East Texas.

Tread Lightly

Please do your part to protect the scenic country that you pass through. Be careful with fire. Be sure to thoroughly put out campfires and cigarettes. Stay on designated roads; the land is fragile. Please don't litter. Don't disturb historic sites, such as old forts and ghost towns. Most of the land in Texas is privately owned, so unless you are within a park or other public land, stay within the highway right-of-way.

Lastly, use this guide as an *introduction*. Follow that intriguing side road that disappears into the pines. Stop at a state park and hike along a trail or swim in a lake. Browse through a small-town antiques shop or pull into a roadside barbecue stand and sink your teeth into some ribs. Stay at a bed-and-breakfast and meet the hosts and other guests. Take your time and discover the real Texas.

Trans-Mountain Highway

El Paso & Franklin Mountains

General description: An 11-mile paved highway through the rugged Franklin Mountains, around which the city of El Paso forms a horseshoe shape.

Special attractions: Franklin Mountains State Park, Wilderness Park Museum, Border Patrol Museum, Wyler Aerial Tramway, hiking, views.

Location: West Texas. The drive starts in El Paso.

Drive route number: Texas Loop 375.

Travel season: All year. The drive is hot in summer, although afternoon thunderstorms sometimes provide relief. The rest of the year is usually more pleasant, with fall most ideal. On rare occasions, short-lived winter storms make the road icy and treacherous.

Camping: The Tom Mays section of Franklin Mountains State Park allows limited camping with no water or hookups.

Services: All services are available in El Paso.

Nearby attractions: Hueco Tanks State Park; Chamizal National Memorial; historic missions and churches at Ysleta, Socorro, and San Elizario.

For more information: Franklin Mountains State Park, 1331 McKelligon Canyon Rd., El Paso, TX 79930; (915) 566-6441; www.tpwd.state.tx.us/spdest/findadest/parks/franklin. Greater El Paso Chamber of Commerce, 10 Civic Center Plaza, El Paso, TX 79901; (915) 534-0500; www.elpaso.org.

The Drive

El Paso lies at the far western tip of Texas, squeezed between Mexico to the south and New Mexico to the north. The Rio Grande has cut a pass through a north-south mountain range, dividing the Franklin Mountains of Texas from similar mountains across the river in Mexico. In that cut, or river pass, sprawls the heart of El Paso. Two horns of the city curve up to the north, flanking the Franklin Mountains on both east and west, forming a large horseshoe-shaped urban area. Across the river, Juarez, Mexico, stretches for miles.

More than two million people live in the combined cities of El Paso and its larger twin, Juarez. As with any big urban area, traffic, crime, pollution, and other problems are common. But an easy escape is found in the Franklin Mountains, the rugged backbone of El Paso. To ease travel between the west side of the city along the Rio Grande and the east side in the flat desert basin called the Hueco Bolson, Texas Loop 375 was built across the heart of the mountains.

To begin, drive north of downtown El Paso about 12 to 13 miles on I-10 West to exit 6 for Loop 375, the Trans-Mountain Highway. Turn right, toward the

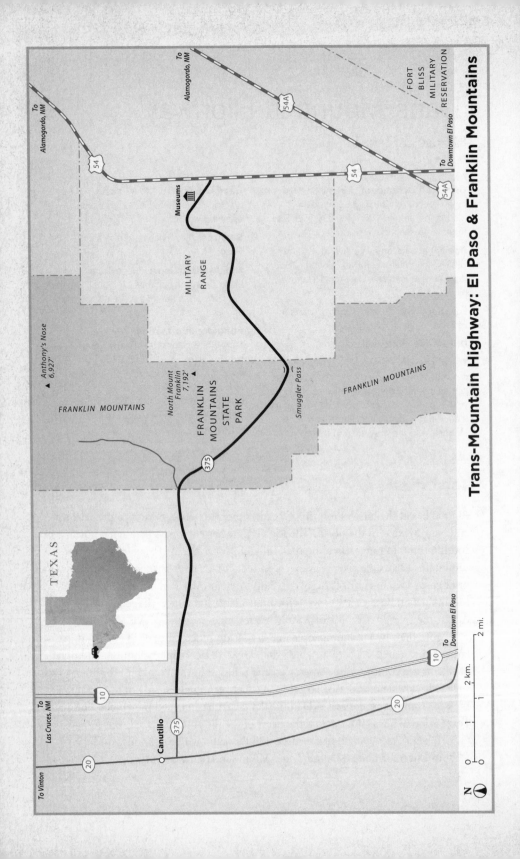

Trans-Mountain Highway: El Paso & Franklin Mountains

Loop 375 climbs toward Smuggler Pass in the Franklin Mountains.

mountains. The broad two-lane road climbs steadily up the desert slopes to the mountains and enters Franklin Mountains State Park.

The Franklins are not a large range; the highest point is North Franklin Peak at 7,192 feet. Yet they still rise an impressive 3,400 feet above downtown El Paso and dominate the skyline. To Anglo-Americans who visited here early in the 19th century, the mountains were full of menace and hidden dangers. The Franklins were a "chain of frowning mountains" to George Kendall, who was taken prisoner by Mexicans along with 300 others when the Republic of Texas sent them on an expedition to Santa Fe in 1841.

In 1951, noted artist and author Tom Lea wrote of the mountains: "Mount Franklin is a gaunt, hardrock mountain, standing against the sky like a piece of the world's uncovered carcass. The plants that grow along Mount Franklin's slopes are tough plants, with thirsty roots and meager leaves and sharp thorns that neither hide nor cover the mountain's rough rock face. Mount Franklin is a lasting piece of our planet, unadorned."

The Franklins still stand, but little remains to menace visitors. No Apaches haunt the slopes waiting to raid parties of passing travelers, no outlaws hide out in the canyons, no fearsome animals lie in wait for unsuspecting prey. The mountains hide their secrets well, but those who persevere will find the flowing water and lush vegetation of springs tucked out of sight in narrow canyons. Old mines mark the site of prospectors' searches for mineral wealth buried deep within the rocky heart of the mountains. Other secrets, such as tremendous views from the high peaks, are more obvious but reward only those willing to hike.

Because of their small size and resulting inability to capture much extra rain, these fault-block mountains are blanketed almost entirely by Chihuahuan Desert vegetation. The dry climate and steep rocky slopes are sparsely vegetated.

Spiny green rosettes of lechuguilla plants, whose stiff, daggerlike leaves seem designed to spear the ankles of unwary hikers, grow in much of the mountain park. Its tough fibers were once used by Indians to make ropes and sandals. Because the plant is common throughout the Chihuahuan Desert of Texas, New Mexico, and Mexico, biologists consider it an indicator plant for that specific desert.

The tall, crooked stalks of the ocotillo appear lifeless until rains come, then small leaves sprout all along the woody stalks. Another common Chihuahuan Desert species, the sotol, clings to rocky inclines. Long, thin leaves radiate out from the center of the large, bushy plant. Small hooklike thorns line the leaf edges like the teeth of a saw blade.

Cacti, such as the common prickly pear, have thick waxy skins and no leaves to better conserve water. The barrel cactus, common in Arizona's Sonoran Desert, finds its easternmost outpost in the United States in the Franklin Mountains. This distinctive cactus grows into ponderous individual stems up to 4 feet tall and 2 feet in diameter. The idea that the stem can be cut open to reveal a reservoir of water to thirsty travelers is only a myth. Many very old plants have been damaged or destroyed by people cutting into them, only to find a thick, unpalatable sap. People frequently steal barrel cacti and other cactus species from the state park for use in gardens. Consequently, large cacti are becoming rare in the Franklins.

Franklin Mountains State Park

The main entrance to Franklin Mountains State Park is on the left after about 3.5 miles. The park was created by the Texas legislature in 1979 after development began to encroach on the mountains. The 24,000-acre state park, one of the largest in Texas, contains most of the mountain range. The short side road leads to the Tom Mays area, with picnic tables and trailheads.

A strenuous but spectacular trail leads from the picnic area to the summit of **North Franklin Peak.** It follows an old road up the large canyon to the east of the

Hikers that reach the summit of North Franklin Peak are rewarded with spectacular views, including this view to the north.

picnic area to a gap in the mountains. From there the old road climbs the ridge to the top of the peak. Views stretch for miles, from mountains far to the south in Mexico to 12,000-foot Sierra Blanca Peak 100 miles north in New Mexico. Be aware of weather conditions; the peak is very exposed. Storms are infrequent but can build quickly, especially in late summer. I got caught in a vicious lightning and hail storm on the summit several years ago. With no cover to be found, I ended up running down the mountain. For an easy ride to the top of Ranger Peak farther south in the mountain range, take the Wyler Aerial Tramway.

After Loop 375 passes the entrance to the picnic area, it widens to four lanes and begins to climb in earnest. In a little more than 2 miles, the highway tops out at 5,250-foot **Smuggler Pass.** Shelters and picnic tables provide a lunch spot with tremendous views of the Rio Grande Valley below. The site is particularly nice at sunset.

Just past the large road-cut of the pass on the other side lies a large gravel parking area on the right. Signs mark the trailhead for trails leading south along the crest of the Franklin Mountains.

The Wyler Aerial Tramway carries visitors to the summit of Ranger Peak on the south end of the Franklin Mountains.

About a mile below the pass the road leaves the state park and enters a military reservation. The former artillery range is no longer used but, because of fears of unexploded ammunition, is still posted against trespassing. However, several trails on the left side of the road lead to interesting sites, including lush, hidden springs. The military apparently does not enforce the entry restrictions, because cars are often parked at the trailheads. The Texas Parks and Wildlife Department eventually hopes to obtain the property from the Department of Defense. Before entering these areas, check with Fort Bliss or Franklin Mountains State Park.

Last Stop: History

Near the end of the drive at the eastern edge of the mountains is the **El Paso Museum of Archeology.** This excellent museum offers exhibits on early human history of the area inside and extensive cactus gardens outside. Excellent large-scale dioramas show cliff dwellers and other early Indian cultures from the area.

If this appeals, be sure to visit **Hueco Tanks State Park** on the far east side of El Paso. It contains hundreds, if not thousands, of Indian pictographs, plus excellent hiking and rock-climbing opportunities.

The National Border Patrol Museum stands next door to the Museum of Archeology. It contains exhibits and historical materials about the Border Patrol, appropriate here, the largest urban area on the US border. The drive ends just beyond the museums at the junction with the US 54 freeway, Gateway Boulevard.

2

Guadalupe Pass

Salt Flat to McKittrick Canyon

General description: A 21-mile drive through a mountain pass below the highest peak in Texas to the state's best fall colors.

Special attractions: Guadalupe Mountains National Park, Guadalupe Peak, fall colors, the only reproducing trout population in Texas, hiking, camping, views.

Location: West Texas. The drive starts at the junction of US 62/180 and TX 54 about 100 miles east of El Paso and 55 miles north of Van Horn.

Drive route number: US 62/180, McKittrick Canyon Road.

Travel season: All year. The drive is pleasant most of the year, but winter brings occasional snows and treacherous road conditions. Spring can be windy at times. Summers are hot but still cooler than most of the rest of the state. Late summer, when rains turn the mountains lush and green, and fall, with its cool days and autumn color

changes, are probably the best times to visit.

Camping: The National Park Service maintains a campground at Pine Springs.

Services: Services are few and far between around Guadalupe Mountains National Park; be prepared. Limited gas and food are available west of the drive along US 62/180 at the tiny outpost of Cornudas. The closest full services are in Whites City and Carlsbad, New Mexico, and Van Horn, Texas.

Nearby attractions: Carlsbad Caverns National Park (New Mexico), Lincoln National Forest (New Mexico), Hueco Tanks State Park.

For more information: Guadalupe Mountains National Park, 400 Pine Canyon Rd., Salt Flat, TX 79847; (915) 828-3251; www.nps.gov/gumo. Carlsbad Convention and Visitor's Bureau, P.O. Box 910, Carlsbad, NM 88220; (505) 887-6516 or (800) 221-1224; www.2chambers.com/carlsbad1.html.

The Drive

The route over Guadalupe Pass is one of the highest highways in Texas, surpassed only by TX 118 in the Davis Mountains. It climbs up out of the desert into the foothills of the Guadalupe Mountains, a rugged mountain range dominated by the sheer cliffs of El Capitan Peak.

The drive starts in the Chihuahuan Desert at the junction of US 62/180 and TX 54. To the west are the tiny outposts of Salt Flat and Cornudas. The small farming village of Dell City, located in a desert valley about 30 miles northwest of the junction, is the only settlement for many miles. Residents raise cotton and other crops using groundwater to irrigate the arid land.

A short side trip on US 62/180 a few miles west of the junction is worthwhile. The road crosses a broad, white flat of salt and gypsum at the low point of the

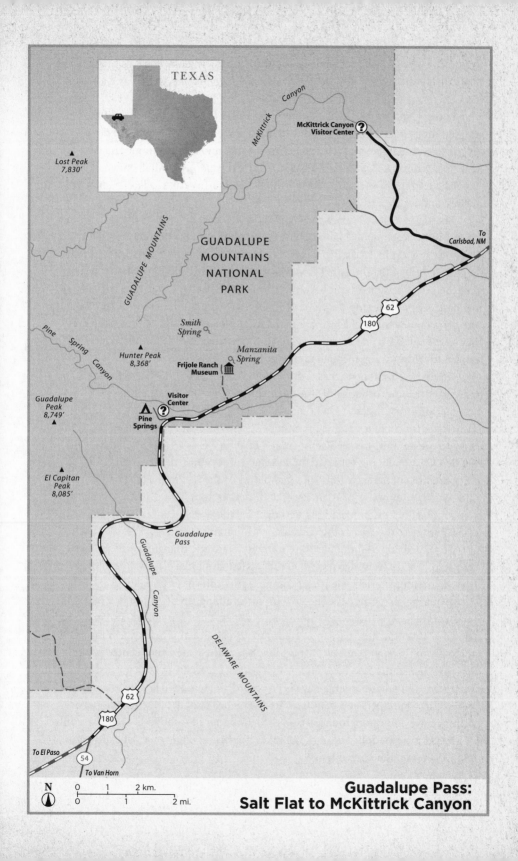

TEXAS

Lost Peak
7,830'

GUADALUPE MOUNTAINS

McKittrick Canyon

GUADALUPE
MOUNTAINS
NATIONAL
PARK

McKittrick Canyon
Visitor Center ?

To
Carlsbad, NM

Smith
Spring

Manzanita
Spring

Pine Spring Canyon

Hunter Peak
8,368'

Frijole Ranch
Museum

62
180

Guadalupe
Peak
8,749'

Visitor
Center

Pine
Springs ?

El Capitan
Peak
8,085'

Guadalupe
Pass

Guadalupe Canyon

DELAWARE MOUNTAINS

62

180

To El Paso

54

To Van Horn

N

0   1   2 km.
0   1   2 mi.

**Guadalupe Pass:
Salt Flat to McKittrick Canyon**

valley. In late summer, if the rains have been good, a shallow lake fills much of the flat. During the last ice age, the region was much cooler and wetter, and a large, deeper, permanent lake inundated the valley.

In the 19th century the flats were an important source of salt for El Paso and surrounding areas. In the 1860s and 1870s, disputes over control of the deposits led to considerable violence, including murder and assassination. The violence peaked in 1877 with the Salt War. Before the bloody conflict ended, it had involved citizens of Mexico and the United States, army troops, Texas Rangers, judges, and legislators.

The sheer western wall of the Guadalupes towers almost a vertical mile above the salt flats, reaching its highest point at the summit of 8,749-foot Guadalupe Peak, the highest in Texas. Turn back east on US 62/180 and head for the mountains. After the junction with TX 54, the highway begins climbing, slowly at first and then steeply right after it becomes a four-lane road. A picnic area partway up the pass is a popular stop for views of El Capitan. The prominent peak, probably the most notable natural landmark in Texas, is a massive bluff of limestone that marks the southern end of the Guadalupe Mountains. It rises like the bow of an enormous ship cutting through a vast desert sea.

About 250 million years ago, during the Permian Period, an ancient sea filled the area now occupied by the Guadalupe Mountains. At the edge of this sea, marine creatures created the massive Capitan Reef by depositing calcium carbonate, which later became limestone. The 400-mile-long reef ringed much of the ancient sea and stretched across much of West Texas and southeastern New Mexico. Eventually the sea dried up and the reef was buried under thousands of feet of sediment. Later, faulting uplifted blocks of the reef in the Guadalupe, Glass, and Apache Mountains of West Texas and southeastern New Mexico. As the living Capitan Reef once dominated the Permian sea, today its fossilized remnants once again dominate the area as the Guadalupe Mountains.

The Guadalupe Mountains were uplifted in a large, triangular wedge. The southern part of the wedge was lifted the highest and today lies in the national park. Limestone of the ancient reef composes the cliffs of El Capitan.

From the picnic area the road continues climbing steeply through large road-cuts before opening onto more gentle slopes. The air is cooler, and grasses take over from the desert scrub of creosote bush and cacti. The road climbs more gradually to the high point of the pass just before the park visitor center at Pine Springs. Guadalupe Pass is noted for high winds, especially in spring. Gusts of more than 120 miles per hour have been recorded; 60 miles per hour is common.

Scattered junipers and oaks indicate the higher rainfall of the foothills. The visitor center and campground are on the left. Be sure to stop in to view the exhibits and get information. The park is a hiker's paradise; many miles of trails penetrate deep into the rugged range.

El Capitan and other peaks of the Guadalupe Mountains tower thousands of feet above the desert.

The mountains are deceiving from the highway. They appear dry, desolate, and waterless. But those willing to hike will discover the mountains' secrets. Four of the state's highest peaks crown the range. A relict forest of ponderosa pine, Douglas fir, southwestern white pine, and even aspen grows in the high country. Elk, mule deer, mountain lion, wild turkey, and black bear roam the mountain slopes. Unlike most of Texas, several snows usually blanket the mountains every winter.

A number of trails start from the campground, including the strenuous but rewarding climb to Guadalupe Peak. Other trails lead to the Bowl, one of the most lush areas of forested high country in the park, and to the narrow slot of Devils Hall in Pine Spring Canyon.

On the left, just past the visitor center turnoff, rests the remains of the old Butterfield stage station, built in 1858. For about a year, stages lumbered over the pass. Even though there was water here, Apache raids soon forced the stage line to move to another route farther south. Only crumbling walls remain today. Walk

The rest area ramada along the old highway frames El Capitan and Guadalupe peaks.

out to the ruins on a quiet moonlit night and listen closely. Maybe you'll hear a faint rumble of horses' hooves and the crack of a whip.

Frijole Ranch

About a mile farther down the highway, a marked gravel road on the left leads a short distance to the old **Frijole Ranch** house, named for the local diet which tended to be heavy on beans. As the last Indians were forced out of the Guadalupe Mountains late in the 19th century, a few hardy ranchers moved into the area. The Rader brothers built a ranch house at Frijole Spring in the 1870s. The house, greatly enlarged by the Smith family in later years, still stands, shaded by large, spreading oak trees. The park service converted the building into a museum chronicling the history of the area.

If Frijole Ranch seems empty and lonesome even today, consider **Williams Ranch** on the other side of the mountains. The dry, desolate western side of the mountains remained unsettled until early this century when Robert Belcher decided to graze cattle on the thick grama grass. Since Bone Spring provided the only water on the west side, Belcher was forced to lay almost 2 miles of pipe down rugged Bone Canyon to obtain water for his stock.

To provide a home for his wife, Belcher spent a week hauling lumber from Van Horn by wagon and built, in the middle of nowhere, a clapboard house that would look more appropriate on the coast of New England. He brought Mrs. Belcher out, and she took one look around, stayed the night, then headed back East.

Belcher soon followed, leaving his ranch to his brother, who lasted 7 years before overgrazing and drought ended his stay. A sheep rancher, Dolph Williams, took over the ranch with a partner and stayed until his death in 1942.

A 2.3-mile loop trail leads from the Frijole Ranch house to Manzanita and Smith Springs. A plaque at **Manzanita Spring,** only a quarter-mile down the trail, describes a battle fought there.

After the end of the Civil War, the US Army made a concerted effort to halt the raiding of Mescalero Apaches. Finally on December 30, 1869, Lieutenant Howard B. Cushing raided the large winter camp of the Apaches at Manzanita Spring.

"Abandoning everything but their ponies," recounted Cushing, "they [the Apaches] rapidly scaled the steep slopes in scattered parties, driving their stock ahead of them. Keeping some of my men after the Indians, I put others to work to destroy the rancheria. By hard labor, a little after dark, the destruction was complete."

The survivors of the raid were forced to live on the run for the next 11 years, when the remnant band was finally ambushed at Hueco Tanks, many miles to the west.

The trail leads from Manzanita Spring into a narrow canyon that hides the oasis of Smith Spring. The spring feeds a small bubbling brook shaded by a dense canopy of oaks, colorful bigtooth maples, smooth-barked madrones, and ponderosa pines. On a hot summer day, the spring provides a cool sanctuary.

McKittrick Canyon

About 8 miles down the highway from the visitor center, turn left onto the marked McKittrick Canyon Road. The canyon is open only during the day, so be sure to note when the gate closes in the evening. The road winds through the grassy foothills for about 4.5 miles and ends at the mouth of **McKittrick Canyon.** A small visitor center here has restrooms, water, and information.

The canyon mouth appears dry and not especially appealing, but don't be deceived. The deep, rugged canyon harbors many surprises. A well-maintained trail with only minimal climbing leads into the heart of the canyon. Soon trees

Snow blankets the old line camp in McKittrick Canyon, reached by an easy 3.4-mile trail.

appear on the north-facing slopes and the sound of flowing water echoes from the canyon walls. A permanent stream flows down much of McKittrick Canyon, hosting the only reproducing population of trout in Texas. Tall ponderosa pines reach skyward from the canyon bottom. Far above float endangered peregrine falcons, which nest high on the sheer canyon walls.

Bigtooth maples dot the canyon and turn brilliant gold, orange, and scarlet in the fall, creating the best fall color display in Texas. Usually the color peaks in late October. If possible, avoid visiting during fall color weekends. The canyon is crowded and the park service limits entry once the parking lot fills. Enjoy your hike through what has been called "the prettiest spot in Texas."

3

Davis Mountains Loop

Fort Davis

General description: A 74-mile loop through the lush Davis Mountains, the second-highest range in Texas.

Special attractions: Fort Davis National Historic Site, Davis Mountains State Park, McDonald Observatory, hiking, camping, views.

Location: West Texas. The loop drive starts and ends in Fort Davis.

Drive route numbers: TX 17, TX 118, and TX 166.

Travel season: All year. Summer and fall are the most pleasant times, although the drive is usually enjoyable all year. The Davis Mountains are one of the coolest places in Texas during long hot summers. Occasional short-lived snows in winter can make the drive icy and treacherous.

Camping: Davis Mountains State Park contains a large, attractive campground.

Services: All services are available in Fort Davis and nearby Marfa and Alpine. A very popular CCC-vintage lodge is in the state park.

Nearby attractions: Balmorhea State Park, Marfa Mystery Lights.

For more information: Fort Davis National Historic Site, P.O. Box 1379, Fort Davis, TX 79734; (432) 426-3224; www.nps.gov /foda. Davis Mountains State Park, P.O. Box 1707, Fort Davis, TX 79734; (432) 426-3337; www.tpwd.state.tx.us/spdest/finda dest/parks/davis_mountains. Fort Davis Chamber of Commerce, P.O. Box 378, Fort Davis, TX 79734; (800) 524-3015; www .fortdavis.com.

The Drive

Unlike the rugged Guadalupe Mountains to the northwest and the Chisos and other rough desert ranges of the Big Bend area to the south, the Davis Mountains are rounded and heavily vegetated. Thick grasses and patchy forests of oak, juniper, and pine blanket the slopes. The Guadalupe Mountains are higher, but the Davis Mountains seem more lush, possibly because of greater rainfall and more fertile volcanic soil. Late summer rains turn the mountains and surrounding grasslands a rich green.

The Davis Mountains originated 35 to 39 million years ago from a series of volcanic eruptions that extended from the present-day course of the Rio Grande to I-10. Molten rock oozed forth, creating extensive lava flows, and blasted skyward in violent eruptions of ash and cinders. Erosion has smoothed the extinct volcanoes and lava flows, but dark igneous rock is still exposed in scattered outcrops and cliffs.

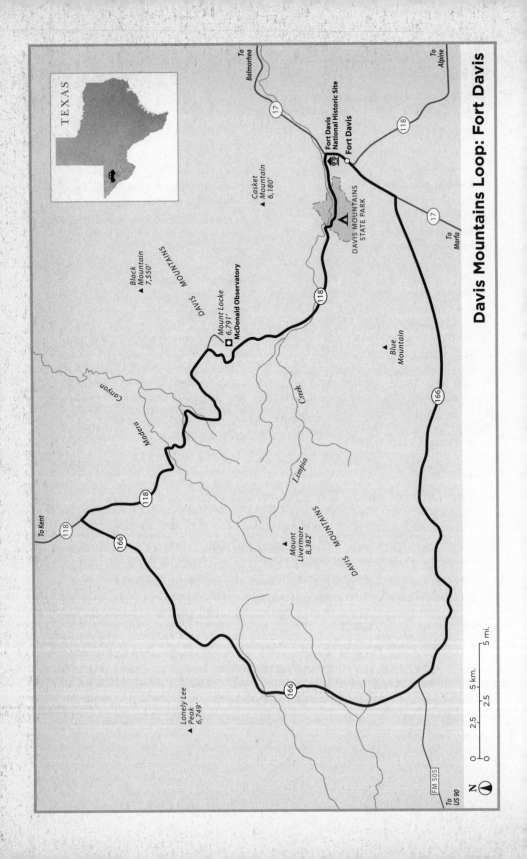

Davis Mountains Loop: Fort Davis

Snow dusts a trail at Fort Davis National Historic Site.

The drive starts in Fort Davis, a small, charming town founded with the establishment of the nearby fort. At an elevation of 5,050 feet, Fort Davis is the highest town in Texas. The dry air and high altitude make for a pleasant escape from the Texas heat in summer. Winters are generally mild and sunny, giving the town possibly the best climate in the state.

The interesting, recently renovated Jeff Davis County Courthouse is surrounded by trees in the courthouse square. Turnstiles in the fence surrounding the grounds keep out stray cows.

Industrial tourism has not yet discovered Fort Davis. The restored Hotel Limpia and a few other small lodging places welcome guests. A handful of shops and restaurants on the main street cater to tourists, but franchised chains are notably absent. Unpaved back streets lead past old homes, bed and breakfast establishments, and churches.

Texas Highway 118 follows Limpia Canyon upstream past golden fall cottonwoods.

Fort Davis National Historic Site

Begin the drive by going to the **Fort Davis National Historic Site** on the north side of town along TX 17. In 1854 the army built the fort to protect western travelers from raids by Apaches and Comanches. The trickle of immigrants became a flood after the Southwest was acquired during the Mexican-American War in 1848 and gold was discovered in California in 1849.

The soldiers operated out of a crudely built fort of pine slabs and stone. The Confederates took over the fort after the start of the Civil War but abandoned it in less than a year. In 1867, after 5 vacant years, federal troops reoccupied the fort. The wrecked outpost was rebuilt in solid stone and adobe. More than 60 structures were built on the small plain at the foot of the mountains, making it one of the largest army installations in the Southwest.

Troops from Fort Davis, many of them black "buffalo soldiers," fought Apaches throughout West Texas. The last skirmish with Apaches in Texas occurred in 1880 along the Mexican border. The last Indian wars in the United States ended in 1886 with the surrender of Geronimo in Arizona, so the fort was abandoned in 1891. The installation slowly crumbled until an effort was made to preserve it for its historical value. In 1961 it was designated a national historic site. The National Park Service has restored about 25 structures, including a fully outfitted enlisted men's barracks and several of the officers' quarters. Restoration work on the post hospital is currently underway.

Davis Mountains State Park

To continue the drive turn left onto TX 118 just north of the fort. TX 118 follows Limpia Creek, a permanent flowing stream shaded by large cottonwoods that are colorful in fall. About 6 miles west of the town lies **Davis Mountains State Park.** An attractive campground is tucked in oak trees along a canyon bottom. A scenic drive climbs to a ridgetop overlooking the town of Fort Davis and a vast sweep of mountains and grasslands. A good hiking trail leads from the ridge to the old fort.

The Civilian Conservation Corps built Indian Lodge in the park in the 1930s on a grassy mountainside. The small hotel was built of adobe in the pueblo style and many of the furnishings are original. The lodge, with pool and restaurant, is very popular, especially on weekends, so reservations are suggested.

Beyond the state park entrance, the highway continues to follow Limpia Creek upstream. On the right is the Prude Ranch, a well-known resort, dude ranch, and RV park. It offers hiking, mountain biking, horseback riding, swimming, tennis, and many other activities.

McDonald Observatory

Beyond the Prude Ranch the highway leaves the creek and begins to climb steeply toward Mount Locke. The white domes of **McDonald Observatory** are visible on the summit. The highway passes the turnoff to the observatory on the right, about 11 miles northwest of the state park. Be sure to stop at the visitor center near the junction before driving up to the observatory.

The observatory road climbs steeply through a thick forest of pinyon pine, juniper, and oak to a parking lot on the 6,791-foot summit of Mount Locke. The road to the top is the highest state road in Texas. Two large domes dominate the summit; the first holds an 82-inch telescope and the second dome houses a 107-inch telescope. The site was selected for its high elevation, clear air, southern location, distance from city lights, and large number of cloudless nights. The larger dome has a visitors' gallery to allow viewing of the 107-inch telescope. A third telescope, the large Hobby-Eberly telescope, crowns an adjoining summit. The

A 107-inch telescope crowns the summit of snowy Mount Locke at the McDonald Observatory.

observatory hosts "star parties" on selected nights to allow the public to view planets, galaxies, and other celestial objects through smaller telescopes.

Enjoy the spectacular views from the summit. Mount Livermore, the highest peak in the Davis Mountains, rises prominently to the west. It reaches an altitude of 8,382 feet; in Texas only a few peaks in the Guadalupe Mountains are higher. The rest of the drive makes a large loop around Mount Livermore. Take a deep breath of cool mountain air before leaving Mount Locke.

Beyond the observatory the highway winds northwest over wooded ridges and rocky canyons. Oaks, junipers, pinyon pines, and even a few tall ponderosa pines shade a large roadside picnic area in the bottom of Madera Canyon, one of the most attractive roadside stops in Texas. The highway cuts through the Nature Conservancy's Davis Mountains Preserve at the rest area. Although most of the preserve is only open to the public for selected events and dates, a nice trail starts at the picnic area that is open all the time. A trailhead sign marks the 2.5-mile trail which loops through mountain woodland on a bluff above the canyon. The easy walk offers a nice break from the drive. A few miles past Madera Canyon the highway drops down a long grade to the junction with TX 166.

Turn left onto TX 166 and head south, around the west side of Mount Livermore. The road passes well-named Sawtooth Peak, one of the most rugged summits in the Davis Mountains, on the left. After circling around Sawtooth Peak, the road drops to a noticeably lower elevation. Trees become more scarce and grasslands dominate. After passing the junction with TX 505, TX 166 turns east, back toward Fort Davis. Pronghorn antelope roam freely on the grasslands surrounding the Davis Mountains. Watch closely; they're quite common, although not as common as they used to be because of drought and disease. The drive crosses a mix of grasslands and southern foothills of the mountains during the 20-plus miles to Fort Davis from the TX 505 junction. A roadside park or two lie in scenic spots along this leg of the loop. TX 166 joins TX 17 just south of Fort Davis.

4

Ghost Town of Shafter

Marfa to Presidio

General description: A 61-mile drive through the Chinati Mountains and the old silver-mining town of Shafter.

Special attractions: Ghost town of Shafter, Chinati Mountains, Presidio County Courthouse, Chinati Foundation, pronghorn antelope.

Location: West Texas. The drive starts in Marfa.

Drive route number: US 67.

Travel season: All year. Late summer and fall are probably the most pleasant times. Occasional short-lived snows can make the drive icy in winter.

Camping: There are no public campgrounds along the route.

Services: All services are available in Marfa and Presidio.

Nearby attractions: Fort Davis National Historic Site, McDonald Observatory, Marfa Mystery Lights, Fort Leaton State Historic Site, Big Bend Ranch State Park.

For more information: Marfa Chamber of Commerce, Box 635, Marfa, TX 79843; (432) 729-4942; www.marfacc.com.

The Drive

The drive starts in Marfa, a small town of about 2,500 located in the high grasslands on the south side of the Davis Mountains. The route crosses the Chinati Mountains, passing the ghost town of Shafter, before descending into the Rio Grande Valley at Presidio.

Marfa lies at an elevation of 4,688 feet, surpassed in Texas only by Fort Davis, a few miles north. The town boasts the highest golf course in the state. The altitude and dry climate make for relatively cool summers and mild winters, an uncommon find in Texas.

Even though Marfa lies in an open area of rolling grasslands, it is mostly hidden from view because it is nestled in a shallow depression along Alamito Creek. The architecturally impressive 19th-century courthouse at the north side of downtown dominates the town. The Renaissance-style dome on top of the building, open to visitors during weekday office hours, provides a good view of Marfa. The economy of this clean, well-kept town depends on area ranchers and tourists. Thermals (rising air currents) created by the surrounding terrain and weather conditions have made Marfa popular with sailplane pilots. Several national soaring championships have been held here.

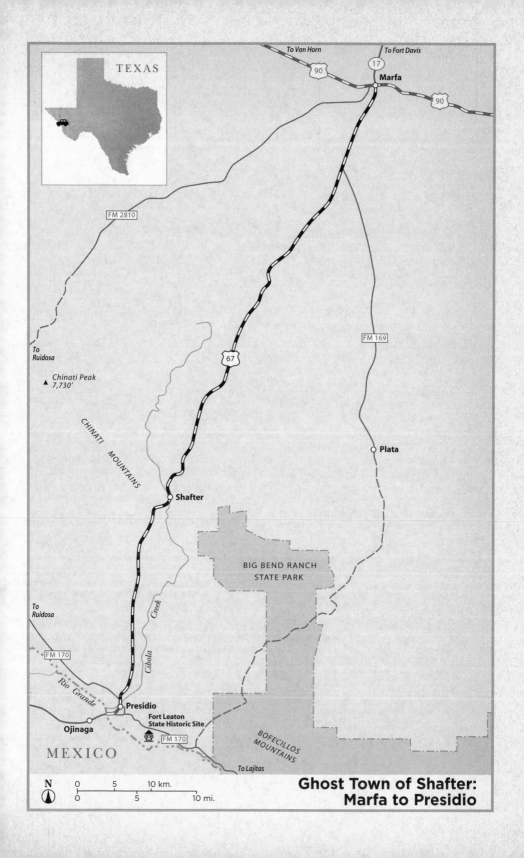

TEXAS

To Van Horn   To Fort Davis
90   17
Marfa
90

FM 2810

To
Ruidosa

FM 169

67

Chinati Peak
7,730'

CHINATI MOUNTAINS

Plata

Shafter

BIG BEND RANCH
STATE PARK

Cibola Creek

To
Ruidosa

FM 170

Rio Grande

Presidio

Fort Leaton
State Historic Site

Ojinaga
FM 170

BOFECILLOS
MOUNTAINS

MEXICO

To Lajitas

N

0   5   10 km.
0   5   10 mi.

Ghost Town of Shafter:
Marfa to Presidio

Marfa is probably most famous for the mysterious lights frequently seen on the grasslands southeast of town. Sightings of the strange lights are common. The highway department maintains a viewing site along US 90 about 9 miles east of town. Scientists are still unable to explain the lights with certainty, even though they have been studied extensively. Popular theories include UFOs, Indian ghosts, and atmospheric reflections of automobile headlights. A historical marker at the viewing site gives additional details.

Begin the drive by taking US 67 south from Marfa. Note the modular concrete structures on the right side of the highway on the south side of town. They are the works of sculptor Donald Judd, housed by the nonprofit Chinati Foundation on the site of former Fort D. A. Russell. His and other artists' works are displayed in both indoor and outdoor exhibits.

South of Marfa the highway crosses a broad swath of high desert grasslands. More rain falls on these higher elevations than on the lower desert areas to the south along the Rio Grande. In late summer warm rising columns of air spur creation of dramatic thunderstorms. Towering cumulonimbus clouds march across the sky, trailing shafts of rain. Lightning bolts arc from the clouds and thunder rumbles across the uplands. In late afternoon, rays of sun bend rainbows over green, grassy plains.

Pronghorn antelope roam the rolling countryside in large numbers. Until drivers stop and approach the fleet-footed animals, the pronghorn seem oblivious to traffic whizzing by on the highway.

The highway climbs slightly as it proceeds south, finally cresting on a low ridge that divides the grassy plains around Marfa from the broken, mountainous terrain to the south. A few juniper trees dot the slopes of the ridge.

After the ridge the highway descends, ultimately losing more than 2,000 feet by the time it arrives in Presidio. The grasses become less lush and desert plants begin to dominate as the highway winds through the foothills of the Chinati Mountains. To the west Chinati Peak rises to 7,730 feet, making the mountain range one of the highest in Texas. Tucked into its foothills lies Cibolo Creek Ranch, a very expensive resort built at a beautifully restored, historic fort.

Shafter

Finally, about 40 miles south of Marfa, the highway crosses cottonwood-lined Cibolo Creek at the ghost town of Shafter. The creek usually has permanent water, a rarity in this desert country. Although Shafter still has a few residents, it is only a shadow of its former self. Old adobe buildings lining the valley bottom slowly crumble and melt away under the assault of wind and rain. Heaps of rock on the surrounding hills mark the site of mines that once supported the town.

FM 2810 crosses high grassland as it approaches the Chinati Mountains from Marfa.

Grassland blankets the high plains around Marfa.

Although economically significant deposits of hardrock minerals are rare in Texas, silver was discovered in the Chinati Mountains in the 1860s and small amounts of ore were mined and smelted in Mexico. In 1882 John Spencer found a large enough ore body to expand the mining operation. Using capital from California investors, he created the Presidio Mining Company.

This mining district was extremely isolated, requiring long wagon trips for supplies to be brought in from Marfa and Presidio. The town of Shafter boomed as miners tunneled their way along the ore veins. At times the mines employed as many as 300 men. Although the mines were not especially large or rich, miners ultimately removed more than 20 million dollars in silver from more than 100 miles of tunnels. As the ore bodies were depleted, the mines closed and the town dwindled. Today the church still stands, along with several other buildings and a few residences. Cibolo Creek trickles quietly through the village, accompanied by the rustling leaves of the cottonwoods. High silver prices in recent years have led mining companies to investigate reopening the mines.

Presidio

After Shafter the road climbs out of the Cibolo Creek Valley and begins the final segment of the drive to **Presidio.** After the highway leaves the foothills of the Chinati Mountains, it enters the broad desert valley of the Rio Grande. The road crosses broad alluvial slopes as it slowly descends to the river. Creosote bush, lechuguilla, ocotillo, prickly pear, and other scrubby desert plants grow in spite of the harsh, dry conditions. Summer heat in the valley can be brutal; temperatures of 110 degrees are not uncommon. Presidio is often the hottest spot in Texas. To avoid discouraging visitors, local boosters try to prevent temperatures from being reported to news services.

Presidio and its larger twin town across the river, Ojinaga (or "O.J." to locals), lie at the confluence of the Rio Grande and the larger Rio Conchos of Mexico. The headwaters of the Rio Conchos lie in the massive Sierra Madre Occidental, the mountain backbone of northern Mexico. The Rio Conchos has always had a higher flow rate, but intensive upstream development has greatly reduced the flow of the Rio Grande. Large cities, such as El Paso, Juarez, and Albuquerque, plus massive lakes and the irrigation of several hundred thousand acres of farmland have depleted the river's flow. Sometimes the Rio Grande is dry above the confluence. Logging in the Sierra Madre, increased irrigation, population growth, drought, and development have greatly diminished the flow of the Rio Conchos, too. In some recent drought years Mexico has been accused of holding back water in violation of its treaty with the United States.

Presidio is a poor, rough-edged border town, but it has most services needed by travelers. For more of the history of Presidio, see the description for Drive 5, the River Road. For an interesting return route to Marfa, drive west on FM 170 to the tiny village of Ruidosa and turn right onto the county dirt road that leads to Marfa. In recent years, a 2-mile stretch of the road in Pinto Canyon has been quite rough, requiring a high-clearance vehicle. It climbs up the Canyon before topping out in the grasslands surrounding Marfa. The last 30 miles or so are on paved RM 2810.

5

The River Road

Lajitas to Presidio

General description: A winding, 50-mile paved highway through spectacular canyon and mountain country along the Rio Grande.

Special attractions: Big Bend Ranch State Park, Colorado Canyon, Fort Leaton State Historic Site, hiking, river trips, views, camping.

Location: West Texas. The drive starts in Lajitas, a small town on the Rio Grande about 95 miles south of Alpine.

Drive route number: FM 170.

Travel season: Oct through Mar. The drive can be extremely hot in summer; temperatures can exceed 110 degrees.

Camping: Big Bend Ranch State Park maintains primitive campsites along the Rio Grande.

Services: All services are available in Lajitas and Presidio.

Nearby attractions: Big Bend National Park, ghost towns of Shafter and Terlingua.

For more information: Big Bend Ranch State Park, P.O. Box 2319, Presidio, TX 79845; (432) 358-4444; www.tpwd.state.tx.us/spdest/findadest/parks/big_bend_ranch. Fort Leaton State Historic Site, P.O. Box 2319, Presidio, TX 79845; (432) 229-3613; www.tpwd.state.tx.us/spdest/findadest/parks/fort_leaton.

The Drive

The highway between Lajitas and Presidio may well be the most scenic drive in Texas. The road follows the Rio Grande through Colorado Canyon, a rugged defile cut through the lava flows of the Bofecillos and Sierra Rica volcanoes. The road twists and winds and has very steep grades of 15 percent in places; drivers of large RVs or vehicles with trailers should make sure that their brakes and engines are in excellent operating condition.

The drive starts in Lajitas, a small village on the Rio Grande. Because the town lies on a stretch of the river not hemmed in by deep canyons, it has long been a river crossing, used by everyone from early Indians to modern tourists. The western leg of the great Comanche War Trail crossed the river at Lajitas. For more than 100 years, Comanches raided deep into Mexico from their homes on the southern Great Plains. Every fall the appearance of the Comanche moon struck fear in the hearts of Mexicans and Indians as far south as Durango. The Comanches swept south, raiding Mexican ranches and villages and taking livestock, captives, weapons, and other loot back with them. The Comanche raids were finally stopped by American troops in Oklahoma and the High Plains of Texas. For many years afterward a bare scar across the desert littered with bones marked the War Trail.

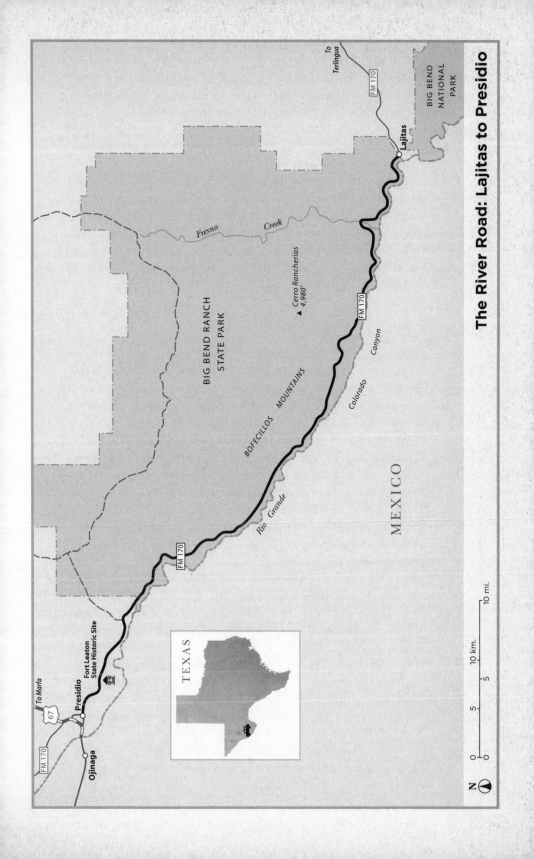

The River Road: Lajitas to Presidio

The Lajitas Trading Post has operated for many years out of an old adobe building above the river. The trading post is probably most famous for its beer-drinking goat, Clay Henry. The original goat has since departed for that great grazing ground in the sky, but its descendants carry on the tradition.

In recent years developers have built a resort community at Lajitas. Although the development is still relatively small, its homes, hotels, shops, golf course, and air strip overwhelm the original settlement.

The town is a popular starting point for river trips through Santa Elena and Colorado Canyons. Outfitters are located here and in nearby Terlingua and Study Butte. If time and water levels permit, consider taking a float trip down one of the Big Bend canyons. It's the only easy way to see some of the most spectacular country in Texas. Unfortunately, with frequent droughts and Mexico periodically withholding much of the Rio Grande's water in violation of treaty obligations, the river is only sporadically high enough to float.

Big Bend Ranch State Park

The Texas Parks and Wildlife Department purchased 400 square miles of mountains and desert just west of Lajitas in 1988. Christened **Big Bend Ranch State Park,** the acquisition approximately doubled the size of the state park system. The park contains most of the rugged Bofecillos Mountains and fronts many miles of the Rio Grande in Colorado Canyon.

Before beginning the drive be sure to stop in at park headquarters at the Barton Warnock Environmental Education Center on the east side of Lajitas. Permits for hiking, camping, and river trips can be obtained here, along with general information. The center has exhibits on the area's human and natural history, a bookstore stocked with titles of regional interest, and a desert botanical garden.

From Lajitas FM 170 follows the Rio Grande and soon enters Big Bend Ranch State Park. Except for occasional inholdings, most of the next 30 miles lie within Big Bend Ranch. The rusty red canyon walls quickly close in, pinching the river and highway into a narrow corridor. About 25 to 40 million years ago, large volcanoes erupted on both sides of the river, creating the Bofecillos Mountains of Texas and the Sierra Rica of Mexico. Over many millennia the river cut Colorado Canyon through the mountains. Cliffs formed of ancient lava flows tower over the river. Erosion has carved deposits of white consolidated volcanic ash, or tuff, into pinnacles and fanciful shapes. The remains of the **Contrabando movie set** lie between the highway and the river, looking like an abandoned adobe village.

The highway makes a detour away from the river where it crosses the large tributary of Fresno Canyon. This canyon often has a small trickle of water, rare in

The Rio Grande has carved deep Colorado Canyon, shown here at the Big Hill.

Big Bend Ranch offers about 300,000 acres of rugged desert in the Bofecillos Mountains to hikers.

this dry country. Two marked river access points are on the left at Grassy Banks and Madera Canyon; primitive car camping is allowed with a permit at Madera Canyon. The transportation department has constructed an interesting picnic area with large, painted tepee shelters along the road just before the narrowest part of the canyon.

Just past the picnic area, the road climbs steeply out of the canyon bottom to the top of what locals call the **Big Hill.** Be sure to stop at one of the broad pullouts on either side of the road-cut at the top of the hill for the view stretching many miles up and down the river. The steel-gray outline of the Chisos Mountains lies far to the east in Big Bend National Park. Across the river to the south rise the desolate, forbidding peaks of the Sierra Rica, while above the road stand the gaunt cliffs of the Bofecillos Mountains. Those with stout hearts and stomachs can scramble up the bluff between the river and the highway. The far side of the bluff drops directly into the river 500 feet below in a vertigo-inducing plunge. It's not recommended for acrophobes. Use great caution near the lip of the drop; there are no railings or official trails.

Beyond the Big Hill the road descends steeply again and leaves the river for a few miles. The marked trailheads for the **Rancherías** and **Closed Canyon Trails** are found shortly before the highway rejoins the river. Closed Canyon is a short, interesting trail into a narrow slot of a canyon. The Rancherías Trail has two sections, both starting from the same trailhead. The terrain at the trailhead appears uninteresting, but don't be deceived. The Rancherías Canyon Trail leads almost 5 miles into a deep, rugged canyon to a 75-foot waterfall that is usually dry except after good rains. The larger loop trail traverses 19 miles of rugged desert terrain and passes springs, steep-walled canyons, and high-desert plateaus. All of the trails follow narrow canyon bottoms at times and are vulnerable to flash flooding during heavy rains. This is rugged, empty country; be sure to get maps, permits, and information at park headquarters in Lajitas or at Fort Leaton before hiking.

Fort Leaton to Presidio

A long dirt road leads into the heart of the park, past springs, Indian shelters, and other sights. A ranch house and bunkhouse can be reserved for overnight stays at the center of the park. Inquire at park headquarters for information.

Just past the West Rancherías trailhead is another river access point. Beyond the access point the mountains begin to pull back from the river, creating a wider and wider valley. Near the small village of Redford, the floodplain becomes broad and farms line the river. Shortly before Presidio the highway passes **Fort Leaton State Historic Site** on the left.

In 1848, at the end of the Mexican-American War, Ben Leaton and two partners purchased land on the north side of the Rio Grande in what had just become part of the United States. He built a large, heavily fortified adobe ranch house to protect against Apache and Comanche raids. It was the first Anglo settlement in the area. Leaton operated a mercantile business with Mexicans, Americans, and Indians. The state maintains the thick-walled building as part of the state park system.

Just beyond Fort Leaton lies the border town of Presidio and across the river its larger sister city, Ojinaga. Neither are tourist cities; their economies depend on ranching, farming, and trade. The broad valley lies at the confluence of the Rio Grande and the larger Rio Conchos of Mexico. Downstream most of the combined rivers' flow comes from the Rio Conchos, although that has greatly declined in recent years.

The floodplain at the confluence may be the oldest continuously cultivated land in the United States. The Patarabueye Indians farmed the land as early as AD 1200 and built adobe villages in the valley. Although little is known about them, they were probably a Pueblo Indian group from northern New Mexico or another group influenced by the Pueblo Indian culture.

Ben Leaton's old fort with its thick adobe walls has been preserved at Fort Leaton State Historic Site.

The ragged remains of Cabeza de Vaca's expedition may have passed through the area in 1535, but the first documented contact with Spanish explorers occurred in 1581 when Fray Agustín Rodríguez arrived. The Spaniards made a number of contacts with the Indians and even attempted missionary work, but they largely ignored the area for many years. In 1760 they established a fort, or *presidio,* at La Junta, the river confluence, to protect their northern frontier. They enjoyed only sporadic success in protecting their lands from Comanche and Apache raids. For a time the Spaniards and Apaches united against the common threat of the Comanches, but Comanche raids continued well into the 19th century.

Today Presidio is a small, poor border town with dusty back streets. In the past decade, the state built new schools and installed curbing along the main highway through town, which helps the town's appearance. Presidio is hot; the average June high temperature is 103 degrees.

Ross Maxwell Scenic Drive

Big Bend National Park

6

General description: A 30-mile paved road through the rugged mountain and desert country of Big Bend National Park.

Special attractions: Big Bend National Park, Santa Elena Canyon, Chisos Mountains, historic ranches, river trips, hiking, camping, scenic views.

Location: West Texas. The drive starts at the Santa Elena highway junction along the main park road about 13 miles west of park headquarters.

Drive route name: Ross Maxwell Scenic Drive.

Travel season: Oct through Mar is the most pleasant time. Summers are usually very hot, especially on the last section of the road from Castolon to Santa Elena Canyon.

Camping: The park maintains pleasant, shady Cottonwood Campground along the Rio Grande near Castolon.

Services: Snacks and limited groceries are available at Castolon. Gas is available at nearby Panther Junction (park headquarters). Food and limited lodging are available in the nearby Basin. All services are available at Study Butte and Terlingua on the west side of the park.

Nearby attractions: Other Big Bend National Park sites, such as the Basin, Boquillas Canyon, Hot Springs, and Mariscal Canyon; Big Bend Ranch State Park; ghost town of Terlingua.

For more information: Superintendent, P.O. Box 129, Big Bend National Park, TX 79834; (432) 477-2251; www.nps.gov /bibe.

The Drive

The Ross Maxwell Scenic Drive, one of the most scenic roads in Texas, was named after the first superintendent of Big Bend National Park. The drive begins in the western foothills of the Chisos Mountains and winds down to the valley of the Rio Grande, ending at the spectacular gorge of Santa Elena Canyon.

Big Bend National Park sprawls across 800,000 acres, an area larger than Rhode Island, in the least-populated part of Texas. Because of its remote location, it is not swamped with visitors even though it is one of the country's premier national parks. At the south side of the park at Mariscal Canyon, the river makes an abrupt turn northeast. The park and the region were named for this big bend in the Rio Grande.

Desert covers the vast majority of the park, but the heights of the rugged Chisos Mountains support a small woodland, and hidden springs hide lush oases. The Rio Grande, the dividing line between Mexico and the United States, winds its way across the desert, creating a narrow ribbon of emerald green vegetation.

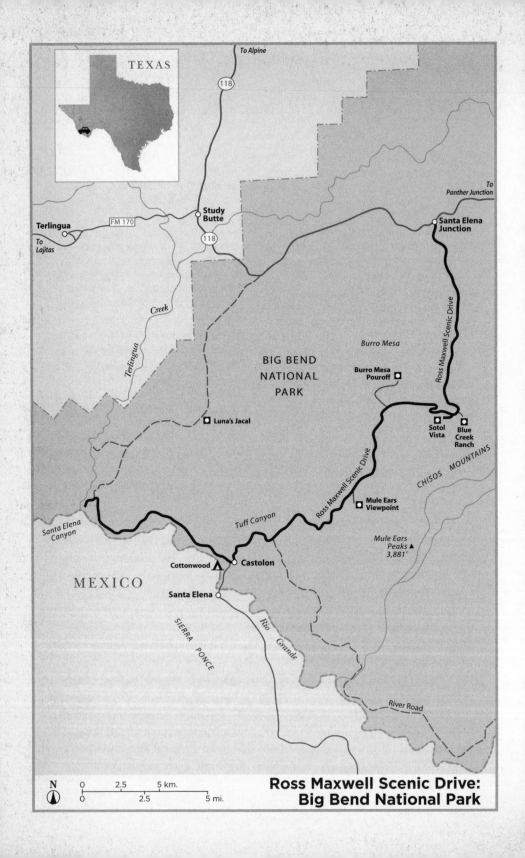

TEXAS

To Alpine

118

To Panther Junction

Terlingua
To Lajitas

FM 170

Study Butte

118

Santa Elena Junction

Terlingua Creek

BIG BEND NATIONAL PARK

Burro Mesa

Burro Mesa Pouroff

Ross Maxwell Scenic Drive

□ **Luna's Jacal**

Sotol Vista □   □ **Blue Creek Ranch**

CHISOS MOUNTAINS

Ross Maxwell Scenic Drive

□ **Mule Ears Viewpoint**

Santa Elena Canyon

Tuff Canyon

Mule Ears Peaks ▲ *3,881'*

MEXICO

Cottonwood ⛺   ○ **Castolon**

Santa Elena ○

SIERRA PONCE

Rio Grande

River Road

N

0	2.5	5 km.
0	2.5	5 mi.

Ross Maxwell Scenic Drive: Big Bend National Park

Big Bend National Park contains the best undeveloped example of Chihuahuan Desert in the United States. The Chihuahuan Desert covers a large area of northern Mexico, West Texas, and southern New Mexico. As with all deserts, it's characterized by annual rainfall of less than 10 inches at the lower elevations. Mountain ranges within the desert generally receive greater amounts of rain, depending upon their elevation. Because this drive starts in the foothills and ends in the river valley, the terrain grows drier as you progress.

One of the most common desert plants along the route is the lechuguilla. Botanists consider it an indicator plant for the Chihuahuan Desert because it only grows here. Its leaves grow in a green rosette of thick fibrous blades tipped with needle-sharp spines. The plants can grow into thick patches that are difficult to cross without spearing an ankle. Overgrazing in years past probably encouraged a thicker growth of lechuguilla than is natural. After growing for as long as 10 or 15 years, the plant sprouts a fast-growing, green, asparaguslike stalk 10 or more feet tall. After the stalk flowers, the entire plant dies, its food supply exhausted.

As you would expect, many species of cacti are common along the drive. April and May are the best times to see the cacti in bloom. Two of the most prominent species are prickly pear and strawberry cactus. Prickly pear grow in masses of flat, round, spine-covered pads. They bloom with large yellow flowers. Strawberry cactus grows in rounded mounds and has brilliant reddish-purple flowers that mature into edible fruit.

From the marked Santa Elena junction along the park highway between headquarters and Study Butte, turn south into a valley between the Chisos Mountains to the left and Burro Mesa to the right. Grasses are slowly recovering in the valley from years of overgrazing before the park was created in 1944, but creosote bush, cacti, lechuguilla, and other desert plants are nonetheless very common. Some areas of soil are still bare of vegetation.

A pullout on the right and a windmill mark the site of the old Nail Ranch. A short trail leads to the ruined adobe ranch house along Cottonwood Creek. Two brothers, Sam and Jim, started the ranch in 1916 and built the house, along with gardens, animal pens, and a well. As were most early settlers in Big Bend country, they were relatively self-sufficient. They raised produce, kept milk cows and chickens, and raised livestock on several sections of land. Water from the windmill still supplies birds and wildlife.

The Chisos Mountains form an impressive wall to the west as you continue south from the old ranch. Several igneous dikes radiate outward from the foot of the mountains like tumbled-down Chinese walls. They formed when molten rock squeezed into cracks in the earth's crust and hardened. The softer surrounding rock later eroded away, leaving only the dikes. A pullout on the left describes them.

The road climbs out of the valley to the highest point of the drive. Another pullout on the left marks a short trail to the Homer Wilson Blue Creek Ranch. From the parking area you can see the abandoned ranch house in the canyon below. The trail leads down to the ranch and then up Blue Creek Canyon into the high Chisos Mountains. For many years the building was a line camp for Homer Wilson's ranching operation and was occupied by his foreman, Lott Felts. The ranch was once a sizable operation. Water for livestock was piped down the canyon from a spring and a cistern system was built for the house. Corrals, a bunkhouse, a storeroom, and pens were once in constant use.

Be sure to stop at **Sotol Vista.** A short spur road leads to one of the best views in the park at the end of a ridge. To the west the mountains drop away abruptly into the lower desert. In the distance a deep notch in Mesa de Anguila marks the downstream entrance of Santa Elena Canyon. Beyond towers the remote Sierra Rica of Mexico.

The omnipresent sotol plant lends the vista its name. This bushy plant grows 3 or 4 feet tall and has long, thin, green leaves radiating from the center of the plant. Hooked thorns line the edges of the leaves like teeth on a saw blade. The sotol, a member of the lily family, thrives at this elevation in the foothills of the Chisos Mountains. Mexicans make a potent drink, also called sotol, by fermenting the heart of the plant and distilling the juice, similar to the way tequila is made from a species of agave plant.

After Sotol Vista the highway descends steeply into the lower, drier desert. Grasses become less common and desert plants dominate. At the bottom of the steep hill, a short side road leads to the base of Burro Mesa. Two short trails start at the end of the road. One leads half a mile up into a hidden box canyon. After heavy rains, water pours off the cliff above into the canyon. Unlike many of the desert trails, canyon walls provide some shade here. The other trail leads to a small desert spring about a mile away.

Just beyond the Burro Mesa Pouroff road is the Chimneys trailhead. The rocky outcrop of the Chimneys to the west appears close in the desert air but is more than 2 miles away. The trail leads to the Chimneys and beyond to the Old Maverick Road, about 7 miles away. It makes a good winter hike, especially if someone can pick you up at the other end.

After the Chimneys the road drops into a twisted landscape of rocky volcanoes and deposits of consolidated white ash, or tuff. A short side road leads to a view of Mule Ears, a distinctive twin peak of eroded volcanic dikes. A trail leads to Mule Ears Spring and other destinations.

Surprisingly, wildflowers can blanket this stark terrain in the spring after a year of good rains. The tall Big Bend bluebonnet in particular can turn the hills purple in late March.

Canoeists paddle through the deep defile of Santa Elena Canyon.

Another pullout beyond the Mule Ears road lies at Tuff Canyon. Short trails lead to overlooks down into the narrow defile carved from white tuff. The rough River Road joins the highway just past Tuff Canyon. It's a long but scenic drive that parallels the river to the east side of the park. It generally requires a high-clearance vehicle and sometimes four-wheel-drive. Check on current conditions and be properly prepared before venturing down this road.

At the base of Cerro Castellan, the highway passes through a short but spectacular stretch of white tuff and dark lava. Look closely at the white ash deposits on the right for a dark volcanic neck that looks like a large petrified tree trunk, complete with a knot hole.

Castolon to Santa Elena Canyon

Just south is the tiny settlement of Castolon, perched on a gravel ridge above the Rio Grande floodplain. The area along the river was settled by ranchers and floodplain farmers around the turn of the last century. Over the years the buildings at Castolon have been residences, a post office, and a trading post. Today the park maintains exhibits and a ranger station here, and a store serves tourists. On a hot day, buy a cold drink at the store and relax under the shady ramada in front.

From Castolon, the road follows the river upstream to Santa Elena Canyon. Along the way it passes Cottonwood Campground and former fields, now grown up in creosote bush, four-wing saltbush, and other plants. Crumbling adobe and stone buildings scattered along the route were once farmhouses.

The road ends at a large parking lot at the mouth of **Santa Elena Canyon.** Thick vegetation of huisache, willow, tamarisk, and mesquite surrounds the parking area. Take a look at the bathroom before walking down to the river. A line on its wall indicates the high-water mark of a major flood, even though the river is some distance below and away.

The hike into Santa Elena Canyon is one of the most spectacular in the park. It includes a short climb, but overall it's an easy round-trip walk of less than 2 miles. The trail leads through the floodplain thicket to the banks of the Rio Grande. Terlingua Creek joins the river here; at times hikers may have to wade across the creek to continue into the canyon. The trail switchbacks up a rock bluff and then descends back to the floodplain inside the canyon. Sheer walls tower 1,500 feet overhead, forming a deep, narrow gorge. The trail winds past house-size boulders and through shady thickets of reeds and tamarisks. The muddy river hisses quietly by, accompanied by the descending trill of canyon wrens.

The canyon is the most popular raft trip at Big Bend, although frequent low river levels can make the trip difficult. Boaters put in at Lajitas and make one- or

Ancient volcanoes left deposits of ash and lava near Castolon in Big Bend National Park.

Ross Maxwell Scenic Drive winds its way through the desert mountains below Sotol Vista.

two-day trips through the canyon, taking out a short distance downriver from the canyon parking lot.

An alternate return route follows **Old Maverick Road** back to the north side of the park. The improved dirt road turns off just before the Santa Elena parking lot. The road is usually passable to all vehicles, but ask about its condition beforehand.

7

Basic Drive

Big Bend National Park

General description: A 10-mile paved road that climbs from the high desert at Big Bend National Park headquarters into the cooler, wooded peaks of the Chisos Mountains.

Special attractions: Big Bend National Park, Chisos Mountains, Lost Mine Trail, hiking, camping, scenic views.

Location: West Texas. The drive starts at park headquarters at Panther Junction in Big Bend National Park.

Drive route name: Basin Drive.

Travel season: All year. Compared to the surrounding desert, the mountains are relatively cool in summer. On rare occasions, snow or ice can close the road for a short time.

Camping: The Park Service maintains a pleasant campground in the Basin.

Services: Food and limited lodging are available in the Basin. Be sure to reserve a room well ahead of time; the lodge is popular. Gas is available at Panther Junction. Nearby Study Butte and Terlingua offer all services.

Nearby attractions: Other sites in Big Bend National Park, including Santa Elena Canyon, Boquillas Canyon, Mariscal Canyon, and Hot Springs; Black Gap Wildlife Management Area; ghost town of Terlingua.

For more information: Superintendent, P.O. Box 129, Box Big Bend National Park, TX 79834; (432) 477-2251; www.nps.gov /bibe.

The Drive

From a distance, the Chisos Mountains of Big Bend National Park seem to float like an island on a desert sea. The rugged mountains rise to 7,835 feet at Emory Peak, about 6,000 feet above the Rio Grande. As in other mountain ranges, the increased elevation makes the high peaks considerably cooler than the surrounding lowlands. Mountains also attract more rainfall as air that flows over the mountains is forced to rise, which cools it, condensing out moisture and creating precipitation. The cooler climate and additional rainfall support a scrubby forest of pinyon pine, oak, and juniper in the Chisos Mountains. In sheltered canyons and on shady north- facing slopes, even a few Arizona pines, Douglas firs, and aspens survive.

This is an excellent drive in summer when the Big Bend desert is baking in the sun. The road is steep and winding, so the Park Service recommends that large trailers not be taken into the Basin. Start the drive at the Panther Junction visitor center, which has exhibits, an excellent bookstore on regional topics, a post office, and park staff to answer questions and issue river and backcountry camping permits.

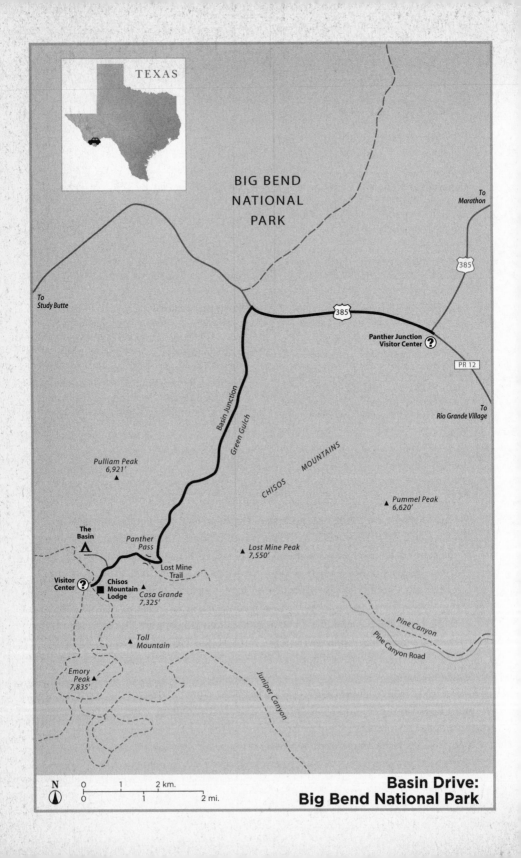

TEXAS

BIG BEND
NATIONAL
PARK

To
Marathon

To
Study Butte

385

385

Panther Junction
Visitor Center ❓

PR 12

To
Rio Grande Village

Basin Junction

Green Gulch

Pulliam Peak
6,921'
▲

CHISOS   MOUNTAINS

Pummel Peak
6,620'
▲

The
Basin
⛺

Panther
Pass

Lost Mine Peak
7,550'
▲

Lost Mine
Trail

Visitor
Center ❓

Chisos
Mountain
Lodge ■

Casa Grande
7,325' ▲

Pine Canyon

Pine Canyon Road

Toll
Mountain ▲

Emory
Peak ▲
7,835'

Juniper Canyon

N

0   1   2 km.

0   1   2 mi.

**Basin Drive:
Big Bend National Park**

Drive west from the junction toward Study Butte, Terlingua, and the Basin. The highway traverses the northern high-desert slopes of the Chisos Mountains for about 3 miles to the marked Basin junction. A mix of grasses, cacti, agave, creosote bush, and other plants blanket the hills. Turn left at the junction and begin climbing into the mountains toward the Basin.

The road soon enters the canyon of Green Gulch. The vegetation changes as the canyon walls rise higher and higher. Desert plants give way to thick grasses and scattered oaks, junipers, and pinyon pines. As the road climbs the woodland becomes thicker. The unique Texas madrone tree, with its distinctive smooth, pale cream, pink, and red bark, grows along this road. This slow-growing species, related to the Arizona and Pacific madrones, is relatively uncommon. In the United States it grows in only a few mountain ranges in West Texas and southeastern New Mexico and in widely scattered areas of the Texas Hill Country.

Lost Mine Trail & The Basin

After a few sharp turns, the road reaches its high point at Panther Pass. Be sure to stop at the parking area on the left, the trailhead for the **Lost Mine Trail.** The rocky ramparts of Casa Grande Peak tower above, while other peaks and ridges jab at the sky in all directions. Although the mountains are quiet now, millions of years ago violent eruptions exploded, ejecting lava and ash across the land. Igneous rocks also pushed up into the mountains from below, rather than erupting. **The Basin,** the large mountain valley visible to the west, looks like a huge crater but was created by erosion, not by a past eruption.

The Lost Mine Trail is strenuous, but this is one of my favorite hikes in Texas. The park has an interpretive booklet for the trail. The 2.4-mile trail climbs onto an exposed ridge near **Lost Mine Peak** from which views extend over a vast spread of mountains and desert. Much of the hike passes through shady woodland. One interesting tree along the trail, the **drooping juniper,** looks permanently wilted and grows only in the Chisos Mountains of the US. A Mexican bird, the **Colima warbler,** also lives only in the Chisos Mountains in the United States. Be sure to watch for **black bears** along the trail. After being almost exterminated years ago, they have begun to return to the Chisos Mountains from the Sierra del Carmen of Mexico.

The well-built trail is very steep for the first few hundred feet, but then it flattens out considerably for the next mile to the Juniper Canyon overlook. If you are not up to the steep climb beyond here, don't despair; the views here are well worth the hike.

The next mile switchbacks steeply up to the ridgetop and finally levels off for the last few tenths of a mile. The trail ends on a rocky point almost surrounded by cliffs. The views are breathtaking, from Lost Mine Peak in the north to mountains

far to the south in Mexico. Experienced hikers can consider taking a flashlight along and staying until sunset. The light show is hard to beat anywhere. If it's warm, watch out for snakes on the way down; they prefer the evening hours.

From the Lost Mine trailhead the road winds down into the mountain valley of the Basin and ends at the lodge. High peaks surround the Basin like a protective castle wall. Creeks drain out of the Basin through a rocky notch in the west wall called the Window. The desert can be seen far below through the narrow gap.

A complex of buildings lies at the end of the road at the lodge, including a store, ranger station, restaurant, and gift shop. Most of the lodge consists of boring motel rooms, but there are several attractive stone cabins tucked away in the pines. Be sure to reserve well ahead if you want to stay at the lodge.

Several excellent trails originate in the Basin from a trailhead at the lower end of the lodge parking lot. Most are strenuous, but all are extremely scenic. The trail to the South Rim may well be the classic Texas hike, with tremendous views and mountain forests. An easy, short paved loop trail gives a great view of the Window at sunset. Be sure to spend some time hiking and enjoying the mountain scenery before descending back to the hot desert below.

Casa Grande Peak towers over the Basin and a century plant high the Chisos Mountains.

8

Rio Grande Village Drive

Big Bend National Park

General description: A 24-mile paved highway from Big Bend National Park headquarters to one of the major canyons of the Rio Grande.

Special attractions: Boquillas Canyon, Hot Springs, Rio Grande Village Nature Trail, birds.

Location: West Texas. The drive starts at Big Bend National Park headquarters at Panther Junction.

Drive route name: Rio Grande Village Drive.

Travel season: Fall through spring. If you do the drive in summer, plan to go very early or late in the day to avoid the heat.

Camping: The Park Service maintains a large, shady campground at Rio Grande Village. A park concessionaire also operates a small RV campground with hookups at the village.

Services: Gas is available at Panther Junction and Rio Grande Village. A small grocery is at the village. The nearest lodging is at the Basin in the park. Reserve rooms there at the Chisos Mountains Lodge well ahead of time; it's very popular. A restaurant is also located in the Basin. All services are available outside the park at Study Butte, Terlingua, and Marathon.

Nearby attractions: Other Big Bend National Park sites such as the Chisos Mountains, Santa Elena Canyon, and Mariscal Canyon; Big Bend Ranch State Park; ghost town of Terlingua.

For more information: Superintendent, P.O. Box 129, Big Bend National Park, TX 79834; (432) 477-2251; www.nps.gov /bibe.

The Drive

This route crosses a vast sweep of the Chihuahuan Desert in its descent from the foothills of the Chisos Mountains to the Rio Grande. Views stretch for many miles, with little sign of human activity. Big Bend National Park occupies more than 1,200 square miles and, combined with two other large tracts of public land (Big Bend Ranch State Park and Black Gap Wildlife Management Area), sets aside an enormous area free of most development. Across the Rio Grande in Mexico, the Mexican government has created two protected areas: Maderas del Carmen and Cañón de Santa Elena. Cemex, a Mexican cement conglomerate, is purchasing private land south of the Rio Grande to be more strictly conserved. But even the unprotected lands across the river are only lightly settled.

In fact the Big Bend region has always been sparsely populated. The rugged land and harsh, dry climate discouraged settlement. Water was scarce and rugged mountains and deep canyons restricted travel. Apaches, Comanches, and other

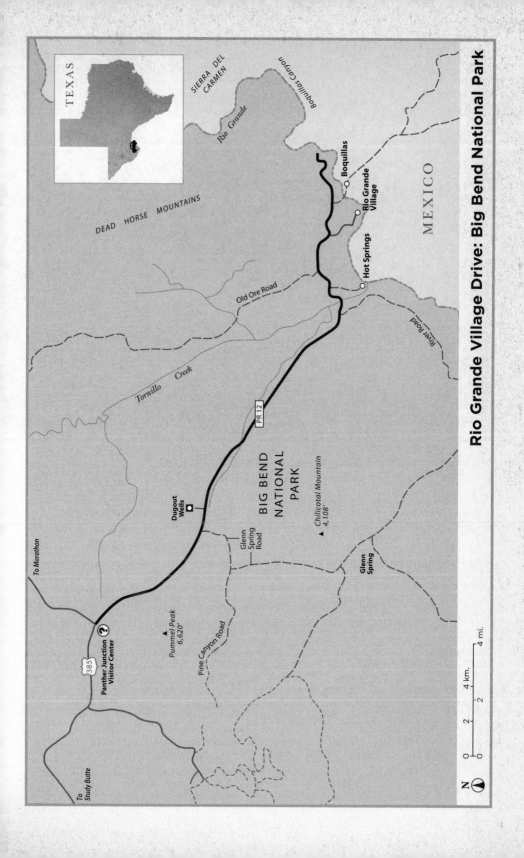

Rio Grande Village Drive: Big Bend National Park

The Rio Grande flows through the desert near Langford Hot Springs.

groups resisted the intrusion of newcomers. Even the plants seemed hostile; spines and thorns covered stalks and stems. For the most part the Spaniards ignored and avoided the area. Attempts to establish missions and forts along the Rio Grande met with limited success. The Spaniards called the area "el despoblado," which means "the uninhabited land."

The United States acquired the land from Mexico in 1848 at the end of the Mexican-American War, but little development occurred until the Apaches and Comanches were defeated later that century. Widely scattered ranches were established to graze livestock on the desert grasses, and irrigated farms were started on the Rio Grande floodplain. Small mining booms brought people to Terlingua, Mariscal Mountain, Boquillas, and Shafter. When the ore ran out, the miners drifted away. When the land was purchased for the park, the ranches and farms closed, leaving few residents in the area.

This drive visits some sites of human occupation, but they seem almost insignificant in the vast, empty land. Except for the lingering effects of overgrazing, the land looks little different today than it did to the eyes of Spanish explorers hundreds of years ago.

This drive starts at park headquarters. A visitor center here provides information and permits and sells books on Big Bend and regional topics. A short nature trail in front of the center acquaints visitors with some common desert plants of Big Bend.

Park headquarters lies on the northern edge of the Chisos Mountains, which tower into the sky behind Panther Junction. The headquarters is low enough on the mountain slopes that grasses and desert vegetation dominate, rather than the forest woodland found high in the mountains. However, the road drops about 2,000 feet by the time it reaches the river. Consequently, the climate grows significantly hotter and drier. Grasses compete heavily with cacti and other desert plants at Panther Junction. As you progress down the road, the grasses thin and desert plants, such as cacti, ocotillo, lechuguilla, and creosote bush, dominate. Even desert plants become more widely scattered, with increasingly large areas of bare rock and soil separating them.

Rio Grande Village Drive

From headquarters drive east on the road to Rio Grande Village. The road drops gradually for most of the drive, making it a fun bicycle ride if you have someone to pick you up at the other end. After about 5 miles the Glenn Spring Road turns off to the right. This is a dirt road requiring a high-clearance vehicle. Glenn Spring was a small settlement early in the 20th century that depended on ranching and wax extraction from the **candelilla plant.**

Candelilla is a common plant in the low-desert country of the Big Bend region. It grows in low clumps with grayish-green, leafless, pencil-like stems. To limit water loss in the dry, hot climate, it secretes a wax coating. By using a relatively simple boiling process, the high-quality wax can be extracted and used for many products, including candles, chewing gum, food products, and wood polishes. With modern use of synthetic, petroleum-based waxes, demand for labor-intensive candelilla wax has declined. Some Mexicans still produce the wax across the river, but little is produced in the United States.

In the early part of the 20th century, the Mexican Revolution raged in Mexico and involved Pancho Villa and others in the northern part of the country. At times violence spilled over into the United States. On the night of May 5, 1916, a party of about 80 bandits raided Glenn Spring and Boquillas, killing several people, taking captives, and looting. The raid, coming soon after a raid of Columbus, New Mexico, by Villa, was a serious international incident. United States troops, led by Major George Langhorne, pursued the bandits into Mexico. The expedition was accompanied by reporters, photographers, and a film crew. The terrain they crossed was difficult. One reporter, James Hopper, quoted a cameraman in an article printed in that July's *Collier's, the National Weekly.* "The country isn't bad," he said. "It's just worse. Worse the moment you set foot from the train, and then, after that, just worser and worser."

Langhorne's troops pursued the bandits deep into Mexico and freed the captives, recovered much of the loot, and killed, captured, or dispersed most of the bandits. The Mexican government was upset at the incursion of American troops, so Langhorne withdrew after 16 days, his mission largely a success. The National Guard was sent to protect the border, but many troops were withdrawn as the United States was pulled into the first World War in Europe. Lesser raids continued for the next few years until the political situation in Mexico stabilized.

Beyond the Glenn Spring turnoff, the road continues to descend. In the distance ahead is the massive wall of the Sierra del Carmen of Mexico. At sunset the towering limestone cliffs turn gold and then pink and purple.

At about 15 miles, just before the large bridge that spans Tornillo Creek, the River Road turns off to the right. This 51-mile road is a rough but scenic route to the west side of the park that parallels the river. A high-clearance vehicle and sometimes four-wheel drive are necessary to drive it. Be sure to check with the park on road conditions before attempting it.

The broad, dry wash of Tornillo Creek drains much of the eastern side of the park. At one time it was a permanent stream lined with cottonwoods that wound through desert grasslands. Overgrazing stripped the grasslands, leading to increased flooding and topsoil erosion. The water table fell and water now runs off quickly, so the creek dried up on most of its route. In time, as the grasslands recover, water and cottonwoods may return.

About a mile east of the creek is the **Hot Springs turnoff.** The 2-mile gravel road is passable to automobiles, but it is too narrow for RVs, trailers, or other large vehicles. The road ends at the Rio Grande, at the confluence with Tornillo Creek.

J. O. Langford homesteaded here in 1909 and developed a small health spa using hot water flowing from a large spring on the riverbank. Violence associated with the Mexican Revolution forced the Langfords to leave temporarily, but they returned to build a general store, motel rooms, and a post office. They left in 1942 after selling their land to the government for the national park. Maggy Smith operated the hot springs for a few more years as a park concession before finally closing it. Several historic buildings still remain from the resort, and hot water still bubbles up into the old bathhouse foundation on the riverbank, attracting many bathers. A hiking trail follows the river from Hot Springs to Rio Grande Village about 2 miles downstream.

Just beyond the Hot Springs turnoff is the Old Ore Road. This rough, high-clearance route follows the foot of the Dead Horse Mountains to the north side of the park. Check on its condition and be properly prepared before trying it.

A storm breaks over the Sierra del Carmen of Mexico beyond where the Rio Grande flows through Hot Springs Canyon.

The main highway soon passes through a tunnel, a rare sight in Texas. The tunnel cuts off a sharp bend in the road known as Dead Man's Curve. Near here Max Ernst, an early settler, was shot in the back on September 27, 1908. His killer was never found.

Below the tunnel lies a road junction. The drive turns left to Boquillas Canyon, but consider a short side trip into **Rio Grande Village.** A small visitor center is here, along with a store, gas station, campground, laundry facility, and showers. The village lies on a broad floodplain of the Rio Grande that was farmed until the 1940s. The fields are gone, but the irrigation system is still used to water the trees that shade the campground and other facilities. The old adobe home of Maria and John Daniel still stands at the end of the road west of the store.

The campground is popular with birders, especially during the spring migration. Many species are attracted to the wooded area and water. A short nature trail leads from the campground to the top of a low bluff overlooking the river. The bluff is an excellent spot to watch the setting sun on the Sierra del Carmen.

The Rio Grande leaves the open desert abruptly where it flows into deep Boquillas Canyon.

Amazingly enough in this dry country, the trail crosses a boardwalk through a dense junglelike swamp fed by a large spring that harbors the Big Bend mosquito-fish, found nowhere else in the world.

Boquillas Canyon

A short distance beyond Rio Grande Village is a short side road to the Boquillas crossing. Between 1909 and 1919 a tramway carried ore across the river into Texas from mines in the Sierra del Carmen. Many of the miners lived in Boquillas. Until September 11, 2001, villagers would ferry you across the river in a rowboat for a small fee. You could eat in the local restaurant or buy souvenirs. Unfortunately, the border crossing is now closed, and many villagers, dependent on tourists, have moved away.

Beyond the Boquillas crossing, a short side road on the right overlooks the mouth of **Boquillas Canyon** and the town of Boquillas. The highway ends at the parking lot at Boquillas Canyon. The gorge cuts through the Sierra del Carmen range, known as the Dead Horse Mountains on the Texas side of the river. It's hard to believe that the quiet Rio Grande could have carved a path through the massive wall of mountains. The canyon is 17 miles long, the longest in the park. I highly recommend the popular two- or three-day float trip through the canyon and some of the most spectacular scenery in Texas, if water levels allow.

An easy 0.75-mile trail climbs over a low ridge above the parking lot and enters the gaping mouth of Boquillas Canyon. A ledge of bedrock above the river contains Indian grinding holes. Against a canyon wall, wind has piled a huge drift of sand that kids are drawn to immediately. The trail ends just beyond where the canyon wall meets the river.

9

Palo Duro Canyon

General description: A 21-mile drive across the High Plains and into the depths of Palo Duro Canyon.

Special attractions: Palo Duro Canyon State Park, "Texas" outdoor drama, Panhandle-Plains Historical Museum, hiking, camping, mountain biking, scenic views.

Location: Texas Panhandle. The drive starts in Canyon, a small city about 15 miles south of Amarillo.

Drive route numbers: TX 217, Park Road 5.

Travel season: All year. The drive is hot in summer but comfortable early and late in the day. Occasional winter snows can make the drive icy and treacherous. Spring and fall are probably the best times.

Camping: Palo Duro Canyon State Park has several campgrounds.

Services: All services are available in Canyon and Amarillo, plus Palo Duro Canyon State Park rents cabins.

Nearby attractions: Caprock Canyons State Park and Trailway, Alibates Flint Quarries National Monument, Lake Meredith National Recreation Area, Buffalo Lake National Wildlife Refuge, Amarillo.

For more information: Palo Duro Canyon State Park, 11450 Park Rd. 5, Canyon, TX 79015; (806) 488-2227; www.tpwd.state .tx.us/spdest/findadest/parks/palo_duro. Canyon Chamber of Commerce, 1518 Fifth Ave., Canyon, TX 79015; (806) 655-1183; www.canyonchamber.org. Panhandle-Plains Historical Museum; (806) 651-2244; www .panhandleplains.org.

The Drive

Most people quickly become bored by the flat, treeless terrain of the Texas Panhandle and respond by pressing harder on the gas pedal. But the High Plains hold notable exceptions to the monotonous terrain, the most famous being Palo Duro Canyon. Here the level plains, dotted with irrigated farms and cattle ranches, abruptly drop 800 feet into the ragged gash of the canyon.

The drive to Palo Duro Canyon starts, appropriately enough, in the small city of Canyon. The city sits in a shallow valley, itself an anomaly on the flat plains, at the confluence of what seem to be two minor creeks. The two creeks form the Prairie Dog Town Fork of the Red River, one of the headwater tributaries of the Red River, the long waterway that marks the boundary between Oklahoma and Texas. At Canyon the Prairie Dog Town Fork seems small and insignificant and gives little hint of its striking metamorphosis a short distance downstream.

Canyon was originally founded in 1878 as the headquarters for the vast T Anchor Ranch. The last of the Comanche Indians had been defeated only a few

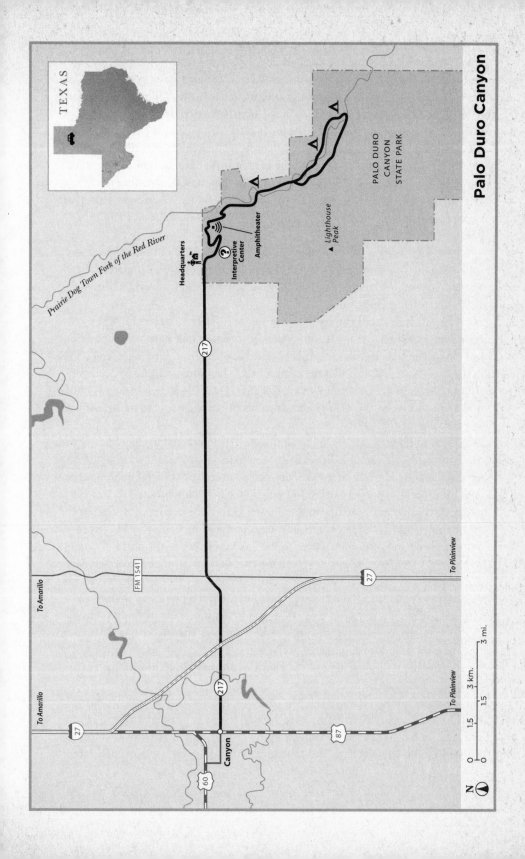

Palo Duro Canyon

years previously, opening the Panhandle for settlement. Development was slow on the High Plains until the railroad arrived. In 1887 the Fort Worth and Denver City Railroad steamed into Amarillo just to the north, followed immediately by the Santa Fe Railway. The Rock Island Railroad arrived a few years later. With the arrival of the railroads, the great cattle drives ceased and the animals were shipped to market via trains. Panhandle settlement accelerated and Amarillo boomed as a commercial shipping center at the intersection of several of the rail lines. Other towns such as Canyon developed in the ensuing growth. The village of Canyon City was named, naturally enough, for nearby Palo Duro Canyon. In 1898 the Pecos and Northern Railroad made Canyon a shipping point.

With increasing settlement many of the largest ranches were subdivided and sold off to the new immigrants. The XIT ranch in the northwestern part of the Panhandle once held more than 3 million acres, making it the world's largest ranch under fence at the time.

The vast spread was conveyed to a group of Chicago investors in 1882 by the cash-poor State of Texas in return for the construction of a state capitol building in Austin. The state legislature, probably still smarting from the Confederacy's loss in the Civil War, specified that the capitol had to be more beautiful and at least 1 foot taller than the US Capitol in Washington, D.C. The state capitol was built, and it long outlasted the XIT. The ranch lands began to be sold in the 1890s, with 90 percent gone by 1912.

Many of the new settlers in the Panhandle tried dryland farming, but frequent droughts made the ventures risky. They soon found that a vast shallow aquifer, the Ogallala, underlaid much of the flat, dry plains. Eventually, several million acres of land came under irrigated cultivation, much of which continues today. Unfortunately the aquifer has been drawn upon faster than it has been replenished, so the long-term viability of much of the farming is in question.

Another major economic factor in the Panhandle, especially north of Canyon, is the oil and gas industry. In 1918 the first natural gas well was drilled near the Canadian River in what would later prove to be one of the world's largest gas fields. Three years later the Panhandle's first successful oil well was completed in Carson County, but transport and refining facilities were slow to develop until drillers brought in a large producing well near Borger. That strike spurred a boom that drew thousands of speculators and workers into the Panhandle. Interestingly, the world's largest known deposit of helium was found mixed in with the gas of the huge Panhandle fields.

Today ranching, farming, oil, gas, and shipping provide the mainstays of much of the Panhandle economy. Canyon's economy is further boosted by the presence of **West Texas A&M University.** Tucked within its attractive campus is the **Panhandle-Plains Historical Museum** (2503 4th Ave.), a surprisingly large and professional museum for the 7,800-student university. Its exhibits range from ranching history to oilfield equipment, from archaeology to Southwestern art. It's probably the most extensive museum in this part of the state.

To start the drive, follow TX 217 east from the center of town to the intersection with I-27, the start of the following mileage measurements. Continue east on TX 217 from I-27, following signs to Palo Duro Canyon State Park. In less than 2 miles, the road crosses FM 1541; FM 1541 and I-27 are two possible routes to Amarillo if you are coming or going from that city. TX 217 continues east across flat plains that seem to stretch to infinity in every direction, broken only by the occasional windmill or farmhouse.

The road passes several playa lakes, shallow depressions with no outlet that dot the High Plains. Over the years clay has coated the bottoms of these depressions, allowing them to hold rainfall for long periods of time, forming ponds and small lakes. The ponds are vital for migrating waterfowl and other wildlife in the dry country of the Panhandle. Nearby **Buffalo Lake National Wildlife Refuge** is a major haven on the Central Flyway. In winter the refuge hosts hundreds of thousands of ducks and geese.

Palo Duro Canyon State Park

After about 10 miles, long enough for the plains to become monotonous, a hint of change appears on the right. A small, narrow canyon cuts into the white caprock just right of the road. Just beyond, after passing a sprinkling of tourist-oriented businesses, the highway ends at the entrance and headquarters building of **Palo Duro Canyon State Park.**

Less than a mile down the park road from the headquarters building, the road reaches the canyon rim at an overlook and interpretive center. The monotony abruptly ends. In stark contrast to the surrounding plains, the canyon cuts a broad chasm deep into the High Plains. Gnarled junipers dot the rocky slopes, softening the outline of the colorful cliffs of red, yellow, and purple. Far below, the Prairie Dog Town Fork of the Red River, seeming so insignificant in the town of Canyon, winds along the bottom, lined by a green ribbon of cottonwoods.

Palo Duro Canyon is one of the most spectacular sights in the Panhandle and one of the premier state parks in Texas. At one time it was even considered by the federal government for national park status. Although the canyon did not become a national park, the state acquired most of the park's 16,400 acres in the 1930s and developed them into one of the largest and most popular state parks in the system. The juniper trees gave the canyon its name; "palo duro" means "hard wood" in Spanish.

Visitors here are sometimes amazed that the little creek at the bottom could have carved the deep, 60-mile-long canyon. However, in the past the area received more rainfall, helping erosion to proceed more quickly. Anyone who has witnessed one of the canyon's notorious floods will not doubt the erosive power of the Prairie Dog Town Fork even today.

The colorful red rocks through which the creek has cut its canyon belong to several different geologic periods. The oldest rocks of the canyon, the bright red shales, clays, and sandstones of the Permian Period, line the bottom and lower slopes. These soft rocks, called the Quartermaster Formation, were formed about 250 million years ago in shallow waters on the edges of ancient seas. Slightly newer Triassic shales and sandstones, called the Trujillo and Tecovas, lie on top of the Permian rocks and are distinguished by their multiple colors, often shades of yellow, pink, and lavender. The Trujillo, the top Triassic layer, is a hard sandstone that resists erosion better than the other rocks, so it forms cliffs and capstones on pinnacles such as the aptly named Lighthouse.

Above the Trujillo lies the 4- to 10-million-year-old **Ogallala Formation,** a mix of sandstone, siltstone, conglomerate, and caliche. The Ogallala is very porous and permeable and is the important Panhandle aquifer. Fossils of many different extinct species of mammals have been found in the formation. There is a gap in time of more than 200 million years between the Trujillo and the Ogallala. Either the intervening rocks eroded away or none were deposited during that time period.

The flat surface of the High Plains resulted when sediment, eroded from the uplifted Rocky Mountains to the west, was carried east and deposited in sheets across the plains. With time the Pecos River eroded northward and stopped mountain streams from flowing eastward across the plains. Eventually the Pecos cut a broad valley far enough north that the High Plains were left as a large, flat, eastward-tilting plateau. Only the Canadian River has managed to cut entirely across the High Plains in Texas, but with time the Prairie Dog Town Fork and other watercourses will erode westward and eventually cut canyons all the way through the plains.

Palo Duro Canyon is more than just a geologic wonder. Its broken country harbors a mix of eastern and western species, such as the Rocky Mountain juniper, left here after the Pleistocene ended and the climate warmed and dried. The Palo Duro mouse lives in the Red River canyonlands and nowhere else. Many different species of birds have been sighted here, almost 200 so far. Mule deer compete for browse with the introduced African aoudad. Before they were exterminated, wolves, bears, and bison haunted the canyon country.

Humans lived in the area as long as 12,000 years ago, hunting extinct ice age animals such as the giant bison and the woolly mammoth. Succeeding groups came and went, ending with the arrival of the Comanches in the 1700s. For many

The Lighthouse, carved from soft sedimentary rock, rises from a ridge within Palo Duro Canyon.

The Lighthouse, reached by an easy 3-mile hike, is the most famous natural landmark of the Texas Panhandle.

years Palo Duro Canyon and the surrounding plains were their domain from which they ventured forth to hunt buffalo and raid other Indian tribes, Mexicans, and Anglos. The last major Indian battle in Texas, the Battle of Palo Duro Canyon, brought the Comanches' reign to a close in 1874.

Coronado was probably the first European to see the canyon when he made his epic journey through the Southwest and across the High Plains in 1541. Although hunting and trading parties ventured occasionally onto the plains, especially from New Mexico, the canyon area was not settled until after the Comanches were defeated. Charles Goodnight established the first large cattle ranch in the area and was soon followed by others. Ranching and farming are still the predominant land uses in the area today.

From the overlook continue along the park road to where it begins its steep descent into the canyon. A riding stable is on the left at the bottom; on the right is the **Texas Outdoor Musical Drama,** an outdoor amphitheater for the "Texas" drama. During summer a large cast presents an elaborate musical drama every evening except Mon. This outdoor performance has been very successful since it started playing in 1966 and has drawn millions of visitors. (Visit www.texas-show .com or call 806-655-2181 to order tickets.)

After the amphitheater, the road passes the first of several camping and picnic areas before crossing the creek on a low-water bridge. The Prairie Dog Town Fork appears quiet and innocent, but heed any flood warnings given out by park staff. The creek is notorious for floods that quickly turn the small creek into a raging, muddy river.

Just across the creek on the right side of the road is a replica of **Charles Goodnight's dugout**, followed by the **B.S. Arnold No. 1 oil well site.** The well was drilled with cable tools in 1919 and blew out when it hit a gas pocket at 2,600 feet. No oil was found, and the site was abandoned.

After the second creek crossing, the road splits into a 5-mile loop that can be driven in either direction. Along the loop are several campgrounds and picnic areas and trails for horses, hikers, and mountain bikers. To cap your visit to Palo Duro Canyon, consider taking the relatively easy hiking and mountain-bike trail to **The Lighthouse,** the 75-foot rock pinnacle that has become the canyon's trademark and one of Texas's most famous landmarks.

10

High Plains to Canyons

Silverton to Caprock Canyons State Park

General description: A 26-mile drive from the High Plains of Texas to the rugged canyons on the edge of the Caprock.

Special attractions: Caprock Canyons State Park and Trailway, hiking, camping, mountain biking, fishing, scenic views.

Location: Texas Panhandle. The drive starts in Silverton about 80 miles southeast of Amarillo.

Drive route numbers: TX 86, FM 1065, state park roads.

Travel season: All year. The drive is hot in summer but is reasonably comfortable in the morning and evening. Occasional winter storms make the road icy and treacherous for a short time. Fall and spring are probably the best times of year.

Camping: Caprock Canyons State Park manages developed and primitive campgrounds.

Services: Food and gas are available in Quitaque and Silverton, along with limited area lodging. Plainview is the nearest town with a broad range of services, including lodging.

Nearby attractions: Palo Duro Canyon State Park, Lubbock Landmark State Historical Park.

For more information: Caprock Canyons State Park, P.O. Box 204, Quitaque, TX, 79255; (806) 455-1492; www.tpwd .state.tx.us/spdest/findadest/parks/ caprock_canyons.

The Drive

This drive traverses the junction between two major landforms in Texas, the High Plains and the Rolling Plains. It starts in Silverton, a small town almost lost in the vast sprawl of the table-flat High Plains of the Texas Panhandle. The town is a small center for the area's farming and ranching, the mainstay of the Panhandle economy.

The Panhandle is noted for its incredibly flat terrain and is sometimes called the "Llano Estacado," or Staked Plains. Before being settled, this featureless plain was a sea of grass grazed by bison. Without any landmarks it must have been disconcerting to early travelers. The flat surface of the High Plains resulted when sediment eroded from the Rocky Mountains to the west was carried east and deposited in sheets across the plains. (See Drive 9 for more geologic history.)

Take TX 86 east out of Silverton across the plains. After a couple of miles, the road forks; stay right on TX 86. The land is not perfectly flat; here and there shallow depressions with no outlets dot the High Plains. Over the years clay has coated the bottoms of these playa lakes, allowing them to hold rainfall for long periods of time. These ponds and small lakes are vital for migrating waterfowl and other

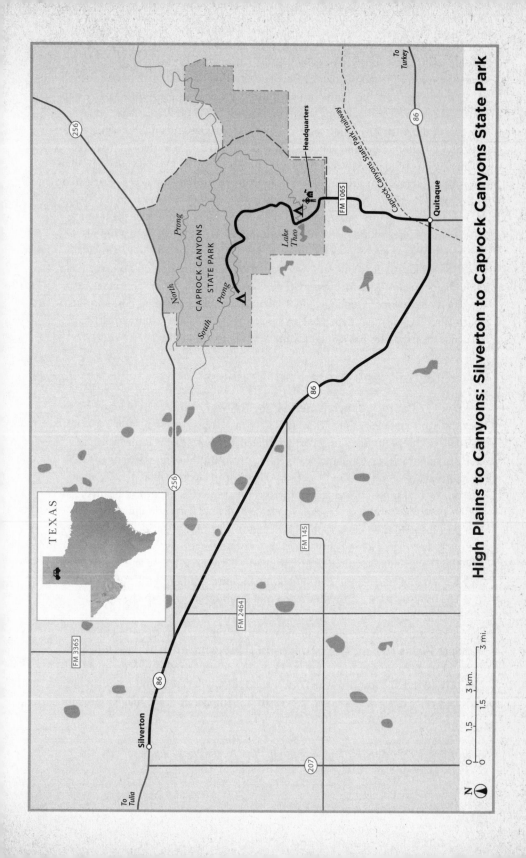

High Plains to Canyons: Silverton to Caprock Canyons State Park

To Turkey

86

Headquarters

Caprock Canyons State Park Trailway

FM 1065

Quitaque

256

North Prong

CAPROCK CANYONS STATE PARK

South Prong

Lake Theo

86

FM 145

TEXAS

FM 2464

FM 3365

86

Silverton

To Tulia

207

N

0   1.5   3 km.
0   1.5   3 mi.

wildlife in the dry country of the Panhandle. Unfortunately, many of the playas have been plowed, breaking the clay seal and limiting their ability to store water.

After a few miles the plains end abruptly at the edge of the Caprock. The Caprock is the rock layer that forms the flat surface of the High Plains. The top layer consists of the 4- to 10-million-year-old Ogallala Formation, a mix of sandstone, siltstone, conglomerate, and caliche. It is well-known for the variety of fossilized extinct species of mammals that have been found in it. The Ogallala also acts as an enormous reservoir for groundwater, supporting several million acres of irrigated cultivation. Unfortunately, the aquifer is being drawn down faster than it is being replenished, calling into question the long-term viability of much of the farming.

From the edge of the plains, the road drops abruptly down onto a broad, lower area of gently rolling terrain known, naturally enough, as the Rolling Plains. These plains lie about 1,000 feet lower than the High Plains and do not have their table-flat character. After dropping off the Llano Estacado, TX 86 continues east into the small town of Quitaque. Since its early origins as a trading post and stagecoach stop, the town has depended on area agriculture. Today, tourism at two related state-park sites has brought some new life to Quitaque.

Caprock Canyons State Park Trailway

The first, the **Caprock Canyons State Park Trailway,** is managed by nearby Caprock Canyons State Park. The trailway is a 64-mile trail converted from a former railroad. In the 1920s, the Fort Worth and Denver South Plains Railway began constructing tracks up Quitaque Canyon to surmount the Caprock and reach the agricultural areas on the Llano Estacado. They completed the line in 1928, after laboriously building a tunnel and numerous trestles across ravines and canyons. By the 1980s tax-subsidized trucking on state highways was eating into the rail line's profits, and the railroad—now Burlington Northern—decided to abandon the track. Through a long, complicated series of negotiations, the Texas Parks and Wildlife Department acquired the right-of-way between Estelline and South Plains and converted it into a combination hiking, mountain-biking, and equestrian trail.

The trailway passes through the town of **Quitaque;** one of the best access points is on the west side of town on the south side of TX 86. The most scenic section of the trail gradually climbs all the way from Quitaque to the small settlement of **South Plains** atop the Caprock. It crosses trestles hundreds of yards long and as much as 50 or 60 feet high. It dives into a tunnel and climbs up Quitaque Canyon, a rugged defile wooded with cottonwoods along the creek and hemmed in by red-rock cliffs. The trail's smooth gravel surface and gentle grade make it probably

Water has carved interesting formations from the soft sandstones, shales, and clays of Caprock Canyons State Park.

A cyclist approaches the old railroad tunnel on the Caprock Canyons State Park Trailway.

the best mountain-bike trail in Texas. If you can arrange a bike shuttle to South Plains (Caprock Canyons State Park can give you shuttle information), you can ride downhill most of the way back to Quitaque.

To continue the drive, turn north on FM 1065 in Quitaque to get to Caprock Canyons State Park. After about 3 miles, turn left into the park. From head-quarters, a bit less than 1 mile into the park, continue into the park toward the red-rock bluffs of the Caprock. Caprock Canyons State Park provides a startling contrast to the flat plains that make up most of the Texas Panhandle. Within this 15,000-acre park, the Llano Estacado gives way to the lower Rolling Plains in a long, serrated, red-rock escarpment as much as 1,000 feet high.

Here tributaries of the **Red River** have slowly cut into the thick red beds of the Llano Estacado. Erosion by the Red River's tributaries have cut deep, narrow canyons into the durable rock, in contrast to the broad valleys carved by the Pecos and Canadian Rivers. Interestingly, the 1,300-mile Red River is one of the longest rivers in North America that does not originate in mountains. It continues to erode the Llano Estacado today, the narrow fingers of its canyons and tributaries slowly cutting westward from the lower plains to the east. The most prominent canyon is Palo Duro (see Drive 9), but Caprock Canyons State Park contains two impressive smaller canyons, the North and South Prongs of the Little Red River.

Humans arrived here at least 10,000 years ago, building campsites near what is now Lake Theo and other areas. The earliest documented people, known as the Folsom culture, are identified by the distinctive design of their projectile points. Their craftsmen carefully chipped a large flake from the base of each side of the point and then mounted it on a spear to kill large animals. These early people were nomadic and followed game across the High Plains, as did many later groups. Contrary to modern myth these hunter-gatherer groups did not leave the land undisturbed. They used fire to encourage grassland growth and to help with hunting. Many archaeologists now believe that they contributed to the extinction of many Pleistocene mammals, including the mammoth, the giant bison, and camels.

More recent cultures utilized pottery and the bow and arrow to improve their standard of living. In the last thousand years or so, some groups established permanent settlements and began cultivating crops of beans, corn, and squash. The Spaniards first appeared in 1541, with Coronado's epic journey across the High Plains. The Comanches arrived from the north in the early 1700s, establishing a nomadic culture centered around bison hunting using horses acquired from the Spaniards. In the late 1800s, Anglo settlers founded towns and vast cattle ranches across the High Plains.

The state park preserves a large area of rugged canyons on the eastern margin of the Llano Estacado. Some of the plants tucked away in the deep canyons, such as the Rocky Mountain juniper, are at the eastern limit of their range. Bison, wolf, and black bear no longer roam the canyon country, but mule deer, bobcats, coyotes, porcupines, jackrabbits, and many other animals are common. The aoudad, a sheep native to northern Africa, was introduced nearby in 1957 and has thrived. Although they are an interesting addition to the rugged canyon country of the Red River, they compete directly with native mule deer.

From headquarters, continue into the park by Lake Theo on the left. The small reservoir, fed by Holmes Creek on the south side of the park, offers fishing and boating opportunities. Bear right toward the campground when you pass a couple of junctions by Lake Theo Dam. The road winds deeper into the park, passing the developed campground, a picnic area, and equestrian and hiking trails before ending at a primitive campground tucked into the mouth of the South Prong of the Little Red River. Those who want to stretch their legs should consider some of the many miles of trail that climb up the North and South Prong canyons to spectacular viewpoints on Haynes Ridge. For the adventurous, two backcountry campsites allow overnight backpacks along the hiking trails.

11

Trail of the Dinosaur

Cleburne to Dinosaur Valley State Park

General description: A 28-mile paved drive through rolling North Texas terrain to a place where dinosaurs once roamed.

Special attractions: Dinosaur Valley State Park, Cleburne State Park, Brazos River, dinosaur tracks, hiking, camping, boating, fishing.

Location: North Texas. The drive starts about 6 miles west of Cleburne, a small city about 25 miles south of Fort Worth, at the junction of US 67 and Park Road 21.

Drive route numbers: Park Road 21, FM 200, US 67, Park Road 59/FM 205.

Travel season: All year. Summers are hot and humid. Spring and fall are the most pleasant times.

Camping: Dinosaur Valley and Cleburne State Parks both maintain campgrounds.

Services: All services are available in Cleburne and Glen Rose.

Nearby attractions: Lake Whitney State Park, Acton State Historical Park, Meridian State Park, Fossil Rim Wildlife Center, Lake Granbury, many city attractions in Fort Worth.

For more information: Cleburne State Park, 5800 Park Road 21, Cleburne, TX 76033; (817) 645-4215; www.tpwd.state.tx .us/spdest/findadest/parks/cleburne. Dinosaur Valley State Park, P.O. Box 396, Glen Rose, TX 76043; (254) 897-4588; www .tpwd.state.tx.us/spdest/findadest/parks /dinosaur_valley. Cleburne Chamber of Commerce, P.O. Box 701, Cleburne, TX 76033; (817) 645-2455; www.cleburnechamber .org. Glen Rose Chamber of Commerce, P.O. Box 605, Glen Rose, TX 76043; (254) 897-2286; www.glenrosechamber.com.

The Drive

Cleburne, a small city of about 29,000 people, was founded around 1854 and was first known as Camp Henderson. In 1867, the name of the town was changed to honor Confederate General Pat Cleburne. To start the drive, go about 6 miles west of the center of Cleburne on US 67 to the junction with Park Road 21 on the left. Follow Park Road 21 southwest through open prairie country for the first 3 or 4 miles. Good views soon open up of the Brazos River Valley to the south. The road then drops abruptly into a narrow wooded valley and passes the entrance of Cleburne State Park on the right 6.3 miles from US 67.

The state park is tucked away in a small valley in the breaks lining the broad Brazos River Valley. In 1934, local businessmen promoted the site as a location for a state park. As with many of Texas's older state parks, Cleburne was developed in the 1930s by the Civilian Conservation Corps. The CCC was created to employ young men during the Depression.

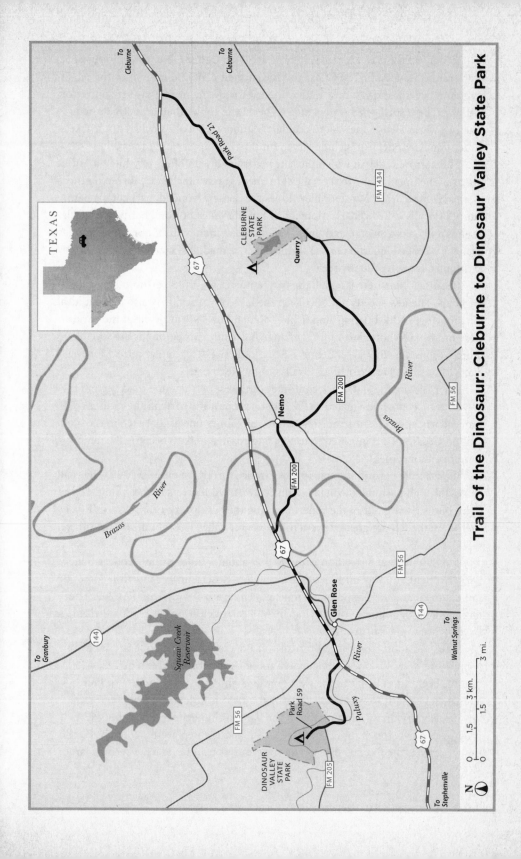

Trail of the Dinosaur: Cleburne to Dinosaur Valley State Park

TEXAS

To Cleburne

To Cleburne

Park Road 21

CLEBURNE STATE PARK

Quarry

FM 1434

FM 200

Nemo

FM 200

Brazos River

FM 56

River

Brazos

FM 56

67

To Granbury

144

Squaw Creek Reservoir

Brazos River

67

Glen Rose

144

To Walnut Springs

River

FM 56

Paluxy River

FM 56

Park Road 59

DINOSAUR VALLEY STATE PARK

FM 205

67

To Stephenville

N

0   1.5   3 km.
0   1.5   3 mi.

Springs feed the clear, cool waters of 116-acre **Cedar Lake,** the centerpiece of Cleburne State Park. The CCC built the earthen dam that impounds this small reservoir. Several springs, now under water, provide the primary water source for the lake. These spring-fed waters tend to be a little cooler than area stream-fed lakes. In winter, when the water is coldest, rainbow trout are stocked in the lake. Other popular sport fish include largemouth bass, crappie, and catfish.

The narrow valley in which the lake lies is lined with bluffs of white limestone. Much of the uplands above the valley are open, grassy ranch land as seen on the first part of the drive, but the valley slopes are densely wooded, particularly with juniper (locally called cedar). Along creeks in the valley bottom, hardwoods such as elms and oaks grow tall and thick. Wildflowers often blanket open, grassy areas near the park headquarters in the spring. Deer, armadillos, raccoons, opossums, and squirrels are frequently seen.

Because Cedar Lake is small, the park enforces a 5-mile-per-hour speed limit for boats. The low speeds not only keep the lake very quiet, they also make it ideal for canoeing, paddleboating, and fishing. Rental boats are available at the park store on the lakeshore. Swimming, hiking, and shady campgrounds are several more reasons why 529-acre Cleburne State Park makes a popular retreat for residents of bustling Fort Worth and Dallas to the northeast.

After leaving the state park continue southwest on the same road beyond the park entrance, now designated as FM 1434. Just past the park on the right is a giant quarry and cement plant. The same white limestone as that seen in the bluffs around Cedar Lake is quarried, crushed, and roasted here to become the main component of cement.

Only a mile beyond the state park entrance turn right onto FM 200. The road passes through pastoral grazing land dotted with wildflowers in the spring. To the right, bluffs rise up out of the valley, marking the edge of the broad Brazos River Valley. To the left are great views across the river valley to far bluffs on the other side.

FM 200 stops at a junction with FM 199 about 9 miles from Cleburne State Park. Go right and stay on FM 200 toward Glen Rose. Another junction comes up soon at the hamlet of Nemo in 0.6 mile; go left, again staying with FM 200. The huge containment domes of the Comanche Peak nuclear power plant are visible in the distance to the northwest.

The road soon crosses the Brazos River on a low bridge, about 3 miles from Nemo. The Brazos is one of the longest and most important rivers in Texas. Its humble beginnings lie far to the west on the High Plains of the southern Panhandle and eastern New Mexico. Initially the river is little more than a few shallow, usually dry draws winding across the flat terrain northwest of Lubbock. As it progresses downstream more tributaries join, and it enters wetter country. By the time it reaches the FM 200 bridge, the river and its tributaries have become large enough to fill several major lakes; the river is also a favorite of canoeists and inner-tubers. Two large and popular nearby lakes are Granbury and Whitney. Downstream from the FM 200 bridge, the river continues to swell in size, finally flowing into the Gulf of Mexico near Freeport after a course hundreds of mile long. Drives 23 and 25 both touch the Brazos at other places in Texas.

About half a mile after FM 200 crosses the Brazos River, the road intersects US 67. Go left onto US 67 to Glen Rose, located about 18 miles from Cleburne State Park. **Glen Rose** was started in 1849 with the establishment of a trading post on the banks of the Paluxy River a short distance upstream from its confluence with the Brazos River. The main route of US 67 through Glen Rose isn't too scenic, so consider detouring through the historic district on the left by following signs marked historic district. The route follows the Paluxy River to the old downtown square centered around the Somervell County Courthouse. The attractive courthouse was built in 1893 of the white limestone so common in the area. Several antiques and gift shops occupy space in the buildings around the square.

Dinosaur Valley State Park

From downtown Glen Rose return to US 67 and continue southwest a short distance to the junction with Park Road 59/FM 205 on the west side of town. Turn right onto Park Road 59/FM 205, following signs to **Dinosaur Valley State Park.** The road winds up the Paluxy River Valley through gentle hills. After 2.4 miles, it passes the Creation Evidences Museum on the right. The museum makes a case for creation science versus evolution. After another 0.5 mile, turn right and enter Dinosaur Valley State Park, the end of the drive.

Although dinosaur tracks are not uncommon in a swath of terrain running through the center of Texas, Dinosaur Valley State Park contains the best display in the state. About 105 million years ago, during the early Cretaceous Period, shallow seas washed over much of Texas. On mudflats near the shore of one of these seas, a giant sauropod called the Pleurocoelus grazed on evergreen foliage. A hungry, carnivorous Acrocanthosaurus spied the larger herbivore and began pursuit, leaving a trail of footprints across the soft mud. The final outcome of the fight is unknown; only the tracks remain. Over time sediment covered the footprints and the mud hardened into limestone. The Paluxy River eroded away the softer, overlying sediments, leaving the tracks exposed today in the riverbed.

The tracks were first discovered in 1908 but did not become widely known until Roland Bird of the American Museum of Natural History investigated the site in 1938. Since then, at least 2,000 tracks have been found in the riverbed of the Paluxy. The most common track is that of the three-toed Acrocanthosaurus. The footprints measure as much as 24 inches long and 17 inches wide. This 20- to

The Paluxy River has exposed many dinosaur tracks in its limestone bed through erosion.

30-foot-long carnivore belonged to the same group as the later, and larger, Tyrannosaurus rex.

The second type of track belonged to one of its prey animals, the 30- to 50-foot-long Pleurocoelus. This massive animal weighed as much as 30 tons and left tracks as large as 3 feet long and 2 feet wide. It was related to the even larger Apatosaurus, one of the biggest land animals of all time. Two full-size models of the Apatosaurus and Tyrannosaurus rex are displayed in the park.

The third type of track found in the park has been harder to identify. Researchers now believe the track belonged to 30-foot, 3-ton dinosaurs called Iguanodons. They were plant-eating creatures like the Pleurocoelus. Iguanodons too were probably pursued by the carnivorous Acrocanthosaurus.

Dinosaur Valley State Park contains one of the best displays of tracks in the world. Other sites are scattered throughout central Texas, from Glen Rose to Utopia, but they lie mostly on private land. The state park visitor center has elaborate exhibits that explain much about the giant reptiles.

Dinosaur tracks are visible in several areas of the Paluxy River bottom. The park is hot in summer, but at least you can wade around in the cool waters of the Paluxy River while you examine the tracks. The tracks attract most of the park visitors, but extensive hiking trails lead from the river to overlooks and primitive campsites in the hills to the north. The upland terrain, wooded with Ashe juniper, live oak, Texas red oak, and other trees, is similar to that of the Hill Country to the southwest. In the creek bottoms, cedar elm, American elm, and green ash dominate. Pecans, cottonwoods, sycamores, black willows, and walnuts thrive in the deep, moist soils along the river.

Many different animals inhabit the park, from wild turkeys to armadillos, raccoons to coyotes. They too leave tracks in the mud, but unless certain conditions act to preserve them, their prints will quickly disappear, unlike those of the dinosaurs that roamed this area millions of years ago.

After seeing the remains of ancient dinosaurs, consider seeing a broad array of modern wildlife at **Fossil Rim Wildlife Center.** This 2,900-acre preserve is home to many species of African wildlife, many rare or endangered. The center concentrates on African wildlife but also manages captive breeding programs for some species of endangered North American animals such as the Mexican wolf. A 9-mile drive allows viewing of many different wildlife species, including the reticulated giraffe, cheetah, Grevy's zebra, and white rhinoceros. The preserve also operates overnight safari camps. Fossil Rim lies off of US 67 about 3 miles west of Glen Rose.

12

Lakes & Caves

Marble Falls to Inks Lake

General description: A 25-mile paved route to several Colorado River lakes and Longhorn Cavern.

Special attractions: Inks Lake State Park, Longhorn Cavern State Park, Lake Marble Falls, hiking, boating, fishing, scenic views, wildflowers.

Location: Central Texas. The drive starts in Marble Falls, a town about 50 miles northwest of Austin.

Drive route numbers: US 281, Park Road 4.

Travel season: All year. Summers are hot, but Longhorn Cavern and the lake waters are cool. Spring and fall are probably the most pleasant times. Spring wildflowers are often excellent around Inks Lake.

Camping: Inks Lake State Park has large developed campgrounds, plus primitive camping for backpackers.

Services: Inks Lake State Park has a small store, and Longhorn Cavern has a snack bar. All services are available in Marble Falls and Burnet.

Nearby attractions: Enchanted Rock State Natural Area, Pedernales Falls State Park, National Museum of the Pacific War, Colorado Bend State Park, LBJ State and National Historical Parks, Fredericksburg, Lake Buchanan, Lake Lyndon B. Johnson.

For more information: Longhorn Cavern State Park, 6211 Park Rd. 4 South, Burnet, TX 78611; (830) 598-2283; www.longhorncavern.com. Inks Lake State Park, 3630 Park 4 West, Burnet, TX 78611; (512) 793-2223; www.tpwd.state.tx.us/spdest/findadest/parks/inks. Marble Falls/Lake LBJ Chamber of Commerce, 801 TX 281, Marble Falls, TX 78654; (830) 693-4449; www.marblefalls.org.

The Drive

The drive starts in Marble Falls, a Hill Country town located on the north shore of Lake Marble Falls. The town and lake were named for a beautiful Colorado River waterfall that once cascaded down a 22-foot-high series of limestone ledges, worn and polished by the water until they looked like marble. Sadly, the falls were drowned under the waters of the lake when Max Starcke Dam was completed in 1951. A side road just across the US 281 bridge from Marble Falls leads to an overlook of the dam and the Colorado River in its narrow limestone canyon.

Lake Marble Falls is one of a series of six lakes built in the heart of the Hill Country on the Colorado River. The Highland Lakes were built primarily for flood control and water conservation. In the 1800s and the early part of the 20th century, Austin and other cities regularly fell victim to massive floods that occurred when heavy rains fell on the overgrazed land of the Hill Country. A calamitous

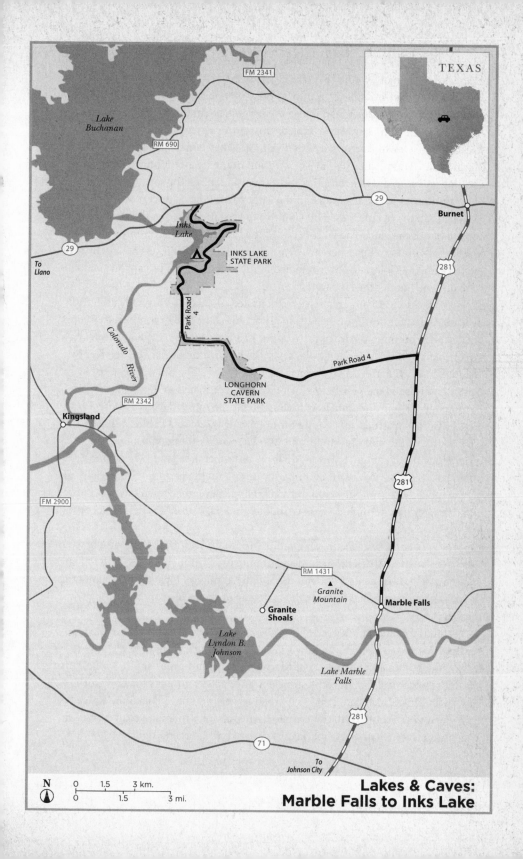

TEXAS

Lake
Buchanan

FM 2341

RM 690

29

Burnet

Inks
Lake

29

281

To
Llano

INKS LAKE
STATE PARK

Colorado
River

Park Road 4

Park Road 4

RM 2342

LONGHORN
CAVERN
STATE PARK

Kingsland

FM 2900

281

RM 1431

Granite
Mountain

Marble Falls

Granite
Shoals

Lake
Lyndon B.
Johnson

Lake Marble
Falls

281

71

To
Johnson City

N

0   1.5   3 km.
0   1.5   3 mi.

Lakes & Caves:
Marble Falls to Inks Lake

flood in 1935 finally spurred the federal government to approve some dam projects. Lake Buchanan was the first lake created when its dam was completed in 1938. At the time the dam—a multiple-arch concrete structure—was the largest of its type in the world. Buchanan is also the largest lake in the chain.

After Buchanan Dam was completed, an entire series of dams was built downstream all the way to Austin, forming five more lakes—Inks, Lyndon B. Johnson, Marble Falls, Travis, and Austin. The creation of the lakes not only halted the flooding and stored water for cities and agriculture, it also opened up recreational opportunities for Central Texans. In the early part of the century, many people had begun to move out of the Hill Country to the cities, tired of the struggle to eke a living out of the land. The lakes reversed the tide and resort communities such as Marble Falls grew and prospered. The price paid was high, however. Very little of the free-flowing Colorado River remains in the Hill Country; its canyons and falls were drowned under the lake waters.

As early as the 1850s, area settlers attempted to create a town at Marble Falls by using the water power of the falls to attract industry. Adam Johnson took up the task of promoting the town in 1854 but had little success for many years. A key element in his development plans was the acquisition of railroad service. By 1882 the railroad had reached Burnet, the county seat. The old state capitol in Austin had burned the year before, necessitating construction of a replacement. Fortunately for Johnson, much wrangling finally led to the decision to use Texas granite for its construction. Granite Mountain, just west of Marble Falls, was an ideal source of the building stone, and its owners offered the state all the granite it needed without charge. Johnson, no fool, and other area landowners quickly offered a free right-of-way for a railroad spur to haul the granite. With a railroad, his town finally began to develop, proving that perseverance often pays off in the end. His later plan to build a massive mill to gin area cotton was never successful, but the town grew anyway.

Today, a somewhat shrunken Granite Mountain is clearly visible on the west side of town, its quarries still producing granite used throughout the United States and the world. It is the first of a number of interesting geologic features along this drive. Lake recreation has become the mainstay of the local economy, along with the quarries.

From the center of Marble Falls, at the junction of US 281 and RM 1431, go north on US 281. The highway slowly climbs out of the Colorado River Valley, leaving the homes and businesses of Marble Falls behind. After about 8 miles, turn left onto Park Road 4, marked by stone entrance gates and signs for Longhorn Cavern and Inks Lake State Parks. The road travels west onto Backbone Ridge with views to the south of the river valley. After about 6 miles the road arrives at Longhorn Cavern State Park, marked by several buildings and signs.

Longhorn Cavern State Park

For many millennia, rainwater has been carving **Longhorn Cavern** from thick beds of Ellenburger Limestone. The cave lies on top of Backbone Ridge, a wedge of sedimentary rocks surrounded by billion-year-old igneous and metamorphic rocks. The limestone was laid down almost 500 million years ago in ancient seas that once covered Central Texas. In West Texas, the deeply buried Ellenburger is an important natural gas and oil reservoir rock.

As rain fell over the years, it picked up small amounts of carbon dioxide and became slightly acidic. It percolated through cracks and faults in the limestone, slowly dissolving chambers and passages. Later, flowing underground streams enlarged the passages, eroding them with suspended sand and silt. The water table fell and eventually dried out the cave. Unlike many caves, conditions were not right for large quantities of stalactites, stalagmites, and other dripstone decorations to form. However, large masses of sparkling calcite crystallized in some areas of the cave, and the erosive action of the water left smoothly sculptured, marblelike walls when it receded.

Fossil evidence indicates that the cave was used by animals that preyed on prehistoric camels, giant bison, and mammoths. Later, after humans appeared, early hunting cultures used the cave as a shelter. More recently Comanches camped in the cave and even, stories tell, battled with Texas Rangers in one of its chambers. During the Civil War, Confederate soldiers manufactured black powder in Longhorn Cavern, and later it was rumored to be a hideout for outlaws, including the notorious Sam Bass. Legend says that he hid a fortune in gold somewhere in the cave or nearby.

By the turn of the 20th century, the Comanches had been defeated and the outlaws routed. A local rancher constructed a wooden dance floor in the cave and created a popular gathering place. At times the cave served as a dance hall, church, nightclub, and restaurant.

The state of Texas acquired the cavern and dedicated it as a state park in 1932. During the Depression the men of the Civilian Conservation Corps made many improvements to the new park. They skillfully used native limestone and timber to construct buildings, retaining walls, an observation tower, and even bridge stonework along Park Road 4. They excavated 2.5 million cubic yards of sediment from cavern passages and chambers, built trails, and installed an electric lighting system. Their projects were built well, and most are still in use today. Interpretive exhibits, housed in the old administrative building, describe their work. Longhorn Cavern State Park does not have spectacular dripstone formations, but it does have attractive, smoothly sculptured passages mixed with an interesting history.

The cave is open all year by guided tour, except Christmas Eve and Christmas Day. The cavern temperature is a constant 64 degrees, so a sweater may be desired on tours. To ensure good footing be sure to wear comfortable, rubber-soled walking shoes. The park also offers interpretive exhibits, a gift shop, snack bar, picnic area, and nature trail.

After returning to the surface world, continue following Park Road 4 west from Longhorn Cavern. Be sure to stop at the **roadside picnic area** on the left after about 2 miles. Broad views of the Colorado River Valley sprawl out to the west, making the stop a great lunch spot. After the overlook, the road drops steeply into the valley. Note the grayish-white limestone beds in the road-cut. Just before you reach the junction with RM 2342 at the bottom of the hill, you cross a fault and the rock abruptly turns into pink granite. Like the granite being quarried at Marble Falls, this granite formed about a billion years ago when molten rock squeezed up into overlying rock layers and slowly cooled and hardened.

Inks Lake State Park

At the junction with RM 2342, stay right on Park Road 4 and travel north toward Inks Lake. The road follows the flat valley bottom for a bit and then climbs into some granite and gneiss hills at the south end of Inks Lake State Park. The small lake soon comes into view on the left, and the road passes the entrance road into the main recreational area after winding through the park for a little less than 2 miles.

The lake and state park are named for Llano businessman and mayor Roy Inks, who worked hard promoting the multiple dam projects on the Colorado River. Unfortunately, Inks did not live to see the projects built; a ruptured appendix plus a bout of pneumonia ended his life in August 1935, 3 years before the first dam, Buchanan, was completed. The Lower Colorado River Authority named the second dam and its reservoir in his honor.

Inks Lake State Park lines much of the eastern shore of Inks Lake on a solid bed of pinkish Valley Spring gneiss. The hard metamorphic rock resembles the pink granite of Marble Falls and nearby Enchanted Rock. The gneiss formed when buried volcanic and sedimentary rocks were recrystallized by intense heat and pressure. The rock is more than 1.3 billion years old and possibly the oldest rock in Texas. Outcrops of it are common throughout the park.

Vegetation cloaks the rocky hills of the state park. Ashe juniper, live oak, and mesquite are common on the rocky slopes; cedar elm, pecan, and hickory prefer the deeper, moister soils along creek bottoms. In spring, arrays of bluebonnets, Indian paintbrushes, and Indian blankets splash color across open fields and hills, seeming to favor the granite and metamorphic soils.

Wildlife thrives at Inks Lake, and in fact, some animals are almost tame. White-tailed deer roam the campgrounds, searching for deer corn and other handouts. At night raccoons brazenly raid food carelessly left out by campers. Wild turkeys, armadillos, opossums, and other animals also frequent the area.

Mist rises from Inks Lake on a chilly spring morning.

To get to most of the recreational facilities, turn into the entrance road and take a break from the drive. Extensive campgrounds hug the lakeshore, tucked into the trees. Fishing piers and a boat ramp make access easy for anglers wanting to pursue striped bass, white bass, catfish, and other species. More than 7 miles of hiking trails wind through hills of ancient gneiss to overlooks and a primitive camping area. Although the lake is relatively small, it is still large enough for water skiers and sailboats. The extensive recreational opportunities at Inks Lake make it one of the state's most popular parks.

After leaving the main recreational area, Park Road 4 continues to wind through the park. After about 2 miles a pullout on the left overlooks the Devil's Waterhole, a rocky canyon carved into the Valley Spring gneiss by Spring Creek. A narrow channel of Inks Lake fills the lower end of it, making it a popular swimming hole.

After another mile, the road passes the nine-hole Inks Lake State Park golf course, a rarity in the Texas state park system. The course borders the lakeshore,

A fishing pier extends out into the calm waters of Inks Lake.

creating a large water hazard for golfers who have not refined their strokes. A short distance beyond the golf course, this drive ends where Park Road 4 terminates at the junction with TX 29.

The large Buchanan Dam is only 2 or 3 miles west along TX 29. Beyond the dam is the town of Llano, the start of Drive 13, another interesting Hill Country route. To the east is Burnet, the northwestern terminus of the **Hill Country Flyer,** a historic steam train that chugs back and forth between Burnet and Cedar Park, a small suburb of Austin. For those returning to Marble Falls, consider retracing Park Road 4 through Inks Lake State Park to the junction of RM 2342. Take RM 2342 to Kingsland on the shores of Lake Lyndon B. Johnson. Turn left onto RM 1431 in Kingsland and follow it back to Marble Falls. Along the way it climbs to a beautiful overlook on the south end of Backbone Ridge, high above the waters of Lake Lyndon B. Johnson, and passes the massive quarry at Granite Mountain.

13

Enchanted Rock

Llano to Fredericksburg

General description: A 42-mile paved highway through the Central Texas mineral region, including Enchanted Rock, to the historic German town of Fredericksburg.

Special attractions: Enchanted Rock State Natural Area, Admiral Nimitz State Historic Site and National Museum of the Pacific War, Fredericksburg, hiking, camping, scenic views, wildflowers, rockhounding, rock climbing.

Location: Central Texas. The drive starts in Llano, about 75 miles northwest of Austin.

Drive route numbers: TX 16, RM 965.

Travel season: All year. Summers are hot, making fall and spring the most pleasant times. Wildflowers are usually abundant in Apr and May.

Camping: Enchanted Rock State Natural Area maintains tent sites and primitive camping, but no RV sites.

Services: All services are available in Llano and Fredericksburg.

Nearby attractions: Inks Lake State Park, Longhorn Cavern State Park, Lake Buchanan, LBJ State and National Historical Parks, Colorado Bend State Park.

For more information: Enchanted Rock State Natural Area, 16710 Ranch Rd. 965, Fredericksburg, TX 78624; (325) 247-3903; www.tpwd.state.tx.us/spdest/findadest/parks/enchanted_rock. National Museum of the Pacific War, 340 E. Main, Fredericksburg, TX 78624; (830) 997-4379; www.pacificwarmuseum.org. Fredericksburg Chamber of Commerce, 302 East Austin, Fredericksburg, TX 78624; (830) 997-6523; www.fredricksburg-texas.com. Llano Chamber of Commerce, 100 Train Station Dr., Llano, TX 78643; (325) 247-5354; www.llanochamber.org.

The Drive

This drive passes through one of the most scenic parts of Central Texas, interesting not only to sightseers but also to geologists. Over the years a vast array of minerals have been found in the Llano area, including gold, silver, asbestos, marble, serpentine, fluorite, molybdenum, and iron. At one time a mine near Burnet was the nation's largest graphite producer. Large quantities of topaz have been produced in adjoining Mason County, mostly by amateur rock hounds. The largest gem-quality topaz in North America was found there and weighed an incredible 1,298 carats, or 2 pounds 13.7 ounces. Granite is by far the most important mineral resource produced in the Llano area. It has been used in everything from the Texas State Capitol in Austin to navigation jetties along the Gulf Coast. The attractive, colorful granite has been exported far beyond Texas—it appears in buildings from Asia to Europe.

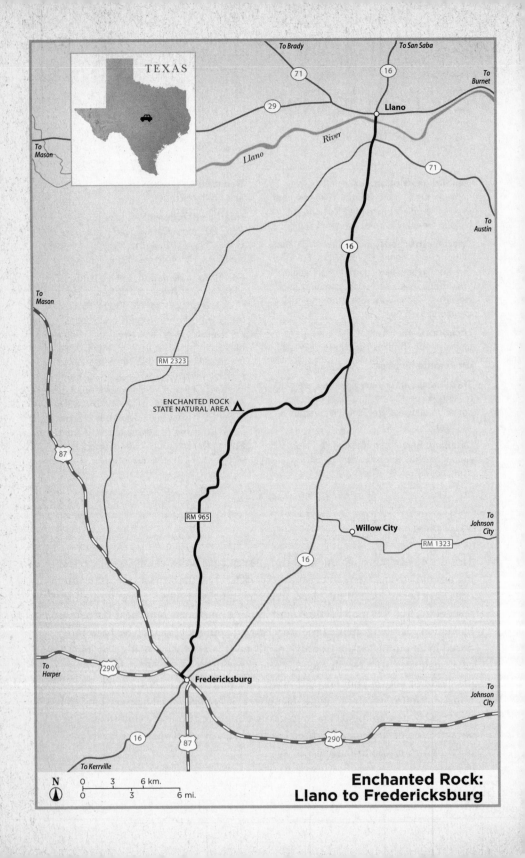

TEXAS

To Brady

To San Saba

71

16

To Burnet

29

Llano

71

To Austin

To Mason

Llano River

16

To Mason

RM 2323

ENCHANTED ROCK
STATE NATURAL AREA

87

RM 965

Willow City

To Johnson City

16

RM 1323

To Harper

290

Fredericksburg

To Johnson City

16

87

To Kerrville

290

N

0   3   6 km.
0   3   6 mi.

**Enchanted Rock:
Llano to Fredericksburg**

One interesting mineral, **llanite,** is unique to the area and was named, appropriately enough, for the town and county. The rock is a striking form of granite with crystals of pink feldspar and bluish quartz floating in a dark background matrix. The rock can be found in a road-cut about 9 miles north of Llano on TX 16 where the road crosses an igneous dike of llanite just before a roadside picnic area on the left. The llanite formed about 1.1 billion years ago when molten magma squeezed into vertical cracks and hardened within an older rock known as Packsaddle schist.

Llano

Much of the early growth of the town of Llano, at the start of this drive, was fueled by mineral speculation in the late 1800s. Before that time Llano was a raw, frontier ranching and farming town. It was founded in 1855 on the banks of the Llano River and soon became the county seat after a hotly contested election. The town name is ironic in this hilly country, because llano means "plain" in Spanish.

Comanche attacks were common in the area, particularly during the Civil War when troops were fighting far away. The Indian conflict did not finally end until after the Battle of Packsaddle Mountain in August 1873. Rustlers and bandits also commonly preyed on travelers and settlers during the town's early years.

In the 1880s deposits of magnetite, a type of iron ore, were discovered near Llano, precipitating a mining boom. Little iron was ever produced, however, in large part because of the lack of nearby coal deposits for use in smelting the ore. In 1894 the speculative boom ended, and Llano suffered through bankruptcies, fires, and even a tornado. Spurred by the building of the State Capitol, granite began to be quarried in the Llano and Marble Falls areas. The granite industry peaked in the 1930s, but large quantities of granite are still removed from the area today.

A number of historic buildings in Llano are of interest. The attractive, tree-shaded courthouse dominates the town square on the south side of the river. This ornate building was completed in 1893, making it one of the oldest county courthouses in Texas. Unlike many courthouses it was not torn down and replaced or added to over the years, so it still retains its architectural integrity. Across the river on the north side of town on TX 71 is the Llano County Museum and the historic Badu House. The Badu House was owned by Professor N. J. Badu, one of Llano's most ardent mineral prospectors and speculators.

Before beginning this drive, consider trying some of Llano's excellent barbecue at Cooper's, Inman Kitchen, or Laird's. I've eaten most recently at Cooper's and was pleased with both the quality and price.

Enchanted Rock

Start the drive at the courthouse and head south on combined TX 16 and TX 71. TX 71 soon splits off to the left; continue south on TX 16. The road quickly leaves town and passes through granite hills and scattered ranches dotted with oaks and mesquites. After about 15 miles, turn right onto RM 965, toward **Enchanted Rock State Natural Area.** RM 965 is narrow and at times crosses open range, so watch for cattle, especially at night. After a little less than 3 miles, watch for the first glimpse of the massive granite dome of Enchanted Rock in the distance ahead.

Rock hounds will want to stop at a low road-cut on the right 5.8 miles from the junction. I have found what appeared to my unpracticed eye to be asbestos ore (don't grind it up and inhale it!) and soapstone, a soft, soapy-feeling rock.

Enchanted Rock looms large when you reach the state natural area entrance on the right after about 3 more miles. Be sure to stop; it's one of the highlights of the entire Hill Country. Legends surround Enchanted Rock, the huge granite dome towering over the entrance road. Early settlers, including Stephen F. Austin, told of Indian ceremonies being held at Enchanted Rock because it was considered sacred. Many Indians feared the rock, believing it to be haunted, and would not climb to its summit. Tales were even told of human sacrifices made by the Comanches, and pioneers reported odd noises emanating from the rock and strange fires on its summit. The many stories swirling around the dome led to it being named Enchanted Rock early in the 1800s.

In 1978 the site came under Texas Parks and Wildlife Department stewardship. The natural area contains Enchanted Rock, an enormous curving dome of pinkish granite that towers 445 feet above Sandy Creek. Several smaller peaks and domes surround the main rock within the natural area, including Little Rock, Turkey Peak, Freshman Mountain, and Buzzard's Roost.

The domes within the natural area are but a small part of the **Enchanted Rock batholith** that is exposed to the surface in an area of more than 60 square miles. The batholith formed when a huge mass of molten rock, or magma, intruded into the Packsaddle schist below the surface and cooled slowly, crystallizing into granite. Over time the area was uplifted and erosion removed the concealing layers of rock, exposing the batholith to the surface. The granite is ancient, approximately a billion years old, and has been buried by new rock layers and exposed repeatedly as seas have come and gone in past geologic ages.

Once the batholith was exposed to the surface, erosion shaped it into its present form. Geologists call Enchanted Rock an exfoliation dome because of the way plates of rock break off the dome, or exfoliate, in thin curving layers, similar to the layers of an onion. The granite formed deep underground under tremendous pressure. As the rock overburden was eroded away, the pressure lessened and the rock expanded a tiny amount, causing it to fracture in thin curving sheets. Freezing and thawing water also helped split the rocks of the dome. The strange noises reported

Large granite boulders lie on the slopes of Enchanted Rock.

at Enchanted Rock may be nothing more than creaks made as the rock heats and cools with temperature changes between day and night.

Other granite outcrops in the area have been heavily quarried for beautiful stone similar to that making up Enchanted Rock. Fortunately, Enchanted Rock, the largest granite dome in Texas and second largest in the United States, escaped such a fate. Since pioneers moved into the Hill Country, it has been an important landmark and tourist attraction. As a state natural area, it continues to increase in popularity.

From a distance much of the rock appears bare and devoid of life. Closer inspection reveals plant communities thriving in pockets of soil eroded from the dome. Colorful lichens grow on the rock itself, while mosses, grasses, ferns, and flowers blanket small pockets of soil. In deeper soils prickly pear cacti and even oak trees find a toehold. Some moist, shady crevices hold rare plants, such as the rock quillwort, basin bellflower, and even a tropical fern. Around the base, cedar elms, mesquites, pecans, hickories, and oaks grow in deep soils.

A rock climber ascends the sheer northwest face of Enchanted Rock late in the day.

The strong, well-consolidated granite of Enchanted Rock draws rock climbers from all over Texas. Only Hueco Tanks State Park in far West Texas offers as good a climbing area. On a pleasant spring or fall weekend, climbers tackle everything from boulders at the base of the rock to the high cliffs on the northwest side of the main dome. A trail system circles Enchanted Rock and some of the smaller domes, also leading to several primitive backpacking campsites. A cave near the summit is also a popular site with park visitors. It was formed when boulders roofed over a deep crack in the dome.

Most people visit simply to make the irresistible climb to the summit, a short but steep walk. Lie back on the smooth granite and enjoy the 360-degree view, one of the best in the Hill Country. Gentle, cooling breezes greet hikers on the bare summit. Vultures circle high overhead, attracted by rising thermals and good roosting sites. As the sun sets to the west and darkness descends, listen for the sounds of the rock and imagine the ancient Indian ceremonies once held here.

The park is very busy on nice spring and fall weekends; try to arrive early at those times or come on weekdays. When all the parking spaces in the park fill up on busy weekends, you have to wait in line outside the park for people to leave before you can enter. Be sure to keep an eye on children near cliffs. Climbers must first register at park headquarters. No bolts, pitons, or other rock-damaging equipment are allowed.

Fredericksburg

From Enchanted Rock continue south on RM 965 toward Fredericksburg. In about 3 miles the road climbs out of the valley surrounding the rock onto a limestone ridge and then drops into another valley. Several historic buildings can be found around the old settlement of Crabapple on a county road on the left.

The road continues south, crossing ridges and valleys with scattered farms and ranches. A little more than 13 miles from Enchanted Rock, another granite outcrop, Bear Mountain, appears on the left side of the road, complete with rock quarries. At one time a short trail led from the small rest area at the base of the mountain to a balanced granite rock. Unfortunately vandals dynamited the formation a number of years ago, leaving only rubble.

After a few more miles, the road drops off a ridge and into the valley containing the town of Fredericksburg. The town was settled by Germans in 1846 after the Republic of Texas had caught the interest of a number of German noblemen. These noblemen established a society, called the Adelsverein, to obtain land in Texas for colonizing. Between 1845 and 1847 thousands of German immigrants landed on the Texas shores and moved inland. Prince Carl of Solms-Braunfels founded New Braunfels in March 1845 but soon returned to Germany, leaving Baron Ottfried Hans Von Meusebach as head of the Adelsverein in Texas. To fit into the new land the baron quickly dropped his title and became John O. Meusebach.

Meusebach purchased 10,000 acres of land near the Pedernales River and started his colonists on their way to the tract in late April 1846. Arrival in the untamed wilderness that was then central Texas must have been a shock to the newly arrived Germans. Although the new settlers were inexperienced in survival on the frontier, they quickly set to work planting crops and laying out the town of Fredericksburg. Hardship and disease made life difficult, but the colonists and subsequent settlers persevered. In the following year a group of Mormons settled nearby and established the community of Zodiac. The Mormons were more experienced at frontier life and helped the greenhorn Germans. Unlike many Texas settlers, Meusebach negotiated a peace treaty with the Comanches, alleviating one of the major threats to frontier life.

In 1848 the military opened Fort Martin Scott on the east side of town to protect the road west to El Paso and California. Because of Meusebach's treaty, the

Snow falls on oak trees along RM 965, an uncommon occurrence in the Hill Country.

fort was little needed for the town's protection, but it did supply hard currency to the town's businesses. Waves of Forty-Niners passing through on their way to California brought not only prosperity to the growing town but also deadly epidemics of cholera and typhoid.

The German settlers of Fredericksburg were conservative and opposed the secession of Texas from the Union at the start of the Civil War. Although the townspeople did not own slaves and most disliked slavery, they believed that a solution could be found to the practice without going to war. There was strong Union sentiment in Fredericksburg and surrounding Gillespie County; 96 percent of the county's electorate voted against secession.

After the war, Fredericksburg competed heavily for a railroad with nearby Kerrville and lost (see Drives 15 and 17). The first train chugged into Kerrville in 1887; Fredericksburg had to wait until 1913 before trains rolled into town.

Today, Fredericksburg remains heavily influenced by its German heritage. Perhaps half of the residents are of German extraction, although very little

German is spoken anymore. During World War II, the townsfolk stopped speaking German or teaching it to their children; after the war the practice never resumed. However, numerous German place names, business names, and family names remind visitors of the town's heritage.

The German settlers built durable, attractive homes and businesses out of locally quarried limestone and granite. The town today is a veritable treasure trove of immaculately maintained historic buildings. Numerous structures sport historic designation plaques; many others could. The second courthouse, now a library, on the west side of downtown is particularly attractive. It was built in 1882 in the Romanesque Revival style of limestone with intricate wrought-iron trim.

The main street through downtown is lined with interesting buildings, many of which host antiques and gift shops and galleries. Bed-and-breakfast inns now occupy a number of the old historic homes. Many restaurants and shops specialize in German fare, including many different types of sausage.

The National Museum of the Pacific War, operated by the Texas Historical Commission, lies on a 6-acre site on the east side of town. It is the only institution in the continental United States dedicated to chronicling the Pacific Theater battles of World War II. The museum comprises numerous buildings, galleries, historic aircraft, tanks and guns, as well as gardens and outdoor memorials.

The Admiral Nimitz Museum, formerly Admiral Nimitz State Historic Site, is on the southeast corner of the museum complex, housed in an odd-looking structure built to resemble the superstructure of a ship. The Steamboat Hotel, as it was known, was first established in 1852 by colonists Charles and Sophie Nimitz. Because of its location on the road west, it quickly grew and became a popular, prosperous place. Over the years, it hosted many famous guests, including Ulysses S. Grant, Robert E. Lee, and the notorious Jesse James.

On February 24, 1885, Chester Nimitz, Charles Nimitz's grandson, was born in a modest home in Fredericksburg. Chester's father died before he was born, and he spent many of his early years at the hotel, making Charles a very important influence in his life. Chester entered the Naval Academy and progressed up the military ladder, finally becoming an admiral. In December 1941, Admiral Nimitz became commander in chief in the Pacific after the Japanese attacked Pearl Harbor. Under his command were thousands of ships and planes and millions of people, more military power than had ever been assembled before under one man. With the skilled leadership of Nimitz and his staff, the United States fought and won a long, brutal war in the Pacific.

Using a strategy of island hopping, American forces led by Nimitz slowly pushed the Japanese back toward Japan, island by island. Massive sea battles such as Midway and Coral Sea, and bitter land battles such as Guadalcanal, Iwo Jima, and Saipan were extremely costly in lives and materials on both sides. Finally, by mid-1945, the Japanese had been driven back to their homeland but were unwilling to surrender. An invasion of well-defended Japan might have cost several million lives before the Japanese military was subdued. To end the war quickly, the agonizing decision to drop newly developed atomic bombs on Hiroshima and Nagasaki was made. Five days after the bombs were dropped, the Japanese surrendered. Admiral Nimitz signed the Instrument of Surrender on the battleship Missouri in Tokyo Bay on September 2, 1945, formally ending World War II.

Behind the Admiral Nimitz Museum is the Japanese Garden of Peace, built using money raised by the people of Japan as a symbol of friendship between the United States and Japan. Within the classic garden is an exact replica of the study of Admiral Togo, the leader of the Japanese fleet. Although they were on opposite sides, Nimitz always had great admiration for Togo.

Also within the complex is the **Pacific Combat Zone.** A trail winds through relics of the war and provides a historical narrative. Exhibits include planes, tanks, guns, parts of ships, and even a bomb casing identical to that of the atomic bomb dropped on Nagasaki. The exhibits of the park chronicle the life of Chester Nimitz and the events in the Pacific Theater of World War II, but the Japanese Garden of Peace symbolizes the hope of the people of the United States and Japan that such a bloody conflict never occurs again. All told, the museum complex covers 9 acres and more than 74,000 square feet of exhibits. Other highlights include a captured Japanese midget submarine and a life-size diorama of a South Pacific army camp.

Look carefully before you leave Fredericksburg and you may notice the first letters of the cross streets heading east along Main Street from the center of town spell "all welcome." Heading west from the center of town, the letters spell "come back." Fredericksburg and the other sites along this drive can easily occupy more than a day. Chances are, you probably will come back.

Willow City Loop

14

General description: A 22-mile paved route through a particularly rugged area of the Hill Country noted for its excellent spring wildflowers.

Special attractions: Wildflowers, scenic views.

Location: Central Texas. The drive starts at the junction of TX 16 and RM 1323 about 13 miles north of Fredericksburg.

Drive route numbers: TX 16, Willow City Loop, RM 1323.

Travel season: All year. The drive is hot in summer. Fall and spring are the most pleasant times of year. The drive can be spectacular from late Mar through May during a good wildflower season.

Camping: There are no camping facilities on this route. The closest public campground is at Enchanted Rock State Natural Area, but it does not have RV sites. Inks Lake and Pedernales Falls State Parks have more elaborate camping facilities.

Services: Food can be purchased during limited hours in Willow City. All services are available in Fredericksburg and Llano.

Nearby attractions: Enchanted Rock State Natural Area, Inks Lake State Park, Longhorn Cavern State Park, Pedernales Falls State Park, National Museum of the Pacific War, LBJ State and National Historical Parks, Fredericksburg.

For more information: Fredericksburg Chamber of Commerce, 302 East Austin, Fredericksburg, TX 78624; (830) 997-6523; www.fredericksburg-texas.com. Llano Chamber of Commerce, 100 Train Station Dr., Llano, TX 78643; (325) 247-5354; www.llanochamber.org.

The Drive

In recent years the Willow City Loop has been discovered as one of the best places in the Hill Country to see fields of Texans' favorite flower, the bluebonnet. Through some fortuitous combination of soil type, rainfall, and grazing practices, bluebonnets seem to thrive in this area. In a good year, preceded by the right amount of rain falling at the right time, bluebonnets blanket the hills.

Bluebonnets first start appearing in mid- to late March and usually peak sometime in early to mid-April. Although the bluebonnet dominates at this time, other flowers, such as the white prickly poppy and a number of yellow flowers, are also common. Indian paintbrush commonly grows mixed in with bluebonnets in other parts of the Hill Country, but it doesn't seem quite as common here.

Although wildflowers are probably the primary attraction of this drive, the rugged setting is almost as scenic as the flowers and makes the drive worthwhile at

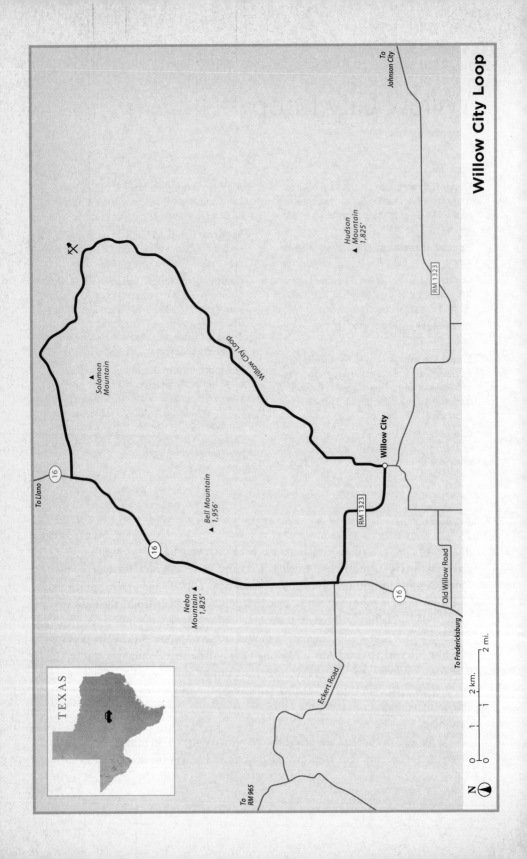

Willow City Loop

other times of the year. Plus, traffic created by other sightseers almost disappears once the wildflowers fade.

Start the drive by heading north from Fredericksburg on TX 16 about 12 to 15 miles to the junction with RM 1323. Although the drive continues north on TX 16, it makes a full loop and returns to this junction on RM 1323.

Llano Uplift

This area of Texas is part of the Llano Uplift, an area in the center of the Hill Country known for its ancient rocks and interesting minerals. Beginning more than a billion years ago, the rocks here began to form. Mountains rose up and were worn down by erosion. Seas came and went, leaving deposits of limestone and other sedimentary rocks. Molten magma forced its way up into older rocks and hardened into granite. Eventually the area was uplifted and the newer rocks were eroded away, exposing ancient granite, gneiss, and schist more than a billion years old. A number of valuable rocks and minerals have been mined over the years in the Llano Uplift area, the most important of which is granite used for building material. Note how the soils and rocks change continuously throughout this drive.

Drive north on TX 16 from the RM 1323 junction, initially through open fields. The road then slowly drops down into a broad valley through several granite hills. About 6 miles north from the junction, turn right onto Willow City Loop, marked with a yellow sign. The road is paved, but it is narrow and winding with wandering cattle and blind curves and hills, so drive slowly and carefully. Large RVs may have some difficulty with the road. Watch for prominent private property and no trespassing signs. As the loop has become better known, thoughtless people have abused the landowners' property. The landowners have become touchy about trespassers, so please stay on the right-of-way and don't enter private land without permission.

In spring the first bluebonnets appear a short distance down the road. For the first 3 miles or so, the road crosses a broad valley, but then it climbs a small divide and drops into a narrow canyon walled in by cliffs of limestone rimrock. The intermittent stream that flows down the canyon is a tributary of Coal Creek. Its deep canyon, dotted with cedar elms and oaks and blanketed with bluebonnets in the spring, is probably the most scenic part of the drive.

As the canyon opens up into a broad valley, a large quarry is visible to the left of the road. Serpentine is mined here, the only such quarry in Texas. This soft, greenish-white rock polishes well and carves easily. It is commonly used in terrazzo floors, sculpture, and interior trim in commercial buildings. There are a number of serpentine outcroppings within the Llano Uplift, but this is the largest. The quarry is privately owned, but you can see what serpentine looks like by examining pieces of it along the shoulder by the quarry entrance road.

Longhorn cattle graze in the bluebonnets along Willow City Loop.

Willow City

After the quarry the road winds through a valley for 3 miles before climbing up through granite outcroppings onto a ridge. The view back across the Coal Creek Valley and the surrounding rocky hills is excellent. The road then crosses a relatively level plateau for a few miles before reaching tiny **Willow City.** It ends at the junction with RM 1323 in the center of the village.

Willow City was founded in the 1870s along Willow Creek. A flood in 1880 almost destroyed the town and encouraged residents to move to the present location on higher ground a little northwest of the original townsite. Willow City is a sleepy settlement today, with the school and most churches and businesses closed. A small store sells snacks, barbecue, and ranch supplies near the junction.

Turn right onto RM 1323 and follow it west about 3 miles to the end of the drive at the junction with TX 16 where you started. This drive can be easily combined with Drive 13 to Enchanted Rock and the interesting towns of Fredericksburg and Llano. For an interesting back road to Enchanted Rock, go right a very short distance on TX 16 to Eckert Road, a paved county road on the left (really almost a continuation of RM 1323).

Follow Eckert Road west, turning right at the intersection with Lower Crabapple Road, and pass through the tiny community of Crabapple. At the junction with RM 965, go right to Enchanted Rock.

15

The Old Tunnel

Comfort to Luckenbach

General description: A 23-mile paved drive through Hill Country back roads from the German-settled town of Comfort along the route of the former Fredericksburg and Northern Railway to Luckenbach, the small village of country music fame.

Special attractions: Old Tunnel Wildlife Management Area, Luckenbach, abandoned railroad tunnel, large bat colony, scenic views.

Location: Central Texas. The drive starts in Comfort, about 50 miles northwest of San Antonio on I-10.

Drive route numbers: RM 473, county roads, RM 1376.

Travel season: All year. The drive is hot in summer, but the evening bat flights at Old Tunnel Wildlife Management Area are best in summer and early fall. Otherwise, spring and fall have the most pleasant temperatures for travel.

Camping: There is no public camping along this route. The closest sites are in Kerrville

Schreiner Park and Enchanted Rock State Natural Area.

Services: All services are available in Comfort and nearby Fredericksburg. Drinks and snacks can be obtained at Luckenbach.

Nearby attractions: Hill Country State Natural Area, Kerrville State Park, National Museum of the Pacific War, LBJ State and National Historical Parks, Guadalupe River State Park, Fredericksburg.

For more information: Old Tunnel Wildlife Management Area, 10619 Old San Antonio Rd., Fredericksburg, TX 78624; (866) 978-2287; www.tpwd.state.tx.us. Comfort Chamber of Commerce, P.O. Box 777, Comfort, TX 78013; (830) 995-3131; www .comfort-texas.com. Fredericksburg Chamber of Commerce, 302 East Austin, Fredericksburg, TX 78624; (830) 997-6523; www.fredericksburg-texas.com. Luckenbach General Store, 412 Luckenbach Town Loop, Fredericksburg, TX 78624; (830) 997-3224; www.luckenbachtexas.com.

The Drive

The drive follows much of the former route of the old San Antonio–Fredericksburg Road and the Fredericksburg and Northern Railway as it climbs over the divide separating the watersheds of the Guadalupe and Pedernales Rivers. At the top of the divide, the drive reaches the high point, literally and figuratively, at a long railroad tunnel cut through a ridge. The tunnel, a rarity in relatively flat Texas, once carried trains under the divide but now hosts a population of up to three million bats.

The drive starts in Comfort, a small town on the Guadalupe River about 20 miles downstream from Kerrville. The town was founded by German immigrants in 1854 who, some stories say, named the town Comfort because it was the first

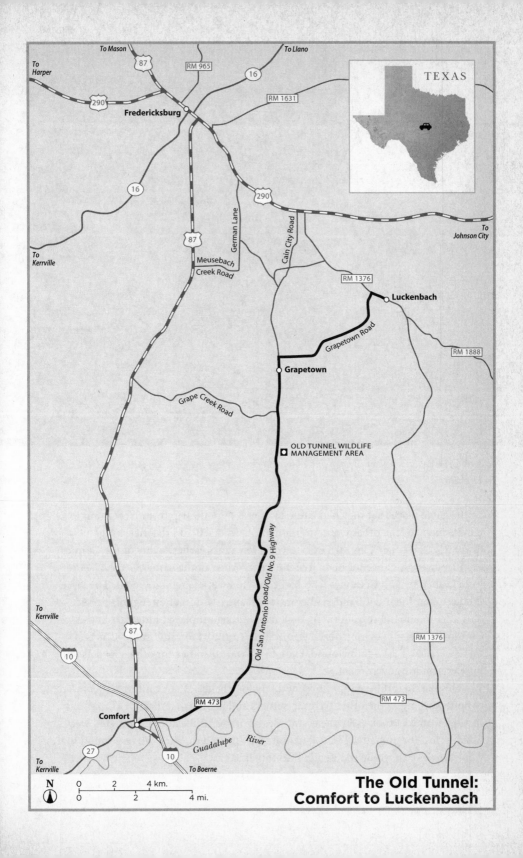

To Mason
To Harco
To Llano
87
RM 965
16
290
RM 1631
Fredericksburg

TEXAS

16

To Johnson City
290

87

To Kerrville

German Lane

Cain City Road

Meusebach Creek Road

RM 1376
Luckenbach

Grapetown Road

RM 1888

Grapetown

Grape Creek Road

OLD TUNNEL WILDLIFE
MANAGEMENT AREA

Old San Antonio Road/Old No. 9 Highway

To Kerrville

87

10

RM 1376

RM 473

RM 473

Comfort

27

10

Guadalupe River

To Kerrville

To Boerne

N

0   2   4 km.
0   2   4 mi.

**The Old Tunnel:
Comfort to Luckenbach**

Hay fields lie on some of the benches above Block Creek along Old San Antonio Road/Old Highway 9.

comfortable place that they had come to after a difficult trip from New Braunfels. Unlike many of the other German immigrants who settled Fredericksburg, New Braunfels, and other Central Texas towns a few years earlier, many of the Comfort founders were highly educated "free thinkers." Most of the earlier German settlers were Lutherans and Catholics who had come to escape unemployment. The "free thinkers," on the other hand, had come to escape political and religious persecution after the liberal revolution of 1848 failed. Religion played little part in the Comfort settlers' lives; no church was built in Comfort for almost 40 years and there were few Bibles to be found. Here there was tolerance for others' beliefs and little esteem for government.

Despite their different political and religious beliefs, the Comfort settlers were as hard working as the other German settlers and soon had a thriving community. In 1860 Comfort took away the county seat from Kerrville after a contested election but lost it again after Kendall County was created in 1862. Surveys found that Comfort was just inside the Kendall County line.

The **Treue Der Union** (True to the Union) monument in Comfort memorializes a sad chapter in the town's history. As with the majority of German settlers, most Comfort residents opposed Texas's secession from the Union and were persecuted by Confederates for their sympathies. On July 4, 1862, men from Kendall, Kerr, and Gillespie Counties founded the Union Loyal League. In response the Confederate government declared the area as being in open rebellion and subject to martial law. To reduce this tension the league dissolved itself. The 68 members, including many from Comfort, who did not wish to live under Confederate rule, met on August 1 at Turtle Creek in Kerr County to flee to Mexico. They left for Mexico that day and made it to the Nueces River near Brackettville about a week later.

Not fearing Confederate action they camped for the night in a poorly defended position with a poor guard. The next morning Confederate cavalry attacked before dawn, killing 19 and capturing nine, who were quickly executed. Forty escaped, of which another six were captured and executed; the rest made it to Mexico or returned home. The men killed at the Nueces were left to rot on the battlefield, and the bones were not retrieved and buried in Comfort until the end of the war.

After the Civil War, cotton farming thrived in the Guadalupe River Valley. The San Antonio and Aransas Pass Railroad arrived in 1887 on its way to Kerrville, making the town an important cotton shipping center. Because Comfort was cooler and drier than much of the rest of Texas to the east and south, it became a summer resort destination after the turn of the century. An ostrich farm was attempted near Comfort in 1914 but was never successful. Later Charles Apelt ran an armadillo farm—probably the only one in the world—a few miles outside of town.

Comfort is one of the largest and oldest unincorporated towns in Texas, part of the heritage of its free-thinking founders. The town has a philosophy of little government and taking care of its own. The schools, parks, fire department, library, and other facilities usually created and managed by city government have all been developed through donations and the efforts of volunteers.

Comfort boasts a wealth of buildings dating from the 1800s and early 1900s centered around the historic business district. A few bed-and-breakfasts and antiques shops have appeared, but Comfort is still a quiet alternative to popular Fredericksburg to the north. One historic building, the **Ingehuett Faust Hotel,** was built in the late 1800s and now houses an antiques shop and a bed-and-breakfast called the Comfort Common. The rooms open off a large veranda that overlooks a shady private courtyard with a gazebo.

From Comfort start the drive by taking RM 473 east from the center of town. After a bit more than 1 mile, the road crosses under I-10. At 0.5 mile farther down the road, watch carefully on the right for a strange structure that looks like a church steeple—without the church—in the back of a fruit orchard. The odd building is a bat roost, created in the early part of the century in an effort to encourage the local bat population. At the time, mosquitoes in Texas commonly carried diseases such as malaria and yellow fever, especially in warm, marshy coastal areas. Because bats eat hordes of mosquitoes and other insects, a number of bat roosts were constructed to control mosquito populations. A side benefit was the guano produced by the roosts; it made an excellent fertilizer. This roost is the only one of its type remaining.

Building of the Railroads

After another 2 miles, by a large old stone house on the left, look to the right for an abandoned railroad trestle crossing the Guadalupe River. The bridge is a visible remnant of the railroad system that once helped bring improved transportation and business prosperity to this part of the Hill Country.

Before the turn of the 20th century, a railroad could bring growth and permanence to a community; lack of rails could eventually spell doom for a town. By the 1880s Kerrville and Fredericksburg needed a railroad for improved transportation and shipping, and both competed heavily for the development of a line. Led by influential businessman Charles Schreiner, Kerrville won the fight and the San Antonio and Aransas Pass Railroad was built up the Guadalupe River Valley to Kerrville, arriving there in 1887. The railroad's route probably was determined in part by the expense and difficulty in laying tracks over the divide between Fredericksburg and Comfort.

Fredericksburg did not give up, however, and after more than 30 years of fund-raising and politicking, construction began on the town's own line, the **Fredericksburg and Northern Railway.** To reach Fredericksburg the railroad had to cross a range of steep hills separating the watersheds of the Guadalupe and Pedernales Rivers. At the top of the ridge, engineers decided to bore a tunnel to get the tracks over the divide. In March 1913, using only mules, blasting powder, and picks and shovels, workers began digging the tunnel through the hard limestone rock. They started on the south side, but crews soon began carving the passage from the north end also. The workers laid bets that the two tunnels would not meet in the middle, but the engineers had surveyed carefully and, on July 15, the two bores met with an error of only 6 inches. After spending $134,000 and six months of hard labor, the 920-foot tunnel was finally completed. To add to the difficulty and expense, two large trestles had to be built across Block Creek Gorge for the railroad to reach the south entrance of the tunnel. The larger of the two was 700 feet long and 60 feet high.

The first train passed through the tunnel on August 26, 1913, and the first train chugged into Fredericksburg that November to a massive welcoming

The abandoned bridge of the San Antonio, Fredericksburg and Northern Railway still spans the Guadalupe River.

celebration. Businessmen were elated; merchandise and produce could now be shipped much more economically and quickly. The railroad was particularly valuable for shipping heavy items, such as granite quarried at nearby Bear Mountain (see Drive 13). The traveler's lot was much improved. Previously, a rough and dusty 25-mile horse or stagecoach ride was necessary to reach the railroad station in Comfort or Waring to board the train to San Antonio.

As welcome as the railroad was to residents of Fredericksburg, it was never very successful. It was poorly capitalized from the start; an extra $134,000 had to be raised to build the tunnel. Only two of the line's engines were owned by the railroad; most of the rest of the equipment was leased. Much of the roadbed was poorly built and soft, causing numerous derailments. Floods frequently washed away bridges and parts of the track. Sometimes the engine would run out of wood, requiring the train to stop while crews cut down nearby trees for fuel. At the tunnel, the train would stop while the crew checked the track for fallen rocks and closed windows to prevent the thick black smoke from billowing into the cars.

Although the train traveled much faster than the old stagecoaches, it still only managed an average speed of about 12 miles per hour and was the butt of numerous jokes. Despite bankruptcies and changes in ownership, the line limped along until 1942, when it was finally done in by the growing network of paved highways and wartime demand for steel and lumber. The railroad was abandoned and the rails, ties, and bridge timbers were sold for scrap, leaving only the tunnel and its old, eroding roadbed.

The rail line to Kerrville was not much more profitable than the Fredericksburg and Northern and was abandoned in the 1950s; the steel bridge over the Guadalupe is one of the most obvious remnants. A little less than 2 miles past the bridge (about 5.5 miles from Comfort), RM 473 turns sharply to the right and crosses a small bridge over Block Creek, while what seems to be the main road continues straight. Leave RM 473 and go straight on the road ahead, Old San Antonio Road, which almost immediately changes to a narrow, winding, paved county road.

Old San Antonio Road follows Block Creek north, initially through a small valley with scattered ranch houses and old stone walls. Look carefully for remnants of the old railroad grade running parallel to the road. The valley slowly narrows and the terrain becomes hillier. Finally, a little more than 8 miles from the junction, the road makes one last steep climb to the top of the divide. A parking area and signs lie on top of the old tunnel, its southern entrance well hidden in the ravine below.

Bats, Grapetown & Luckenbach

A large colony of Brazilian free-tailed bats moved into the tunnel after the railroad's abandonment, and the Texas Parks and Wildlife Department acquired the southern end of the tunnel. The department built a parking lot, observation platform, and small amphitheater to allow people to observe the bats' evening exodus from the tunnel.

The colony of around three million bats arrives at the tunnel every spring and stays until late October, when cool weather forces the bats south. Sometime around sunset each day the bats swirl out of the tunnel mouths in their nightly forays for insects, the clouds of thousands looking, from a distance, like smoke. Although each individual bat is tiny, it will eat roughly half its body weight in insects every night. Thus a large colony can eat millions of tons of insects every year, performing a valuable service to local residents.

The observation platform gives a good view down rugged Block Creek and instills wonder at the hard physical labor necessary to build the railroad. The Old Tunnel nature trail, which goes down the steep decline to the lower viewing area near the tunnel entrance, is open daily from sunrise to sunset during the winter

A large bat colony now dwells in the old railroad tunnel at the Old Tunnel Wildlife Management Area.

months. When the bat colony is in residence, the nature trail closes earlier in the evenings. Do not enter the tunnel—to do so is dangerous and may disturb the bat colony. To view the bat exodus from the amphitheater by the south tunnel entrance, visitors must take one of the guided tours. As of this writing the Texas Parks and Wildlife Department conducts tours from May through September on Thursday through Sunday evenings. Times vary depending on the time of sunset and the bats' inscrutable flying schedule. Before coming, call the Old Tunnel Wildlife Management Area for the current dates and times. Arrive early and grab one of Alamo Springs Cafe's famous burgers before going to watch the bat flight. The restaurant lies just past the Old Tunnel parking lot on Alamo Road.

From the top of the divide at the tunnel, the road slowly descends north through much less rugged country along a fork of Grape Creek. Traces of the railroad grade can be seen here and there. Widely scattered, solidly built stone houses mark the homesteads of some of the early German settlers. Two small communities sprang up here, Bankersmith and Grapetown. The first, Bankersmith, is about

2 miles down the road from the tunnel, near a minor left-hand fork in the road, but not much is visible today. A little more remains of **Grapetown,** another 1.5 miles down the road, including an old schoolhouse, a wooden shooting hall, and a stone house or two. Shooting clubs were organized here and at several other old German towns in the late 1800s for members to compete in marksmanship. The Grapetown group and several others still exist and compete today.

About 400 yards north of the center of Grapetown, turn right onto Grapetown Road, another paved county road, to **Luckenbach.** The road follows South Grape Creek about 5 miles through its sparsely settled valley to a junction with RM 1376. Turn right and drive 0.5 mile and turn right again onto a small paved road that leads right into the heart of Luckenbach.

This tiny town is a sleepy little Hill Country hamlet, settled by Germans in the 1850s, that remained obscure until it was bought in the 1970s by the late Hondo Crouch, a writer, humorist, and true Texas character. It was still only known to a few residents of Austin and surrounding communities until country-and-western stars Willie Nelson and Waylon Jennings brought it fame, crooning ". . . let's go to Luckenbach, Texas, ain't nobody feeling no pain . . ." After the song became popular, people stole the town signs so often that the highway department quit putting up new ones.

The town still remains what it was—a rustic general store selling longneck beers and snacks, a wooden dance hall, and a sometime blacksmith shop. Regulars play dominos in the store while others pitch washers out back, and the "pickers circle" gathers daily to make music under huge old live oaks. On weekends Texas musicians, both famous and local, play live shows, bringing the town to life. The relaxed ambience of Luckenbach makes a great end to the drive.

Springs & Rivers

San Marcos to Guadalupe River State Park

General description: A 53-mile paved route through the Hill Country, from the springs and river in San Marcos to the rushing white water of the Guadalupe River.

Special attractions: Aquarena Center, San Marcos River, Wonder World, Devil's Backbone, Guadalupe River State Park, Honey Creek State Natural Area, Canyon Lake, hiking, camping, canoeing, boating, fishing, scenic views.

Location: Central Texas. The drive starts in San Marcos, a small city about 30 miles south of Austin.

Drive route numbers: RM 12, RM 32, FM 3424, FM 306, US 281, TX 46, Park Road 31.

Travel season: All year. Summers are hot and humid, although there are opportunities to cool off in the San Marcos and Guadalupe Rivers. Spring and fall are probably the most pleasant times.

Camping: Guadalupe River State Park has a campground.

Services: All services are available in San Marcos and nearby Boerne. Gas and snacks can be found at the junctions of FM 306 and US 281, Spring Branch, and the junction of US 281 and TX 46.

Nearby attractions: Wimberley, Cave Without a Name, Blanco State Park, San Antonio.

For more information: Guadalupe River State Park, 3350 Park Rd. 31, Spring Branch, TX 78070; (830) 438-2656; www.tpwd.state.tx.us/spdest/findadest/parks/guadalupe_river. San Marcos Chamber of Commerce, P.O. Box 2310, San Marcos, TX 78667; (512) 393-5900; www.sanmarcostexas.com. Boerne Chamber of Commerce, 126 Rosewood, Boerne, TX 78006; (830) 249-8000; www.boerne.org.

The Drive

This drive starts in San Marcos, a small city located on the eastern, fault-broken edge of the Hill Country. Within the city massive springs gush to the surface and create an entire waterway, the San Marcos River. The driving route goes west from the town, traversing rugged, hilly terrain, and ends at the clear, rushing waters of the Guadalupe River.

The huge springs attracted Indians and early settlers to San Marcos, as they attract tourists today. Their creation began millions of years ago in Cretaceous times when shallow seas covered much of Central Texas and deposited thick beds of limestone. About 10 to 20 million years ago, a large block of the Earth's crust was uplifted 2,000 feet along the Balcones Fault, a fault that started north of Austin, continued southwest through San Marcos and San Antonio, and curved west.

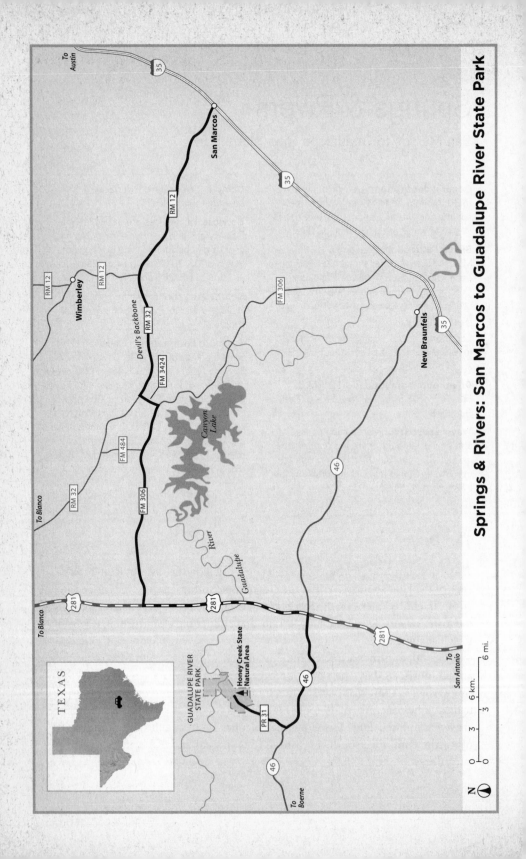

Springs & Rivers: San Marcos to Guadalupe River State Park

The uplifted block is called the Edwards Plateau and has since eroded into a large area of hilly terrain known as the Hill Country. The fault is clearly visible in San Marcos, with an abrupt change between the relatively flat prairies on the east side of town and the steep limestone hills on the west side.

The porous and permeable limestone of the Edwards Plateau acts as an excellent aquifer. The aquifer not only feeds San Marcos and nearby Comal springs, two of the largest springs in the southwestern United States, it also provides water for San Antonio and many other towns and farms. San Marcos Springs is the centerpiece of **Aquarena Center,** the town's flagship tourist attraction. Within the park the spring waters gush into the bottom of a small lake. Glass-bottomed boats glide across its crystalline waters, allowing clear views of the springs, fish, and water plants on the lake bottom. The park was acquired by Texas State University for research and other uses a few years ago, but it is still open to the public.

Archaeological evidence indicates that Indians have lived around the springs for thousands of years. The Spaniards made unsuccessful attempts to settle the area beginning in the 1750s, but it was not permanently settled until the arrival of Anglos in the 1840s. In 1851 William Lindsey, Eli Merriman, and Edward Burleson laid out the townsite that developed into modern San Marcos. The immense water flows of the springs powered mills and cotton gins. In 1899 the San Marcos Normal School was founded on the hills just northwest of downtown to educate teachers. Over time the school became Texas State University-San Marcos, now with an enrollment of more than 32,000 students. The large cluster of university buildings perched on the hills dominates San Marcos physically and economically.

During the warm months of the year, the San Marcos River and springs are the focus of outdoor recreation in San Marcos. The river, which only flows about 50 miles before joining the Guadalupe River, runs through part of the university campus and several city parks downstream from its source. Canoeists, swimmers, and inner-tubers flock to the cool, clear waters, especially on weekends. Outfitters in and around town rent canoes and tubes and run shuttles for river users. The floaters and swimmers share the river with fish and turtles as they glide past banks lined with elephant ears, willows, and endangered Texas wild rice.

Other attractions in the city include historic buildings, particularly along Belvin and San Antonio Streets. **Wonder World** provides an opportunity to see the Balcones Fault from the inside. Wonder Cave was formed when a segment of the fault created a large crack cave in the earth. Although there are not any formations in the cave, its earthquake-formed appearance, multiple rock layers, and plentiful fossils are interesting. Wonder World also offers a small wildlife park, observation tower, anti-gravity house, train ride, and gift shop.

San Marcos hosts a plentiful array of restaurants to fill you up before starting on the drive. Some personal favorites are Grins, with its outdoor, tree-shaded decks; Garcia's, with cheap but good Tex-Mex food; and the more upscale Palmer's, with its shady, peaceful outdoor garden.

To find your way out of San Marcos and onto the drive, start at the courthouse square in the center of downtown, near the university. Signs at intersections mark the route of TX 80 heading west along Hopkins Street. Follow the TX 80 signs closely through the cross streets, turning right at an intersection with a stoplight onto Moore Street/TX 80. Head west to the edge of town and the junction with the newly built RM 12/Wonder World Drive. Go right on RM 12 toward Wimberley. After about 10 miles the route splits, with RM 32 going left and RM 12 continuing right. Our drive follows RM 32 to the left, but the right fork on RM 12 is a worthy side trip to Wimberley, about 5 miles away. Wimberley is a small resort and retirement town tucked into the Blanco River Valley. It features the cypress-lined waters of the Blanco River and Cypress Creek, along with a number of shops and galleries.

RM 32 forges west from the RM 12 junction through rolling Hill Country wooded with live oaks, junipers, and cedar elms before climbing onto a long ridge known as the Devil's Backbone. Broad views open up, especially to the north of the Blanco River watershed. A scenic overlook and picnic area is on the right about 5 miles from the junction. The road drops off the ridge after a bit and intersects FM 3424 about 2.5 miles from the picnic area. Turn left onto FM 3424, toward Canyon Lake. FM 3424 ends in a little more than 1 mile when it intersects FM 306. Turn right onto FM 306 and continue west.

Canyon Lake is visible to the south, its blue waters created by a dam on the Guadalupe River. Numerous lake homes and parks line the shores of this 8,200-acre reservoir. Fishermen, boaters, and water skiers descend on the lake during warm weekends. Below the dam the river roars through a scenic canyon, churning through rapids interspersed with calm stretches of water. By far it is the most popular white water in Texas and attracts many thousands of rafters, kayakers, canoeists, and inner-tubers every summer.

Guadalupe River State Park

FM 306 continues west a little north of Canyon Lake until it finally ends at the junction with US 281. Go left, or south, on US 281 toward San Antonio. After about 4 miles the highway passes through the rapidly growing village of Spring Branch. Just a mile or so farther down the road, the route becomes a four-lane divided highway just before crossing the Guadalupe River. US 281 then climbs out of the river valley and intersects TX 46 after another 4 miles. Turn right onto TX 46, following the signs to **Guadalupe River State Park.** After a little less than

Mist rises above Spring Lake at San Marcos Springs on a cold winter morning.

8 miles, turn right again onto Park Road 31 at the marked junction for the state park.

Park Road 31 travels north and enters the state park after about 3 miles. Just beyond the entrance is park headquarters, the ending point for this drive. After obtaining your entrance permit and information, be sure to explore the park. From headquarters, the park road winds deeper into the park, finally ending on the banks of the Guadalupe River. Across the river from the parking and picnic areas, limestone cliffs rise sheer above the river bank.

The cool, sparkling waters of the Guadalupe River drain from a large area of the Hill Country. The river has cut deeply into the limestone hills, carving narrow canyons and broad valleys. Tall bald cypresses thrive in the wet soils of the river's banks and grow into massive trees that line the waterway.

Guadalupe River State Park provides access to an upper section of what may be the quintessential **Hill Country River.** The river rises in the hills west of Kerrville, fed by a series of springs. It flows eastward through the Hill Country, slowing gaining volume. Well before it reaches the state park, it usually has enough volume to attract canoeists, kayakers, and tubers. Occasional rapids punctuate long calm stretches of the river in and near the state park. Because most land along the river is privately owned, the state park has become a popular site to put in and take out canoes and other small watercraft. Fortunately, however, this section of the river does not have the crowds and attendant problems of the section of the river below the Canyon Lake Dam.

Vegetation typical of the Hill Country blankets the state park. Upland areas are covered by a mix of grasslands and extensive groves of Ashe juniper and live oak. Plants that favor more moisture, such as cypresses, sycamores, and pecans, thrive along creeks and beside the river. One interesting inhabitant of the state park is the rare golden-cheeked warbler, a small, colorful bird that needs strips of mature Ashe juniper bark for nest construction.

The cool waters of the Guadalupe attract most park visitors. Canoeists, tubers, swimmers, and waders all flock to the park during the heat of summer. Although the river is usually calm and quiet, occasional floods sweep down the Guadalupe with surprising ferocity. A tremendous flood in 1978 crested at 63 feet above normal levels, uprooting trees and washing out river banks. The flow volume was at least 240,000 cubic feet per second (cfs), far more than the typical 150 to 200 cfs usually found at the park. Fortunately, adequate upstream warnings of impending floods usually prevent any danger to people within the park. Such floods are rare in any case and are unlikely to interfere with visits to this 1,938-acre state park, one of the Hill Country's jewels.

Sunrise lights up the sky above the Blanco River in Wimberley.

Honey Creek State Natural Area

In the dry, rocky Hill Country next to the state park lies 2,294-acre Honey Creek State Natural Area, one of the hidden gems of the state park system. The sparkling spring waters of Honey Creek tumble down a narrow canyon lined with tall bald cypresses and sycamores to the Guadalupe River. The clear stream bubbles over small cascades and calms in long, deep pools dotted with a species of pond lily, spadderdock. With Spanish moss draping the trees and palmettos dotting the banks, the creek would seem more in place in wetter East Texas than in the Hill Country. The stream and surrounding uplands form the state natural area.

Various Indian tribes used this land until the mid-1800s, when the area was settled by German immigrants. It was used as a ranch by a succession of owners until it was purchased by the Texas Nature Conservancy in 1980 and later conveyed to the Texas Parks and Wildlife Department. Since that time efforts have been made to return the land to its original state as live-oak grassland.

As in the adjoining state park, Ashe juniper and live oak dominate the drier hills, along with several species of grasses. Cedar elms, red oaks, pecans, and other trees are more common on moister slopes and in creek bottoms. Because of the perennial water supply, the narrow floodplain along Honey Creek is a very lush area with many water-dependent species, from maidenhair ferns and palmettos to bald cypresses.

Three major sedimentary rock formations of the Cretaceous Period make up the hills of the natural area. The most important is the Glen Rose Limestone, a rock well-known for its many caves. One cave within the natural area, **Honey Creek Cave,** is the longest known in Texas. One particularly notable geological feature is an igneous dike formed when molten rock squeezed into vertical cracks in the Glen Rose Limestone. It cooled and solidified into a hard, black basalt of uncommon composition.

Wildlife such as white-tailed deer, armadillos, wild turkeys, raccoons, and opossums are common within the natural area and state park. Of particular interest are such rare species as the golden-cheeked warbler and Honey Creek Cave salamander. The creek contains several species of fish, including the native Guadalupe bass.

Because the Honey Creek environment is very fragile, access is limited to guided tours offered by Guadalupe River State Park personnel and volunteers. The guides are knowledgeable and offer an excellent opportunity to see a beautiful, undisturbed Hill Country stream. Trips are usually offered every Sat at 9 a.m., but be sure to call the park ahead of time to verify times.

17

Lost Maples

Kerrville to Lost Maples State Natural Area

General description: A 49-mile paved drive along the scenic upper Guadalupe River and over a divide to the narrow canyons and fall color of Lost Maples State Natural Area.

Special attractions: Lost Maples State Natural Area, Kerrville-Schreiner Park, Museum of Western Art, Schreiner Mansion/Hill Country Museum, fall colors, hiking, camping.

Location: Central Texas. The drive starts in Kerrville, a small city in the center of the Hill Country about 70 miles northwest of San Antonio.

Drive route numbers: TX 27, TX 39, RM 187.

Travel season: All year. The drive is hot in summer. Spring and fall are ideal. Lost Maples State Natural Area is one of the few places in Texas that has excellent fall colors.

Camping: Lost Maples State Natural Area, Kerrville-Schreiner Park.

Services: Limited food, gas, and lodging in Vanderpool, Hunt, and Ingram. All services available in Kerrville.

Nearby attractions: Garner State Park, Hill Country State Natural Area, Fredericksburg.

For more information: Lost Maples State Natural Area, 37221 FM 187, Vanderpool, TX 78885; (830) 966-3413; www.tpwd .state.tx.us/spdest/findadest/parks /lost_maples. Kerrville-Schreiner Park, 2385 Bandera Hwy., Kerrville, TX 78028; (830) 257-7300; www.kerrville.org. Kerrville Chamber of Commerce, 1700 Sidney Baker Street, Suite 100, Kerrville, TX 78028; (830) 896-1155; www.kerrvilletx .com. Museum of Western Art, 1550 Bandera Hwy., Kerrville, TX 78028; (830) 896-2553; www.museumofwesternart.com.

The Drive

The drive starts in Kerrville, a small Hill Country city set on the banks of the Guadalupe River. Kerrville has become a popular vacation destination and retirement community. It was first settled in 1846 by Joshua Brown, who set up a shingle mill using bald cypresses that lined the river. Indians quickly ran him off, but he returned again in 1848. Initially the community was known as Brownsborough, but in 1856 Kerr County was created and the town became Kerrsville, the county seat, and later Kerrville. The town of Comfort soon took the county seat from Kerrville in an election but lost it again when Kendall County was formed and Comfort was found to be within Kendall County.

Kerrville grew slowly, hindered by Indian attacks and the depredations of livestock rustlers and other outlaws. Lawlessness was so bad the area ranchers formed a vigilante group that carried out a harsh frontier justice. Charles Schreiner, a

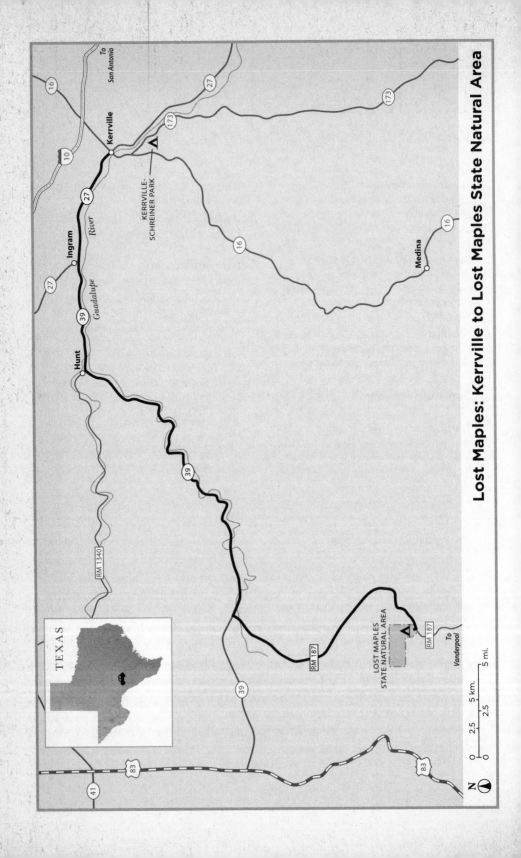

Lost Maples: Kerrville to Lost Maples State Natural Area

former Texas Ranger and Civil War veteran, led much of the town's growth after the war. He opened a mercantile company and bank and built up an enormous 600,000-acre ranch that specialized in sheep raising. In 1887 the railroad arrived after Kerrville competed heavily for it against Fredericksburg. Although ranching is still important in the Kerrville area, tourism is now the mainstay of the local economy. The rolling hills and clear running rivers draw people year-round to Kerrville, making it the largest city in the Hill Country.

Kerrville has a number of attractions. One of the most interesting is the **Museum of Western Art.** The museum, housed in an impressive building featuring mesquite-wood floors and Mexican brick ceiling domes, showcases the works of contemporary and historic artists devoted to western art. The museum, at 1550 Bandera Hwy., also offers seminars, changing exhibitions, and many other activities.

The historic **Schreiner Mansion,** a massive 2-story limestone building at 226 Earl Garrett St., holds the Hill Country Museum. The home, built by Charles Schreiner, has been restored and contains a collection of historic items.

The well-known **Kerrville Folk Festival** attracts droves of people to the area in May and June. The 18-day event features live music every day and night and, contrary to its name, has a broad array of music.

Kerrville-Schreiner Park

Kerrville-Schreiner Park is a pleasant Hill Country retreat on the banks of the Guadalupe River on the southeast side of Kerrville. The park is split into two segments by TX 173. The north side borders the Guadalupe River, one of the Hill Country's largest waterways. Campgrounds, screened shelters, and a picnic area lie on the flat floodplain above the river, shaded by large pecans and other trees.

The south side of the park, across TX 173 from the river section, is much larger. It climbs up and out of the river floodplain into typical Hill Country terrain wooded with Ashe juniper, Spanish red oak, live oak, and cedar elm. Shrubs such as sumac, mountain laurel, and redbud are mixed in with the trees and add colorful blooms in spring and splashes of color in the fall. Wildlife found in the park include armadillo, raccoon, coyote, jackrabbit, and white-tailed deer that seem almost tame at times.

Like most of the Hill Country, a bedrock of limestone underlies the park, exposed in rocky ledges. The limestone was laid down in ancient seas that covered Central Texas millions of years ago during the Cretaceous Period. Later a large block of the Earth's crust, called the Edwards Plateau, was uplifted about 2,000 feet along a large fault. Creeks and rivers such as the Guadalupe have carved the plateau into a land of rolling hills and valleys.

Several miles of hiking and biking trails wind through the hilly terrain, from wooded creek bottoms to bare hilltops, but the Guadalupe River is probably the most popular place in the park, especially on hot summer days. Swimmers, anglers, and canoeists are all attracted to the clear, cool waters.

Ingram to Lost Maples State Natural Area

From Kerrville, head west on TX 27 and follow the heavily developed river valley about 6 or 7 miles to Ingram. The small town was founded at the confluence of the Guadalupe River and Johnson Creek in the 1870s by the Reverend J.C.W. Ingram. Its economy was based on ranching, shingle making, and cedar cutting. In the early days the backcountry along Johnson Creek was known as a rustler and outlaw hangout. Many German settlers in the Hill Country opposed the secession of Texas from the Union during the Civil War and this led to area conflicts. Three German Union sympathizers were hanged on the banks of the creek during the war and their bodies were tossed into the creek.

In Ingram turn left onto TX 39. The building on the right at the junction has murals depicting area history. The highway follows the narrowing river valley about 6 miles west to Hunt. Development lessens somewhat and the natural beauty of the river becomes more apparent. Tall bald cypresses that turn rust-colored in autumn line the banks of the river's sparkling waters. Occasional low-water dams create long pools interspersed with small cascades and rapids. At Hunt the river forks, with TX 39 continuing up the South Fork.

TX 39 follows the South Fork upstream for miles, winding through the narrow, scenic canyon. The road crosses the rushing, cypress-lined river several times, passing occasional homes, resorts, and camps. Springs feed the river so the riverbed is often dry for the last few miles upstream from the springs.

About 21 miles from Hunt, turn left onto RM 187 and leave the Guadalupe River watershed. The highway passes through empty, rolling Hill Country as it crosses the divide into the Sabinal River drainage area. Watch for a picnic area along the highway at a high point after about 12 miles. After the picnic area the terrain gets more rugged, with deep canyons cutting into the upland plateau. The highway soon drops steeply down into a tributary canyon of the Sabinal through a large road-cut. Soon thereafter the highway reaches the entrance of **Lost Maples State Natural Area** at the mouth of another canyon on the right. The park is one of the highlights of the Hill Country.

Lost Maples State Natural Area

Some people believe that fall color in Texas is a contradiction in terms. But hidden deep in these remote Hill Country canyons lies a fall color display that rivals any found in New England. Lost Maples State Natural Area contains several of the most scenic of these canyons.

Some of the most rugged terrain of the Texas Hill Country lies along the southern margin of the Edwards Plateau. Rivers, such as the Sabinal, Frio, Medina, and their tributaries have cut deep canyons into the southern edge of the plateau near the towns of Leakey, Vanderpool, and Medina. Because these canyons are deeper and more steep-walled than in most other areas of the Hill Country, they provide more shelter from the sun and drying winds. Within this moist environment grows a unique community of plants, the most famous being the bigtooth maple.

Bigtooth maples grow in the Rocky Mountains, from Idaho through West Texas and into northern Mexico. Biologists believe that the trees at Lost Maples are relics left by the last ice age. During this cooler and wetter time, the trees migrated eastward across Texas. When the climate became more hot and dry, the trees retreated west, surviving only in isolated pockets such as the state natural area, where they receive extra shade and moisture. Small numbers of the maples also survive at Fort Hood, the Wichita Mountains of Oklahoma, and some West Texas mountains.

The fall color at Lost Maples is dependent on weather conditions during the preceding months. A combination of sunny days, cool fall nights, and adequate rainfall will spark a blazing display of gold, scarlet, and orange maple foliage from mid-October to mid-November. Another tree that favors the deep moist canyons of Lost Maples, the black cherry, adds its share of color during good years.

Other rare and interesting plants found at Lost Maples include the American smoketree, sycamore-leaf snowbell, common witchhazel, and canyon mockorange. One particularly interesting tree, the Texas madrone, thrives here. It boasts a distinctive smooth, thin, peeling bark that ranges in color from cream to maroon, complemented by bright red berries and evergreen leaves.

Other more common trees grow with the maples in the canyon bottoms, including sycamores, pecans, oaks, and hackberries. Dense woodlands of Ashe juniper, red oak, and Lacey oak cloak the upper slopes, mixed with a sprinkling of Texas ash, black cherry, and other trees and shrubs. Grassland blankets most of the more exposed uplands, along with scattered mottes of live oak, juniper, and other trees. Mountain laurel thrives here, blooming with fragrant purple flowers every year. This hardy and attractive evergreen shrub has become a popular native landscaping plant in Texas.

Wildlife thrives in the rugged, undeveloped terrain. White-tailed deer are abundant, as are armadillo, raccoon, opossum, fox squirrel, and striped skunk. Bobcat, gray fox, and ringtail are common but rarely seen. Large predators, such as bear, wolf, and mountain lion, are very rare or extinct in the area. Many bird species flourish at Lost Maples, including the endangered black-capped vireo and golden-cheeked warbler.

Early peoples lived in the area possibly as long as 12,000 years ago. These early groups were nomadic and lived by hunting and gathering. In the 1700s, Apaches and Comanches moved into the area from the north and west. The Spaniards established two short-lived, unsuccessful missions west of the natural area near Camp Wood in 1762. The first Anglo settlers arrived in the mid-1800s to cut cypresses for shingles, grow crops in the flat river bottoms, and raise livestock in the rugged hills, but the area is still only lightly populated, unlike areas of the Hill Country to the east.

Call ahead if you plan to visit Lost Maples during the fall color period. Peak time for color varies from year to year as does the quantity and brilliance. The park is very crowded during this time, especially on weekends. Come on weekdays if possible, arrive early, and reserve campsites or area lodging well ahead of time. A nature trail plus 10 miles of hiking trails allow extensive backcountry exploration and primitive camping for backpackers. Be sure to walk at least a short distance along the trails; some of the park's best color lies within the first quarter mile of the easy Maple Trail. Although the park doesn't have dramatic fall color during other times of the year, it also doesn't have the crowds. Even without fall foliage the steep, narrow canyons and clear streams are worth the visit.

Water seeps from the canyon walls in Hale Hollow and nurtures ferns and maples on the East Trail at Lost Maples State Natural Area.

18

Canyons & Rivers

Medina to Garner State Park

General description: A 46-mile paved drive from Medina to Garner State Park through some of the most rugged parts of the Texas Hill Country.

Special attractions: Garner State Park, scenic views, fall colors, hiking, camping, swimming, fishing, boating.

Location: Central Texas. The drive starts in Medina, a small town about 65 miles northwest of San Antonio.

Drive route numbers: RM 337, US 83, RM 1050.

Travel season: All year. Summers are hot, so spring and fall are the most pleasant times. The drive has some areas of fall color, a rarity in Texas.

Camping: Garner State Park and nearby Lost Maples State Natural Area maintain developed campgrounds.

Services: Limited food, gas, and lodging are available in and near Vanderpool and Leakey. Limited food and gas can be found in Medina. All services are available in Kerrville.

Nearby attractions: Lost Maples State Natural Area, Hill Country State Natural Area, Medina Lake.

For more information: Garner State Park, 234 RR 1050, Concan, TX 78838; (830) 232-6132; www.tpwd.state.tx.us/spdest /findadest/parks/garner.

The Drive

This drive crosses some of the most rugged parts of the Texas Hill Country as it climbs in and out of three major river valleys, the Medina, Sabinal, and Frio. It starts in Medina, a small town located on the banks of the Medina River. The river flows southeast out of the Hill Country, eventually joining the San Antonio River south of San Antonio. Spanish explorer Alonso de León named the river in 1689 for the noted Spanish scholar and engineer Pedro Medina. During much of the 1700s, the river was considered the western boundary of Texas by the Spaniards.

On August 18, 1813, Spanish troops defeated the forces of the Gutiérrez-Magee Expedition at the Battle of Medina River. Earlier, after Mexican revolutionaries led by Father Miguel Hidalgo y Costilla failed to free Mexico from Spain in 1810–1811, one of his supporters, José Bernardo Maximiliano Gutiérrez de Lara, attempted to free the northern part of Mexico—modern-day Texas. He allied with American army officer August Magee and organized a small army that quickly seized poorly defended Nacogdoches, Goliad, and San Antonio. Magee died, allowing Gutiérrez to assume command of the "Republic of the North." He soon lost support after becoming dictatorial and was replaced by a Cuban leader.

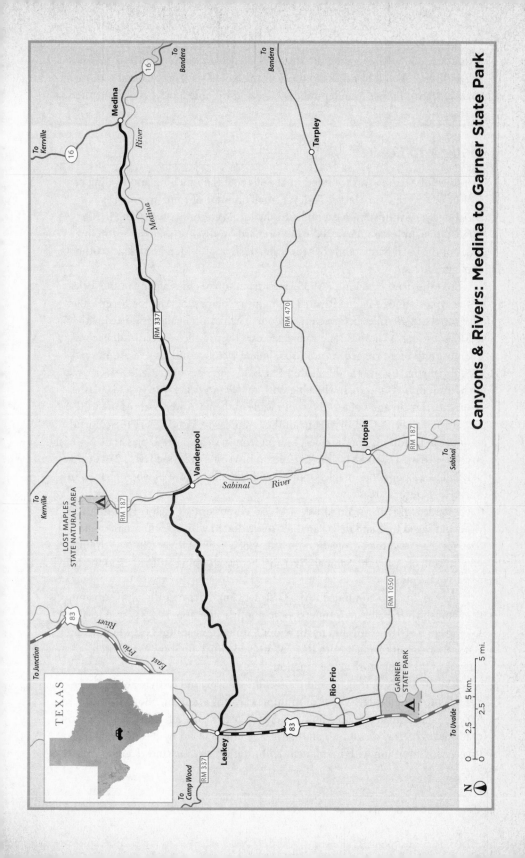

Canyons & Rivers: Medina to Garner State Park

After the Medina River battle, the short-lived republic came to an end. Possibly a seventh flag should be added to those of the fabled six flags of Texas—those of Spain, Mexico, France, the Republic of Texas, the Confederacy, and the United States.

Medina to Leakey

The town of Medina was founded in about 1880 as a ranching and trading center but never grew very large. Today a small amount of tourism and Texas's fledgling apple industry give a boost to the local economy. Beginning in late August, the apples are harvested from orchards and sent to market. Stop in at some of the local fruit stands or stores for fresh apple cider, apples, and other apple products.

Start the drive by taking RM 337 west from town, crossing one of the forks of the cypress-lined Medina River. The highway follows the Medina River Valley west for about 10 miles before climbing out. The pastoral valley is dotted with fields and scattered homes. The valley narrows toward the western end, becoming more and more rugged. Some years, in late October and early November, fall color brightens the river and hillsides. The bald cypresses hugging the riverbanks turn burnt orange and rust, while bigtooth maples and cherry trees add splashes of bright crimson and gold to the south walls of the narrower parts of the valley. This area of the Hill Country is one of the few areas in Texas where the colorful maples can be found. They are best known from nearby Lost Maples State Natural Area (see Drive 17) and McKittrick Canyon in West Texas (see Drive 2). A nursery in Medina sells bigtooth maple saplings; with care, they do well when planted in most Hill Country areas.

After leaving the Medina River, RM 337 climbs onto a high ridge with great views of rugged hills and deep canyons, some dotted with colorful maples and cherries. The road then drops into the valley of a Sabinal River tributary and follows it west, crossing the Sabinal River just before stopping at RM 187 in the hamlet of Vanderpool.

Turn right onto combined RM 337/RM 187 and drive north a mile or so up the Sabinal River Valley in Vanderpool to another junction. RM 337 and RM 187 split again; RM 187 continues north about 5 miles to beautiful Lost Maples State Natural Area, but turn left onto RM 337 instead. Stock up if necessary on food and gas at the small store at the junction.

RM 337 turns west again and soon climbs steeply out of the Sabinal River Valley onto a high ridge. Views of multiple canyons are tremendous from the highway and a small rest area on the ridgetop. After only a few miles, the narrow road snakes its way down into another valley, this one cut by the West Sabinal River. As is common with permanent Hill Country streams and rivers, cypresses

Kids love to play in the cool waters of the Frio River at Garner State Park.

thrive on its banks. The road climbs out of that valley and winds up onto another ridge with great views. RM 337 is steep, narrow, and winding, and it has old-fashioned guardrails along big drop-offs; the guard rails may be nostalgic but probably aren't terribly effective. Plan to take it slow on this road.

The highway soon drops yet again into another valley, this time the Little Dry Frio River. The highway follows it most of the way to Leakey, crossing the Frio River on the east side of the small town. RM 337 intersects US 83 in the center of Leakey, about 16 miles from Vanderpool. The small town was founded by John and Mary Leakey when they built a cabin here in 1857. It eventually became the Real County seat and remains so today.

Garner State Park

RM 337 continues west to Camp Wood and is quite scenic; however, for this drive turn left onto US 83 in Leakey and head south toward **Garner State Park.** US 83

Large bald cypress trees thrive along the banks of the Frio River at Garner State Park.

follows the clear, cold Frio River south along its west bank (*frio* means cold in Spanish). The Frio River flows southeast for many miles, out of the Hill Country and across the South Texas plains. Along the way it is joined by the Sabinal and Leona Rivers before finally becoming part of the Nueces River between San Antonio and Corpus Christi.

About 10 miles south of Leakey, turn left onto RM 1050. This drive ends at the entrance to Garner State Park on the right. Garner is one of the classic state parks of Texas, well demonstrated by its enduring popularity. The Frio River pools in a small lake and tumbles over cascades and boulders as it flows through the park. It swirls and eddies as it washes over smooth, polished white limestone bedrock. Tall bald cypresses cling to the banks below rocky bluffs covered with live oak, cedar elm, and Ashe juniper.

The 1,420-acre park lies on the southwestern edge of the Hill Country, between Leakey and Uvalde. Millions of years ago, the Edwards Plateau was uplifted along a curving fault that stretched from north of Austin southwest to San

Antonio and westward, to north of Uvalde. The plateau was uplifted 2,000 feet and has been eroding ever since. Rivers and streams, such as the Frio, have cut the once-flat plateau into a particularly rugged land of hills and canyons in the part of the Hill Country traversed by this drive.

Garner State Park was named after John Nance Garner, vice president under Franklin Roosevelt and former resident of nearby Uvalde. The park was developed during the 1930s to preserve a section of the Hill Country for public use and to put unemployed young men to work during the Depression. In 1935, the Civilian Conservation Corps set up camp at the park site and began construction. CCC workers used native materials, such as cypress, oak, and limestone, to build durable park facilities that are still in use today. The large, central concession building, with its adjoining open-air pavilion, is the park's premier structure. Using excellent craftsmanship, the CCC built it in the French-Alsatian style with stone walls and massive exposed wooden beams. The corps also built cabins, roads, and trails in the park.

Garner State Park officially opened in 1941 and has been welcoming increasing numbers of visitors ever since. The state park is the most popular camping park in the state park system, evidenced by its enormous campgrounds. Many people return year after year, drawn by the rugged hills and sparkling Frio River. Water-oriented activities are most popular, with swimmers, tubers, and canoeists filling the river on summer weekends. Cyclists can pedal along park roads, while hikers can climb the heights of Mount Baldy for spectacular views. There is even a miniature golf course in the park.

Saturday night dances were started by the CCC men in the 1930s and have grown in popularity to the point where they happen every evening in summer. As many as several hundred people congregate at the outdoor pavilion by the concession building to dance to jukebox music or live bands. Young and old mix at the dances, both newcomers to Garner and people who have been returning for years to one of the most popular destinations in Texas.

Garner is especially busy in summer and on spring and fall weekends. During those times camping and cabin reservations are highly recommended, especially since the cabins were renovated in the fall of 2010. Probably the best time to visit the park is during weekdays in spring and fall.

19

Rio Grande Valley

Bentsen–Rio Grande Valley State Park
to Santa Ana National Wildlife Refuge

General description: A 24-mile paved drive through agricultural areas of the Rio Grande Valley between two small remaining islands of subtropical forest habitat.

Special attractions: Bentsen–Rio Grande Valley State Park, World Birding Center, Santa Ana National Wildlife Refuge, La Lomita Chapel, hiking, rare species of birds and animals.

Location: South Texas. The drive starts at Bentsen–Rio Grande Valley State Park, along the Rio Grande a few miles southwest of Mission.

Drive route numbers: FM 2062, county road, FM 1016, FM 494, TX 336, US 281 East.

Travel season: All year. The drive is hot and humid from late Apr through Sept. The best time for the trip is late fall through early spring.

Camping: Bentsen–Rio Grande Valley State Park has a few primitive campsites.

Services: All services are available in Mission, McAllen, and other Rio Grande Valley cities.

Nearby attractions: Los Ebanos hand-operated river ferry, Falcon State Park, Laguna Atascosa National Wildlife Refuge, South Padre Island, Port Isabel Lighthouse State Historical Park, Sabal Palm Refuge.

For more information: Bentsen–Rio Grande Valley State Park, 2800 S. Bentsen Palm Dr., Mission, TX 78572; (956) 584-9156; www.worldbirdingcenter .org. Santa Ana National Wildlife Refuge, Route 2, Box 202A, Alamo, TX 78516; (956) 784-7500; www.fws.gov. McAllen Chamber of Commerce, 1200 Ash Ave., McAllen, TX 78501; (956) 682-2871; www.mcallen.org. Mission Chamber of Commerce, 202 W. Tom Landry, Mission, TX 78572; (956) 585-2727; www.mission chamber.com.

The Drive

Deep in the Rio Grande Valley lies one of the southernmost state parks in the United States, the starting point for this drive. **Bentsen–Rio Grande Valley State Park** abuts the Rio Grande near the city of Mission in South Texas. Unusual, rarely seen animals such as the ocelot and jaguarundi roam thick, brushy woodlands of cedar elm, Rio Grande ash, black willow, anaqua, ebony, huisache, mesquite, and many other species. At one time even jaguar, the largest cat in the western hemisphere, stalked prey on the banks of the Rio Grande.

The state park's unique avian life draws even more people than the animals. The park provides a home for a tremendous variety of birds, leading to its becoming the headquarters for the World Birding Center. The Center features nine city

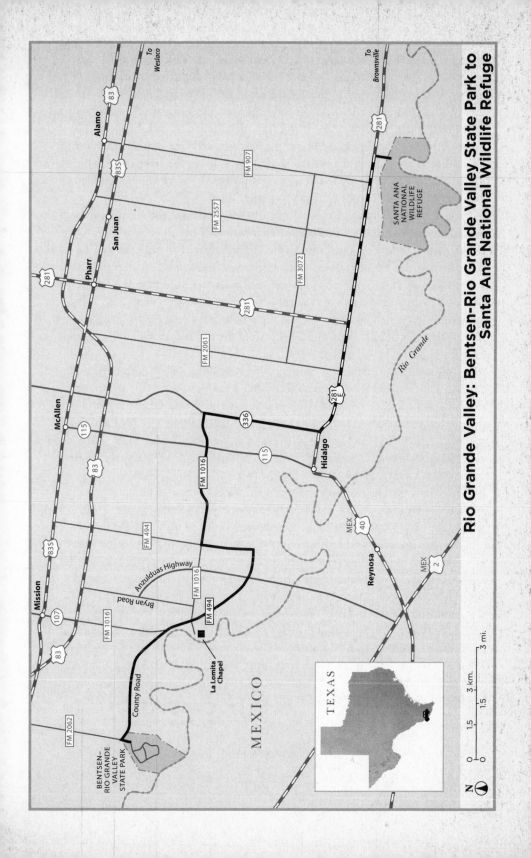

Rio Grande Valley: Bentsen-Rio Grande Valley State Park to Santa Ana National Wildlife Refuge

To Weslaco

To Brownsville

Alamo

San Juan

Pharr

McAllen

Mission

Hidalgo

Reynosa

FM 907

FM 2557

FM 3072

SANTA ANA NATIONAL WILDLIFE REFUGE

Rio Grande

FM 2061

FM 1016

FM 494

FM 1016

FM 494

Anzulduas Highway

Bryan Road

County Road

La Lomita Chapel

FM 1016

FM 2062

BENTSEN-RIO GRANDE VALLEY STATE PARK

MEXICO

MEX 40

MEX 2

TEXAS

N

0   1.5   3 km.
0   1.5   3 mi.

and state public lands sites across the Lower Rio Grande Valley known for their bird and wildlife populations. Some 296 species have been recorded in the state park; another 74 have been sighted elsewhere in the Rio Grande Valley. Two major flyways, the Central and Mississippi, converge here, funneling large numbers of migrants through the area. Many tropical species, limited by climate, reach the northern limit of their range here, and the nearby Gulf Coast draws many shore-birds. Birders come from all over the United States to see the green jay, Altamira oriole, chachalaca, white-tipped dove, pauraque, groove-billed ani, hook-billed kite, ringed kingfisher, and many other species.

The lower Rio Grande Valley's warm climate, combined with its proximity to Mexico, forms a unique ecosystem found nowhere else in the United States. Before the area was heavily developed into farms and urban areas on both sides of the river, the Rio Grande shifted constantly, creating a broad, fertile floodplain. The valley's southern location near the Tropic of Cancer and its proximity to the warm Gulf of Mexico creates a subtropical climate with a 320-day growing season. Rain-fall is only moderate and evaporation is high, however, so the river supports only a narrow corridor of lush woodlands. Away from the river the woodland grades into brushland more adapted to dryness.

Unfortunately, urbanization and farming have destroyed 99 percent of the original habitat of the Rio Grande Valley. Only a few islands remain of the once extensive subtropical woodland. Many species such as the ocelot and jaguarundi have become endangered because of habitat loss and hunting. The state and federal government have an ongoing program to protect the remnants in a system of state parks, state wildlife management areas, and national wildlife refuges. Because of the valley's many unique species and the tremendous habitat loss, this is the highest priority acquisition area in the United States for the US Fish and Wildlife Service. Private entities such as the Audubon Society, the Nature Conservancy, and Valley Land Fund have also protected pieces of the remaining habitat.

Even native woodland protected in the 760-acre Bentsen–Rio Grande Valley State Park and other refuges has suffered. Many trees have died, particularly cedar elms and ash trees. Dams, upstream irrigation and water use, and flood control projects have ended periodic flooding along the river and lowered the water table, drying out areas along the river. The state park and the US Fish and Wildlife Ser-vice undertook a large irrigation project to water much of the park and an adjoin-ing Fish and Wildlife tract. Not only was the vegetation watered, but also one of the park's resacas, an old cut-off river channel, was refilled. Two hiking and nature trails that wind through the state park's woodland provide an excellent intro-duction to the habitat of the Rio Grande Valley. Spanish moss drapes the trees,

Spanish moss cloaks trees at Bentsen-Rio Grande Valley State Park, part of the World Birding Center.

Palm trees line the shore of a resaca (oxbow lake) at Bentsen-Rio Grande Valley State Park.

creating a tropical, primeval atmosphere. Observant hikers will see many plants, birds, and animals found nowhere else in the United States. A very lucky person might even see a beautiful spotted ocelot as it slips silently through the brush.

When Bentsen—Rio Grande Valley State Park became part of the World Birding Center a few years ago, its developed campground was closed and park roads were limited to a tram, bicycles, and pedestrians. Before you start the drive, be sure to walk or ride the shady park trails and roads. If you're observant, you're sure to see species of birds found in few other places in the United States.

The state park and other areas of the valley are popular from December through April when "Winter Texans" come south to escape harsh northern winters. Reserve hotels well ahead during this time. From the park the drive roughly follows the Rio Grande east toward the Gulf of Mexico.

From the World Birding Center headquarters by the park entrance, drive north a very short distance to the first paved road (an unmarked county road) on the right, just north of the river levee. Follow it east through fields and onto the river levee. The road passes fields of sugar cane and other crops. Note the lack of natural habitat along the drive between the state park and the national wildlife refuge. The vast majority of land has been cleared for agricultural use. Many crops are grown in the valley that require a warm climate with little freezing weather. Sugar cane, lettuce, aloe vera, and many vegetables are grown here. The most famous valley crop is probably citrus, especially grapefruit. A very hard freeze in the early 1980s followed by a later milder freeze destroyed many citrus orchards. Today most of the orchards have recovered and are producing again.

Although agricultural land clearing destroyed much of the original habitat, urbanization is now taking over increasing amounts of farmland. High birth rates and heavy immigration from Mexico have given the Rio Grande Valley a rapidly growing population.

The county road intersects FM 1016 3.6 miles from park headquarters; turn right (effectively, straight ahead) onto FM 1016. Turn right again in 0.7 mile onto FM 494. For a short side trip, turn right again after only 0.1 mile to go to **La Lomita Chapel.** The side road climbs over the river levee to the chapel on the left.

La Lomita Chapel was first built of adobe in 1865 as an overnight way station for Oblate fathers traveling between Brownsville and Roma. The tiny structure was rebuilt in 1889 of stone with brick floors and heavy wooden ceiling beams and moved to its present site 10 years later. The chapel is still used for marriages and other private services. Ancient, gnarled mesquites and other trees shade the surrounding 7-acre grounds. Picnic tables, restrooms, and historic plaques make the site a pleasant stop along the drive.

Just south and in view of the chapel is a popular restaurant on the banks of the Rio Grande. The outdoor decks overlooking the river are particularly popular during the cooler times of the year when the Winter Texans arrive.

Continue the drive by returning to FM 494 and going right. In less than 0.5 mile an interesting old brick building caps a low hill on the right. It was originally established by the Catholic Church to provide a mission for La Lomita Ranch workers. It later oversaw a large farming operation that was sold when it became a financial burden.

FM 494 turns north after a bit and intersects FM 1016 again a little more than 4 miles from La Lomita Chapel. Turn right onto FM 1016 and go east again, crossing Texas Spur 115 and turning right onto TX 336 after 3.6 miles. After following TX 336 south for 3.3 miles, get on US 281E to Brownsville and turn east again.

Santa Ana National Wildlife Refuge

US 281E passes through farms and small settlements for about 8 miles before arriving at the **Santa Ana National Wildlife Refuge** on the right. Like Bentsen–Rio Grande Valley State Park, 2,080-acre Santa Ana preserves a small remaining

A bridge crosses low ground in the thick, Spanish moss–draped woodland of Santa Ana National Wildlife Refuge.

pocket of the subtropical ecosystem that once lined the Rio Grande and contains many rare and unique plant and animal species. The refuge consists of thick, brushy woodland, much of it draped with Spanish moss, and several small marshy lakes. The visitor center, with exhibits and information, is a worthwhile first stop. Several refuge trails start at the visitor center and are open from sunrise to sunset. A 7-mile loop road is open on weekends, and the visitor center is open daily, except for holidays, although with shorter hours than the trails. During the busy winter season, the refuge road is closed to private vehicles, but during that time the refuge operates an interpretive tram tour of the road.

Rio Grande Delta

Sabal Palm Audubon Center to Boca Chica Beach

General description: A 25-mile paved drive across the Rio Grande delta, from a remnant native palm grove to the beach.

Special attractions: Sabal Palm Audubon Center, Boca Chica Beach, hiking, swimming, beachcombing, fishing, birding.

Location: South Texas. The drive starts at the Sabal Palm Audubon Center a few miles southeast of Brownsville just off of FM 1419 near the intersection with FM 3068.

Drive route numbers: FM 1419, TX 4.

Travel season: All year. The drive is hot and humid from Apr through Sept. The height of summer can be especially uncomfortable. Late fall through early spring is the ideal time for this trip.

Camping: Although there are numerous private RV campgrounds in the area, the only public camping is primitive beach camping at Boca Chica Beach.

Services: All services are available in Brownsville.

Nearby attractions: Laguna Atascosa National Wildlife Refuge, Santa Ana National Wildlife Refuge, Port Isabel Lighthouse State Historic Site, South Padre Island, Gladys Porter Zoo.

For more information: Sabal Palm Grove Sanctuary, National Audubon Society, P.O. Box 5169, Brownsville, TX 78523; (956) 541-8034; www.tx.audubon.org/Sabal.html. Brownsville Convention and Visitors Bureau, P.O. Box 4697, Brownsville, TX 78523; (800) 626-2639; www.brownsville.org.

The Drive

This drive crosses a unique ecological area in the United States, from a lush palm forest to the sandy shores of the Gulf of Mexico on the delta of the 1,900-mile-long Rio Grande. Its location at the very southern tip of Texas gives it a warm, subtropical climate. Only Hawaii and the tip of Florida lie farther south. Because of South Texas's location and its proximity to Mexico, many animal and plant species are found here and nowhere else in the United States. Not only does the warm climate attract many species of wildlife, it also attracts large numbers of tourists and part-time residents during the winter.

Brownsville is both the southernmost city in Texas, with a latitude similar to Miami, Florida, and the largest in the Rio Grande Valley, with a population of more than 100,000. Mixed in with typical Texas trees such as oaks and mesquites are palms, citrus and banana trees, bamboo, and bougainvillea.

Brownsville had a turbulent history during its early years. Its larger sister city Matamoros across the river in Mexico was founded in the mid-1700s, many years

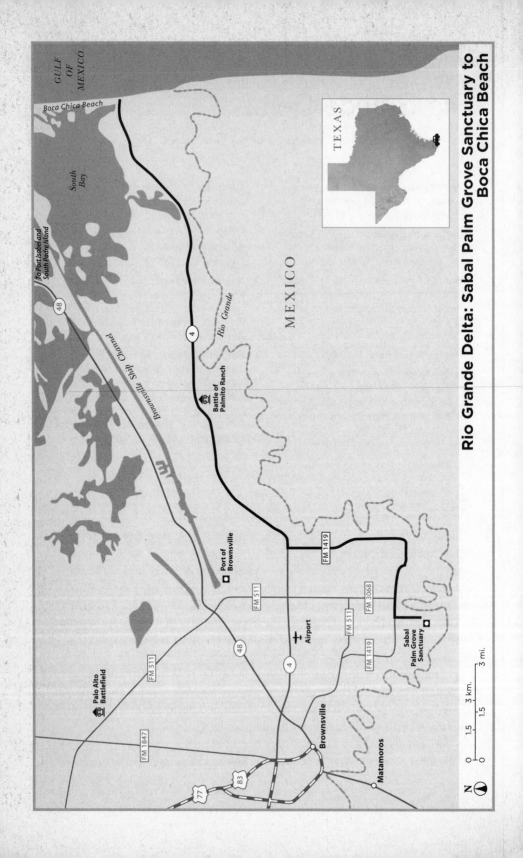

Rio Grande Delta: Sabal Palm Grove Sanctuary to Boca Chica Beach

TEXAS

GULF
OF
MEXICO

Boca Chica Beach

South
Bay

To Port Isabel and
South Padre Island

Brownsville Ship Channel

Rio Grande

MEXICO

Battle of
Palmito Ranch

Port of
Brownsville

Palo Alto
Battlefield

FM 511

FM 1847

FM 511

FM 1419

FM 511

Airport

FM 511

FM 1419

FM 3068

Sabal
Palm Grove
Sanctuary

Brownsville

Matamoros

N

0   1.5   3 km.
0   1.5   3 mi.

before Brownsville. Until Texas joined the United States in 1845, the north bank of the Rio Grande was relatively undeveloped. The annexation of Texas aggravated the unsettled border dispute between Texas and Mexico. After Texas gained independence, Mexico claimed that the Nueces River marked the border, while Texas claimed lands south to the Rio Grande.

In 1846 General Zachary Taylor established a fort across the river from Matamoros to cement the boundary claims of the United States. In response Mexican troops attacked the fort, killing its commander, Major Jacob Brown, and sparking the Mexican-American War. On May 7, 1846, General Taylor left Port Isabel with 2,300 troops to reinforce the fort. The next day his troops clashed with a force of about 6,000 Mexicans at Palo Alto some 10 miles north of the fort. Using light horse artillery the American troops routed the larger Mexican force. By the next day the Mexican Army had dug in closer to the fort at Resaca de la Palma. Once again the American troops proved victorious and inflicted great losses on the Mexican forces. One participant in the battle was Second Lieutenant Ulysses S. Grant. The war raged on for 2 years, with the United States eventually invading Mexico and gaining sovereignty over South Texas and much of the American Southwest.

The city of Brownsville grew up around the fort, but the area remained turbulent. Bandits raided Brownsville and Matamoros and occasional hurricanes pounded the area. In 1851 Matamoros was attacked unsuccessfully by revolutionaries. The Civil War brought additional bloodshed. Until November 1863, when Union troops seized Brownsville, it was the only Confederate port that wasn't blockaded. During that time the two sister cities thrived as supplies poured through the area and the nearby Mexican port of Bagdad. The Confederates recaptured the fort not long after the Union took it. After the turn of the 20th century, banditry and revolutionary unrest in northern Mexico spilled over into Brownsville. Eventually, Brownsville settled into its current role as an agriculture, trade, industry, port, and tourist center.

Sabal Palm Audubon Center

The drive starts at the **Sabal Palm Audubon Center** southeast of Brownsville. To find it, take FM 1419, Southmost Road, southeast from Brownsville several miles and watch for a sign marking the entrance road on the right. The entrance road is only a short distance west of the junction of FM 1419 and FM 3068. Some state road maps do not show these two highways on the main map. But some maps, such as the official Department of Transportation highway travel map, show the roads on the Brownsville city map. Another helpful guide is the detailed map book, *The Roads of Texas* by Shearer Publishing. Most GPS devices should show the roads.

Sabal Palm Audubon Center was acquired in 1971 by the Audubon Society through the generosity of Exxon and many other donors. The sanctuary consists of 527 acres adjoining the Rio Grande, 32 acres of which consist of native palm forest. The Audubon Society is working to restore the remaining acreage, former farms, to palm woodland.

In 1519 the Spanish explorer Alonso Alvarez de Piñeda sailed up the mouth of the Rio Grande and named it the Rio de las Palmas because of the thousands of acres of palms that forested the delta. Before settlers began clearing the subtropical forest for farmland, the palm woodland covered 40,000 acres. Incredibly, except for the 32 acres in the sanctuary and a smaller private tract to the east, the palm forest has been completely removed from the Rio Grande Valley on both sides of the river.

The sanctuary harbors a thick, brushy woodland with a tall canopy of sabal palms, the only native palm in Texas other than the small palmetto of East Texas. An easy loop trail winds through the strange-seeming subtropical forest that appears so out of place in the United States. As with the other parks and wildlife refuges in the Rio Grande Valley, this sanctuary attracts many people hoping to see some of the area's unique wildlife. The endangered ocelot and jaguarundi are now very scarce in the Rio Grande Valley, but their remaining populations survive in remnants of habitat such as the palm grove. Many bird species range only a short distance north of the Rio Grande, including the pauraque, chachalaca, green jay, buff-bellied hummingbird, and kiskadee flycatcher. Most dedicated birders make a trek to the palm sanctuary and other valley refuges sooner or later. The center was closed to the public during the fall of 2010 because of border security issues and the rerouting of the border wall. Once the issues are solved, the center hopes to reopen soon; be sure to call ahead or check the website to determine whether the sanctuary is open.

The tiny remnant of original native habitat found in the sanctuary is, unfortunately, representative of the Rio Grande Valley as a whole. Probably 99 percent of the original forest and brushland of the valley has been cleared for agricultural use. Now high birth rates and immigration are resulting in the urbanization of much of the farmland. Dams and heavy water use have stopped the Rio Grande's periodic flooding, altering what little original habitat remains. The Audubon Society, US Fish and Wildlife Service, Texas Parks and Wildlife Department, and other organizations are attempting to purchase and maintain some of the remaining tracts of native vegetation in a valley-wide refuge system.

Sabal Palm Audubon Center to Boca Chica Beach

From the sanctuary, start the drive by returning to FM 1419 on the entrance road. Turn right and follow FM 1419 east and then north about 7 miles through farmland

A birder walks through the lush palm woodland of the Sabal Palm Audubon Center.

Shore birds congregate where the shrunken Rio Grande flows into the Gulf of Mexico.

to TX 4. Turn right onto TX 4 and follow it east all the way to its end on the beach at Boca Chica. The road leaves the farming area fairly quickly, probably because the land becomes too low-lying and salty. A Border Patrol checkpoint on the highway makes an effort to control illegal immigration and drug smuggling. The terrain is wild, with few homes or side roads, a rarity in the valley. The road climbs up onto a very low, windswept ridge partially covered with mesquite, yucca, ebony, and other shrubs and grasses. Views open up of the surrounding grasslands, marshes, and bays.

A historic marker on the ridge about 14 miles from the palm grove commemorates the Battle of Palmito Ranch. Near this lonely spot the last battle of the Civil War was fought on May 12–13, 1865, 34 days after General Robert E. Lee surrendered at Appomattox. Colonel Theodore Barrett commanded about 1,600 Union troops on Brazos Island miles to the east, while about 300 Confederate troops occupied Fort Brown under the leadership of General James E. Slaughter and Colonel John S. ("Rip") Ford. Barrett's troops attempted to capture the fort and cotton stored in Brownsville warehouses, but the smaller Confederate force prevailed, suffering no fatalities compared to Union losses of 4 officers and 111 men killed, wounded, or missing. Sadly, the casualties were unnecessary. News of Lee's surrender and the end of the war was slow to reach Brownsville.

The road continues east from the marker, mostly following sand ridges and crossing some marshes and tidal areas in the last few miles. Much of the land here has been acquired for the Lower Rio Grande Valley National Wildlife Refuge in recent years. About 2 miles before the beach, a small subdivision and store lie on the left, one of the few signs of development along most of the drive. The road crosses a small ridge of dunes and ends on the broad sandy **Boca Chica Beach.**

The Rio Grande flows into the Gulf of Mexico at the southern tip of Texas known as Boca Chica. Unlike highly developed South Padre Island to the north, Boca Chica is almost devoid of human development. Several miles of empty beach stretch north and south, attracting fishermen and swimmers, campers and birders. Behind the beach lie sand dunes, marshes, and tidal flats populated only by wildlife.

People have tried to settle Boca Chica in the past but little remains of their efforts. Until a bridge was built to South Padre Island, the only easy access to the coast was at Boca Chica. The small town of Brazos Santiago bustled as a port during the Mexican-American and Civil Wars, but Nature did not approve of the settlement. In 1866 cholera struck the community. A harsh winter followed in which snow fell, a rarity in South Texas. Yellow fever hit next, decimating the remaining residents, and the hurricane of 1867 finished the job. The now famous words of General Sheridan were spoken after he was stationed at Brazos Santiago. "If I owned Texas and Hell, I'd lease Texas and go live in the other place."

Before the Great Depression a fairly elaborate beach development was built at Boca Chica, with homes, stores, restaurants, bathhouses, and other structures. In September 1933 a hurricane with 124-mile-per-hour winds and a 13-foot storm surge obliterated the development. Since then other developments and resorts have been proposed and a few were even built, but few have lasted, all hammered by hurricanes or bankruptcy. With most land now part of the wildlife refuge, little development is likely in the future.

Although people have come and gone, rare animals such as the ocelot still prowl the brushy woodlands along the river behind the beach. As at the palm sanctuary, many bird species reach the northern limit of their range here.

With care you can drive on the beach, but be aware of sand and surf conditions. The sand can be soft, making it easy to get stuck. Usually the damp sand near the surf line is most firm. Storms and high tides can also occasionally swamp cars. To the north the beach ends at the pass between Boca Chica and South Padre Island; to the south it ends at the mouth of the Rio Grande, a much shrunken river today. The beach is undeveloped with no facilities, but it and adjoining bays still attract fishermen, campers, beachcombers, and swimmers. The empty coast, where nature has triumphed over man, has a powerful allure.

Padre Island

Aransas Pass to Padre Island National Seashore

General description: A 41-mile drive, beginning with a ferry crossing, along two coastal barrier islands, Mustang and Padre Islands.

Special attractions: Padre Island National Seashore, Mustang Island State Park, Conn Brown Harbor, Aransas Pass–Port Aransas ferry, swimming, hiking, camping, fishing.

Location: The drive starts in Aransas Pass, about 20 miles northeast of Corpus Christi.

Drive route numbers: TX 361, Park Road 22.

Travel season: All year. Summers are hot and very humid, but a swim in the Gulf will cool you off.

Camping: Camping is available at Padre Island National Seashore, Port Aransas Beach, and Mustang Island State Park.

Services: All services are available in Aransas Pass, Port Aransas, and nearby Corpus Christi.

Nearby attractions: Aransas National Wildlife Refuge, Fulton Mansion, Goose Island State Park, Corpus Christi attractions such as the Texas State Aquarium and the USS *Lexington* Museum.

For more information: Padre Island National Seashore, P.O. Box 181300, Corpus Christi, TX 78480; (361) 949-8068; www.nps.gov/pais. Mustang Island State Park, P.O. Box 326, Port Aransas, TX 78373; (361) 749-5246; www.tpwd .state.tx.us/spdest/findadest/parks/mus tang_island. Corpus Christi Convention and Visitors Bureau, 101 North Shoreline Blvd., Suite 430, Corpus Christi, TX 78401; (361) 881-1888 or (800) 678-6232; www.visitcorpuschristitx.org. Port Aransas Chamber of Commerce and Tourist Bureau, 403 West Cotter, Port Aransas, TX 78373; (361) 749-5919 or (800) 452-6278; www .portaransas.org.

The Drive

This drive follows two of many low-lying islands that line the coast of Texas and other Gulf states. They are called barrier islands because they protect the mainland from much of the impact of hurricanes and tropical storms. Waves and wind have built up broad, gently sloping beaches on the Gulf of Mexico side of the islands. Except during storms, the surf here is usually quite mild. A dune ridge lines the back side of the beaches, home to sea oats and other plants adapted to sandy environs. One particularly attractive vine, the goat-foot morning glory, sports large pink to purple flowers from May to December.

Behind the dunes are grasslands and freshwater marshes notorious for mosquitoes. The mainland sides of Mustang and Padre Islands are lined with salt

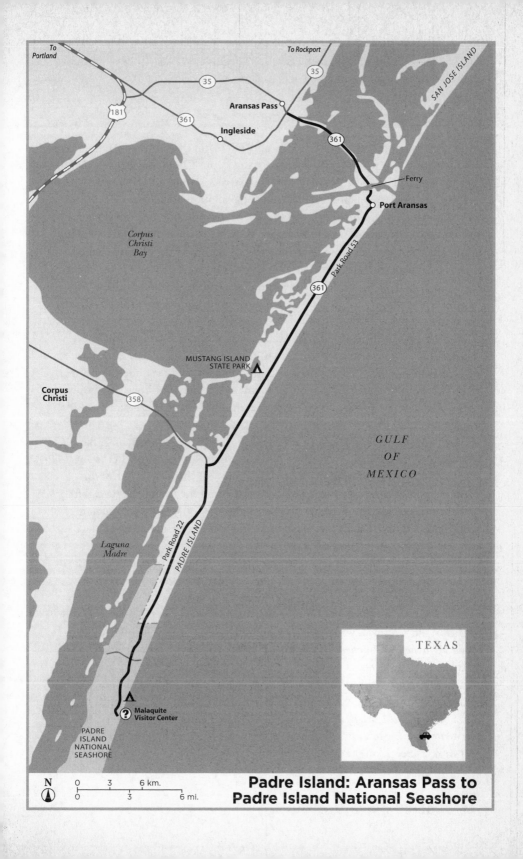

To Portland

To Rockport

SAN JOSE ISLAND

35

35

181

361

Aransas Pass

Ingleside

361

Ferry

Port Aransas

Corpus Christi Bay

Park Road 53

361

MUSTANG ISLAND STATE PARK

Corpus Christi

358

GULF OF MEXICO

Park Road 22

PADRE ISLAND

Laguna Madre

TEXAS

Malaquite Visitor Center

PADRE ISLAND NATIONAL SEASHORE

N

0   3   6 km.

0   3   6 mi.

Padre Island: Aransas Pass to Padre Island National Seashore

marshes along shallow inland bays. This drive begins at the heavily developed area around Port Aransas and ends at a wild national seashore.

Aransas Pass to Port Aransas

Begin the drive at the junction of TX 35 and TX 361 in the center of Aransas Pass. The town was named for the entrance to Corpus Christi Bay between Mustang and San José Islands. The gaps between barrier islands are known as passes. In 1909 Russell Harrison and T.B. Wheeler held a lottery to sell their 12,000 acres on Redfish Bay, which included the site of Aransas Pass. The government intended to dredge a new port in the area, so excitement was high among speculators. The town site was close to an outlet to the gulf, and people expected it to be chosen over Corpus Christi and Rockport. Only 6,000 tickets were sold at $100 each for the 6,000 lots. Everyone won a lot; but the location of the lot was a gamble. Unfortunately for the buyers, the government later chose Corpus Christi for the port.

Before starting the drive to Port Aransas, visit **Conn Brown Harbor,** home of one of the largest shrimp fleets in Texas. Aransas Pass and nearby Port Aransas are centers for deep-sea fishing charters. Fish caught offshore include red snapper, shark, yellowfin tuna, kingfish, marlin, bonito, and tarpon. Fishing is also popular on the beaches, bays, jetties, and piers. Fish commonly caught near shore include redfish, flounder, sheepshead, speckled trout, and drum.

From Aransas Pass drive east on TX 361 on causeways across Redfish Bay. The road ends at the highway ferry in a little less than 7 miles. Huge steel structures often tower into the air just west of the road near the ferry. Some of the world's largest offshore production platforms are built here before being carefully floated to oil and gas fields many miles out in the Gulf of Mexico. Although the structures are built lying on their sides, they still appear enormous, and in fact some are larger than the Empire State Building in New York City.

The ferry runs 24 hours a day and offers a fun 5-minute ride across the Corpus Christi Channel to the funky beach town of **Port Aransas** on the north end of Mustang Island. Except for spring break, when thousands of students descend on Port A, as it's often called, and summer weekends, the wait for the ferry is usually very short. Port Aransas was relatively inaccessible until 1954, when the Mustang Island Highway was opened. Before then the only way to reach town was by boat or railroad.

Port Aransas is still somewhat of a sleepy beach and fishing community. A few luxury condominiums have sprouted here and there, but there are still plenty of beach cottages, bait shops, and motel courts. The franchise chains have yet to take over town. The biggest attraction here, and along the rest of the drive, is the beach. Port Aransas Beach on the north side of town has showers, campsites, concessions,

Sailboats line the harbor at Port Aransas.

restrooms, and the long Horace Caldwell fishing pier. The wide beach is open to driving for most of the island's length. Generally the beach is more attractive south of town.

Fishermen will find many opportunities in Port Aransas. Some favorite spots are the granite jetties that protect the mouth of Aransas Pass, Horace Caldwell Pier, and two smaller city piers on the shipping channel. Numerous party and charter boats offer bay and deep-sea fishing.

Trash is all too common on Texas beaches. It's not that Texans litter any more than anyone else. In fact the state spends millions of dollars cleaning up trash on the coast. But ocean currents carry anything dumped in the Gulf of Mexico to the Texas shore. Litter washes ashore from ships and other countries over which the state has little control.

If you don't mind being surrounded by hordes of exuberant college students, come to Port Aransas between the first of March and early April. Otherwise you may want to visit at another time of year.

The sun sets over Laguna Madre, the long narrow bay between Padre Island and the mainland.

Port Aransas to Padre Island

From Port Aransas drive south on Mustang Island on TX 361 toward Padre Island. Development slowly tapers off south of town. A number of side roads give easy access to the beach. The 3,700-acre **Mustang Island State Park** is about 14 miles south of town along TX 361. The park straddles the island from beach to bay. It offers several miles of wild beach, developed campsites, primitive beach camping, and other facilities.

The highway crosses several passes, including Fish Pass, Corpus Christi Pass, Newport Pass, and 1852 Pass. All were once channels between the gulf and the bay but have since sanded closed. Hurricanes periodically open and close new passes through the barrier islands. Corpus Christi Pass separates Mustang Island from Padre Island.

About 26 miles from the town of Aransas Pass, TX 361 ends at the intersection with Park Road 22. Development has been heavy in recent years in this area.

Eventually a hurricane may discourage it. Turn left onto Park Road 22, toward **Padre Island National Seashore.** Several roads provide beach access from the highway. Development thins and ends before reaching the park entrance after about 10 miles. Like most of the Texas coast, the island is almost treeless. Grasslands and marshes stretch east to the back bay of Laguna Madre. Over the dune ridge to the west lies the beach.

Birds are everywhere. Pelicans patrol the skies above Laguna Madre, hunting fish in the shallow water. Herons and egrets wade slowly through the marshes searching for crustaceans and fish. Sandpipers skitter along the beach, moving just ahead of the rolling surf.

A short loop trail winds through island grasslands and interprets the natural history of the area. Be sure to take insect repellent for this or any other walk inland from the beach. Mosquitoes can be fierce, especially on summer evenings.

The drive ends about 5 miles from the park entrance at the Malaquite Beach Area. The complex includes a visitor center, concessions, campground, showers, and several miles of pedestrian-only beach. South of Malaquite the highway ends, but you can drive along the beach for about 5 miles. Beyond that the sand gets softer and more treacherous. With a four-wheel-drive vehicle and proper supplies, you can drive another 55 glorious, primitive miles along the beach to Mansfield Channel. Fish for flounder, hunt for shells or twisted pieces of driftwood, or just relax at Padre Island National Seashore, one of the longest undeveloped ocean beaches in the United States.

Aransas

Rockport to Aransas National Wildlife Refuge

General description: A 56-mile drive along the Gulf Coast, ending at Aransas National Wildlife Refuge.

Special attractions: Aransas National Wildlife Refuge, Goose Island State Park, Fulton Mansion State Historic Site, Goose Island Oak, Copano Bay Fishing Pier, whooping cranes, alligators, swimming, boating, fishing, hiking, camping.

Location: Gulf Coast. The drive starts in Rockport, a small town about 30 miles northeast of Corpus Christi.

Drive route numbers: TX 35, FM 774, FM 2040, Aransas National Wildlife Refuge roads.

Travel season: Fall through spring. The area is hot and humid in summer, but swimming and boating activities can help in coping with the heat.

Camping: Goose Island State Park has two large, attractive campgrounds.

Services: All services are available in Rockport and Fulton.

Nearby attractions: Padre Island National Seashore, Goliad State Historical Park, Fannin Battleground, Matagorda Island National Wildlife Refuge and State Park, Mustang Island State Park, Corpus Christi attractions including the USS *Lexington* Museum, Texas State Aquarium, and many others.

For more information: Aransas National Wildlife Refuge, P.O. Box 100, Austwell, TX 77950; (361) 286-3559; www.fws.gov /southwest/refuges/texas/aransas. Goose Island State Park, 202 South Palmetto St. (Lamar), Rockport, TX 78382; (361) 729-2858; www.tpwd.state.tx.us/spdest/finda dest/parks/goose_island. Fulton Mansion State Historic Site, 317 Fulton Beach Rd., Rockport, TX 78382; (361) 729-0386; www.visitfultonmansion.com. Copano Bay Fishing Pier, 911 Navigation Circle, Rockport, TX 78382; (361) 729-6661; www .acnd.org/copano_bay_pier.html. Rockport-Fulton Area Chamber of Commerce, 404 Broadway, Rockport, TX 78382; (361) 729-6445 or (800) 242-0071; www.rock port-fulton.org.

The Drive

The area around Rockport is one of the most scenic parts of the Texas coast. In most areas of Texas, the coast is treeless, but around Rockport live oaks grow right on the shores of the bays. The second largest live oak in Texas, the **Goose Island Oak,** grows in sight of St. Charles Bay.

Aransas National Wildlife Refuge is famous as the winter home of the endangered whooping crane. Birders flock here to see not only the crane but also many of the other 350 bird species found at the refuge.

Rockport lies on a peninsula between Copano and Aransas Bays. A barrier island, San José Island, protects the peninsula from storms and tides of the Gulf of

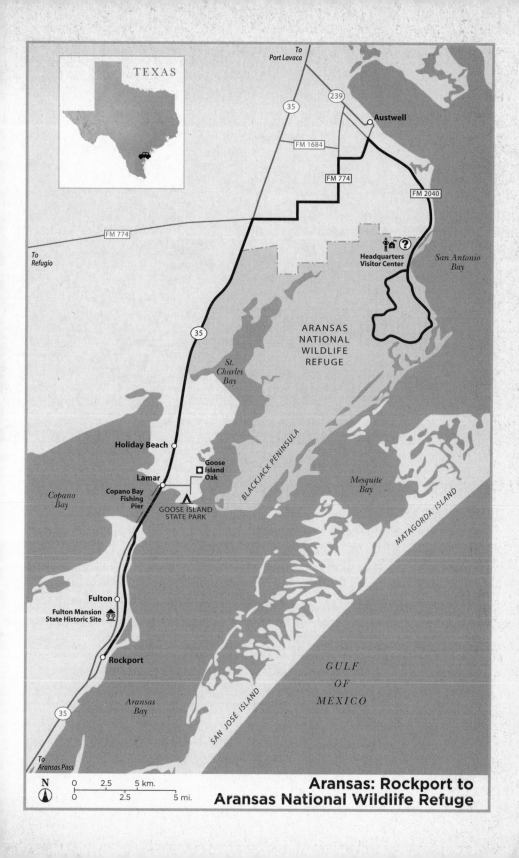

TEXAS

To
Port Lavaca

239

35

Austwell

FM 1684

FM 774

FM 2040

FM 774

To
Refugio

Headquarters
Visitor Center

San Antonio
Bay

35

ARANSAS
NATIONAL
WILDLIFE
REFUGE

St.
Charles
Bay

Holiday Beach

Goose
Island
Oak

Lamar

BLACKJACK PENINSULA

Mesquite
Bay

Copano Bay
Fishing
Pier

GOOSE ISLAND
STATE PARK

Copano
Bay

MATAGORDA ISLAND

Fulton

Fulton Mansion
State Historic Site

Rockport

GULF

OF

MEXICO

35

Aransas
Bay

SAN JOSÉ ISLAND

To
Aransas Pass

N

0   2.5   5 km.

0   2.5   5 mi.

Aransas: Rockport to
Aransas National Wildlife Refuge

The sun rises over shrimp boats at the harbor in Fulton.

Mexico. Rockport was founded in 1867 as a shipping point for hides, wool, bones, and tallow. Huge cattle herds were brought here for slaughter. Surprisingly, the meat was considered a by-product. Some was preserved through salting, pickling, or drying, but most was thrown in the bay as waste. As railroads were built the livestock industry died in Rockport and fishing became the basis of the local economy. The mild climate and attractive coast soon brought tourists. Many artists have also settled here. Rockport and its sister city, Fulton, are still important sport and commercial fishing and resort centers.

Start the drive on the north side of downtown Rockport where TX 35 and Business TX 35 join together at a large grassy traffic island. Both the chamber of commerce and **Texas Maritime Museum** are here. The museum chronicles the maritime history of Texas, from Spanish galleons to the Texas Navy to the commercial fishing industry.

Drive north along TX 35, past Little Bay and the Rockport Beach Park. The park has swimming, picnicking, fishing, and water sports, plus views of the bay for birders. After 0.5 mile a smaller road, Bayshores Drive, forks off to the right. For the fastest route to the wildlife refuge, stay on four-lane TX 35. But take the much more scenic Bayshores Drive if you have time. The road fork is marked with green highway department signs for Fulton Beach and Key Allegro.

Bayshores Drive continues to follow Little Bay. The expensive waterfront homes of Key Allegro are visible a short distance across the water. After 0.5 mile the road crosses a small bridge and forks. Go left toward Fulton Beach on Fulton Beach Road, which follows the shoreline. Except when it's very windy, there isn't much surf on the bay because of San José Island. Note the windswept live oak trees along the drive. Constant gulf winds twist and bend the hardy trees inland. The wind and salty air make survival difficult for the gnarled oaks.

The beach road passes **Fulton Mansion** on the left after 0.6 mile. George Fulton built the 30-room French Second Empire structure in 4 years in the mid-1870s. Not only was the home an architectural showplace, it was very modern for its time, with hot and cold running water, insulation, flush toilets, central heat, and a gas lighting system. Strong construction has allowed it to withstand hurricanes. The Texas Historical Commission conducts tours of the ornate 4-story home Tues through Sun.

Beyond Fulton Mansion the drive continues along the bay, passing the harbor full of shrimp boats and the long Fulton fishing pier. The road finally turns inland a little more than 6 miles from the start and rejoins TX 35.

Turn right onto TX 35 and continue north. The highway soon crosses the long bridge across the mouth of Copano Bay. Paralleling the bridge is the original highway bridge. The Texas Parks and Wildlife Department converted it into a 1.5-mile-long fishing pier cut in the middle for boat traffic. The pier is now managed by the Aransas County Navigation District, so fishing licenses are required. It's accessible at either end of the modern highway bridge.

For a short side trip, turn right onto Park Road 13 at the north end of the bridge and drive to **Goose Island State Park.** The park has campsites on a small islet right on the bay or in thick woods of live oak and other plants. A short, easy hiking trail circles the woodland campground. Even if you don't fish, be sure to take a walk to the end of the quarter-mile fishing pier. It extends into the bay to several tiny islets. Many different birds can be seen in the shallow waters and oyster beds. At night the lighted pier is peaceful, with only lapping water and bird calls to disturb the calm.

Be sure to follow the state park signs to the **Goose Island Oak** at an outlying section of the park. The thousand-year-old tree is enormous, the second largest live oak in Texas. The trunk is 11 feet in diameter, and the tree is 44 feet tall with a crown spread of 90 feet.

Aransas National Wildlife Refuge

From Goose Island continue north on TX 35 through the small resort village of Holiday Beach. The oaks slowly thin and the highway enters coastal plain grassland. The boundary of part of Aransas National Wildlife Refuge is on the right. Turn right onto FM 774 about 23 miles north of Rockport and follow signs to the refuge. After another 9.5 miles of farmland and frequent sharp right-angle bends in the road, turn right again onto FM 2040. As you approach the refuge, oak trees again appear and San Antonio Bay becomes visible to the east. Follow FM 2040 for 6.7 miles until the road enters the refuge. You must first stop at the visitor center a short distance past the entrance to pay an admission fee. The refuge is open from sunrise to sunset.

Aransas National Wildlife Refuge is most famous as the winter home of the whooping crane, the largest bird in North America. The 115,000-acre refuge was created in 1937 to protect the whooping crane and other vanishing wildlife of the Texas coast. About half of the refuge occupies a peninsula between San Antonio, Mesquite, and St. Charles Bays. The rest lies on Matagorda Island and elsewhere. The terrain is a mix of freshwater and saltwater marshes, grassland, and oak woodland. Legend says that notorious pirate Jean Lafitte buried "enough treasure in those woods to ransom a nation."

The visitor center has extensive exhibits and information about the refuge. Continue the drive by following the loop road through the refuge and back to the visitor center. Although not always necessary, insect repellent can be a lifesaver when mosquitoes are thick. Watch carefully as you drive. Although Aransas is noted for its birds, other residents such as deer, javelina, raccoons, and armadillos are common here. There is even some evidence that the jaguarundi, a small, endangered member of the cat family, lives at Aransas.

Several short, easy trails lead to interesting parts of the refuge. The Heron Flats Trail is on the left only a short distance down the road from the visitor center. It's a scenic trail through marshes and small patches of woods along the edge of San Antonio Bay. This is a great trail to see alligators, common in the refuge marshes. Do not approach the large reptiles and, for obvious reasons, keep your pets tightly leashed.

A short spur road on the left leads to Dagger Point and an excellent view of the bay. The short hiking trail climbs a surprisingly high old sand dune now wooded with twisted live oaks and red bays. Waves are slowly eroding the dune, cutting a steep face on the dune, causing the trees to eventually fall into the bay.

The pullout at Jones Lake is worth a stop. A pier extends out into a marshy body of water, another excellent place to view birds, alligators, and other wildlife. Just past Jones Lake, the Big Tree Trail starts on the other side of the road and goes to some very large live oak trees and the shoreline.

Just beyond the Big Tree Trail is the parking lot for the prominent observation tower. From late October to mid-April, this is the best place in the refuge

Alligators are common in the freshwater marshes at Aransas National Wildlife Refuge.

to see whooping cranes without taking a boat tour. The cranes almost became extinct, with only 15 birds left in 1941. Today more than 200 cranes winter at Aransas and summer in Canada. Two smaller flocks have been established in Florida. The larger of the two stays in Florida year-round; the smaller one migrates to Wisconsin in the summer. The tower looks out over marshlands favored by the big birds.

From the observation tower the road winds through grasslands, marshes, and woodlands before arriving back at the visitor center and the end of the drive.

23

Bluewater Highway

Surfside Beach to Galveston

General description: A 40-mile drive along the Texas coast from the sleepy beachtown of Surfside Beach to the bustling port and tourist center of Galveston.

Special attractions: Galveston Island State Park, Bolivar Point Lighthouse, Bishop's Palace, Moody Mansion, The Strand, Moody Gardens, Seawolf Park, Galveston–Port Bolivar ferry, beaches, fishing, camping, hiking, birding.

Location: Upper Gulf Coast. The drive starts in Surfside Beach, a small coastal town about 65 miles south of Houston.

Drive route number: CR 257, FM 3005.

Travel season: All year. The drive is hot and humid in summer, but a swim at one of the beaches will cool you off.

Camping: Galveston Island State Park and San Luis Pass County Park.

Services: Gas and food are available at San Luis Pass. All services are available in Galveston and Surfside Beach.

Nearby attractions: Bryan Beach, Varner-Hogg Plantation State Historic Site, Brazoria National Wildlife Refuge, Brazos Bend State Park.

For more information: Galveston Island Convention and Visitors Bureau, 2428 Seawall Blvd., Galveston, TX 77550; (409) 797-5145 or (866) 505-4456; www.galveston.com. Brazosport Area Chamber of Commerce, 300 Abner Jackson Pkwy., Brazosport, TX 77566; (979) 265-2505; www.brazosport.org. Galveston Island State Park, 14901 FM 3005, Galveston, TX 77554; (409) 737-1222; www.tpwd.state.tx.us/spdest/findadest/parks/galveston.

The Drive

The drive follows the coast, starting in a section that is relatively empty and quiet and ending in the busy tourist city of Galveston. As along most of the Texas coast, there are few trees near the shore except where they have been planted. Wind, salt, and occasional hurricanes make it difficult for trees to become established. But the beaches and dunes have a stark beauty of their own. Nothing beats watching the sun rise over the Gulf of Mexico on a cool, quiet morning. Behind the beaches are low dune ridges that are often covered with flowers such as the purple goat-foot morning glory. Marshes flank the back bays and harbor a tremendous variety of birds, fish, and other creatures.

The drive starts near Freeport in the small town of **Surfside Beach.** The section of coast around Freeport is one of the few places in Texas where the coast lies on the mainland. Most of the coast, including most of this drive, consists of barrier islands and peninsulas separated from the mainland by bays and estuaries.

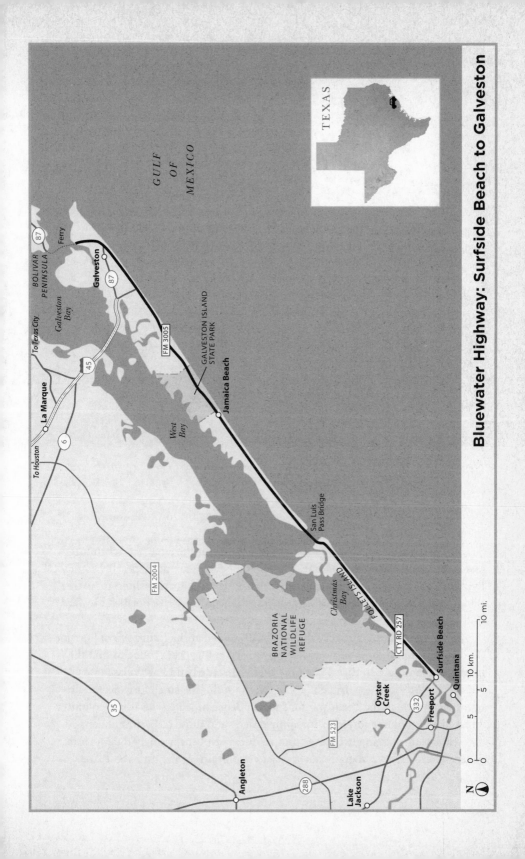

Bluewater Highway: Surfside Beach to Galveston

TEXAS

GULF OF MEXICO

BOLIVAR PENINSULA

Ferry

87

Galveston

87

Galveston Bay

To Texas City

45

La Marque

To Houston

6

FM 3005

GALVESTON ISLAND STATE PARK

Jamaica Beach

West Bay

San Luis Pass Bridge

FOLLETS ISLAND

FM 2004

Christmas Bay

BRAZORIA NATIONAL WILDLIFE REFUGE

35

CTY RD 257

Surfside Beach

Quintana

Oyster Creek

Freeport

332

FM 523

Angleton

288

Lake Jackson

N

0   5   10 km.
0   5   10 mi.

Wooden posts march into the Gulf of Mexico at Surfside Beach.

Possibly the large volume of sediment deposited by the Brazos River somehow alters this section of coastline.

The Freeport–Clute–Lake Jackson area is noted for the large petrochemical plants that drive the local economy. Although the plants are not especially scenic, they have no effect on recreational activities like swimming and fishing at Surfside Beach. The plants quickly disappear from view as you drive northeast toward Galveston.

In 1821 Stephen F. Austin's first colonists landed at the future site of Surfside Beach at the mouth of the Brazos River by mistake; they were trying to find the mouth of the Colorado River. Later the area was settled and Fort Velasco was built by the Mexican government at the river mouth. The small fort was the site of the first battle of the Texas war for independence in 1832. The Texan colonists attacked and took the fort after its commanders, and those of Fort Anahuac to the east, began charging excessive customs duties. Not surprisingly the Mexican government sent several gunboats to exact retribution. At the time the Texans were unhappy with the Mexican president and supported the efforts of a Mexican general to wrest power from him. To their good fortune the commander of the gunboats supported the efforts of that general, so the Texans peacefully returned control of Fort Velasco to the Mexicans. The general eventually did seize power in Mexico but did not remain popular with Texans for long. His name? General Antonio Lopez de Santa Ana. Four years later Santa Ana was brought here after his defeat at the Battle of San Jacinto to sign the treaty granting Texas independence.

Today Surfside Beach is a small, rustic town with plentiful beach rental properties and several motels. The several miles of beach in town are well kept and controlled. Part of the beach allows only pedestrians. One-way driving is allowed on the rest of the beach, but parking requires an inexpensive permit that helps pay for maintenance, toilets, and trash pick-up.

The beach ends on the south side of town where the Freeport ship channel cuts inland at the former mouth of the Brazos River. The Brazos River channel was moved some miles south many years ago. You can watch everything from motorboats to oil tankers slide through the deep waterway. The two granite jetties that protect the channel are capped with broad sidewalks. An attractive park with concessions, a playground, and exercise stations has been built at the north jetty. The jetties extend about half a mile into the gulf and make a great place for an evening stroll. Fishermen love the jetties and are found on them any time of day or night. Common catches are redfish, flounder, and speckled trout. Freeport and Surfside Beach are also centers for shrimping and deep-sea fishing.

Across the channel from Surfside Beach is the village of **Quintana** and the empty shoreline of Bryan Beach. If Surfside Beach is too busy for your tastes, drive over to the other side of the channel via Freeport.

To start the drive, from Surfside Beach follow CR 257 (previously FM 3005) north along the coast. The beach continues for miles, all the way to San Luis Pass. At 2.4 miles, Stahlman Park has a marsh boardwalk on the inland or left side and access to the beach on the right. The beach houses thin out and the beach becomes quiet and empty. The coast resumes its normal character and becomes a peninsula with a bay between it and the mainland. Several small side roads lead down to the beach on the right and tidal marshes on the left.

The peninsula is called **Follets Island,** perhaps because it was once separated from the mainland by a natural waterway. Today it is separated by the man-made channels of the Intracoastal Waterway. The waterway is an important shipping route along the entire Gulf Coast, from Brownsville, Texas, to Florida.

San Luis Pass, reached at a little less than 14 miles, is a narrow channel connecting the Gulf of Mexico with West Bay and separating Follets Island from Galveston Island. A toll bridge crosses the channel. On the west or Follets Island side, Brazoria County maintains San Luis Pass County Park in conjunction with the Texas Parks and Wildlife Department. Fishing, camping, boating, and beach-combing are popular activities at the small 15-acre park. Swimming is not allowed, however; strong currents flow through the pass, induced by tidal changes.

Galveston Island State Park & Galveston

The road, now FM 3005, becomes a four-lane divided highway for a few miles beyond the bridge to Galveston Island. Development and beach houses become more common as the road continues northeast across Galveston Island. At 18 to 20 miles along, development becomes fairly dense. In 2008, Hurricane Ike did severe damage to homes and businesses on the island, including the newer, more expensive developments on the southwest end of the island. Occasional side roads allow access to public beaches. At 27.5 miles the road enters **Galveston Island State Park,** a welcome break in the development. This 1,950-acre park offers a broad beach with swimming, fishing, sailboarding, and other water activities, plus a quiet area of bayside marshes with hiking trails, boardwalks, and wildlife observation platforms. The park has been mostly repaired from the hurricane damage, with campgrounds and picnic areas open.

Beyond the state park the road approaches the heart of the popular resort and port city of **Galveston.** At 34.5 miles the road climbs up onto the seawall, a raised concrete-and-fill structure that lines the beach for miles, protecting the city from hurricanes. The remaining few miles into the heart of the city follow the seawall past numerous hotels, restaurants, and shops.

Cabeza de Vaca first discovered Galveston Island the hard way in 1528 when he was shipwrecked there. After being imprisoned for some time by Karankawa Indians, he made a brutal overland journey back to Mexico City, arriving several years after the shipwreck. In the mid-1700s Spanish troops stationed on the island named it after Count Bernardo de Galvez, the viceroy of Mexico. In 1817 the pirate Jean Lafitte established his base, a true den of thieves, on the island. He became an American hero after assisting General Andrew Jackson at the Battle of New Orleans in the War of 1812, but he was no favorite of others. He preyed on Spanish ships, slave ships, and other vessels in the gulf until 1821 when he made the mistake of attacking a US ship. The American government soon forced Lafitte and his fellow buccaneers to leave Galveston.

Over time Galveston steadily grew and gained importance as a port. During the Texas war for independence, Galveston served as a temporary capital and home port of the Texas Navy. During the Civil War, Union troops took Galveston but were later ejected until the war's end by Confederate troops led by General John Magruder. The town endured a devastating yellow fever epidemic after the

Bishop's Palace is one of many historic structures in Galveston.

The sun rises over the beach at Galveston Island State Park.

war but then thrived, becoming the third largest seaport in the United States by the late 1800s. A busy commercial district, known as the Strand, developed. Extravagant homes of various styles, from Greek Revival to Victorian, sprouted, fed by the vast sums of money pouring through the city.

With the growing wealth, city residents forgot that Galveston was literally a city built on sand only a few feet above sea level. The island is a low-lying barrier of sand created by wind and wave action on the shallow ocean floor. On September 8, 1900, a hurricane swept across Galveston with howling winds and a storm tidal surge that drowned the entire island. The land virtually disappeared under the waves of the Gulf of Mexico. At least 6,000 people died and thousands of homes and buildings were destroyed. The bridge to the mainland disappeared into the waters of Galveston Bay. Even today the Galveston hurricane of 1900 stands as one of the worst natural disasters to befall the United States.

To protect the island from future storms, the survivors began the daunting task of building the seawall, a tall concrete-and-fill structure that originally lined

4 miles of the beach but has since been extended. In addition, massive volumes of sand were dredged from the bays to raise the elevation of the entire city from 3 to 17 feet. In 1915 the residents' labors were severely tested by another hurricane purportedly stronger than the 1900 one. The seawall held and there was significant damage, but only a few people died and the city survived. Numerous hurricanes have struck since then, but none has wrought the damage of the hurricane of 1900. During Hurricane Ike, the seawall protected Galveston from being flattened like in 1900, but severe flooding and wind did affect much of the city. Many homes and businesses were damaged and salt water killed many large live oaks in the historic district. More recent developments along the shore southwest of the seawall were heavily damaged and the beach suffered heavy erosion.

After surviving numerous hurricanes the city suffered again when Houston dug a ship channel inland and stole away much of the city's port trade. Gambling brought new life to Galveston in the 1930s and 1940s, but the city slumped again in the 1950s after authorities cracked down on the activity. Although the city was suffering an economic depression, civic leaders came to the realization that tourists would come to see the historic homes and buildings, in addition to the beaches. A big push was made to restore the old bank buildings of the Strand and the wealth of Victorian homes in the city. Today the Strand bustles with a mix of galleries, shops, and restaurants. Hotels, from modest to luxurious, line the seawall. Major sources of economic activity include tourism, the port, the University of Texas Medical Branch, and a variety of banks and insurance companies.

Galveston offers several days' worth of activities for visitors. There are literally hundreds of historic buildings. Three particularly impressive homes open for tours are the **Bishop's Palace,** the **Moody Mansion,** and **Ashton Villa.** The Strand deserves some time, if for nothing more than viewing the carefully restored commercial buildings. Other worthwhile sights include the extensive **Moody Gardens** with its recreated tropical rain forest, **Seawolf Park** with a World War II submarine and destroyer escort, and the elaborate **Railroad Museum** at the west end of the Strand. Another guidebook is needed to fully describe the many attractions of Galveston. If you tire of the city, head for the quiet marshes of Galveston Island State Park or catch the free car ferry across the mouth of Galveston Bay to the Bolivar Peninsula. An old iron lighthouse that once guided ships into the bay still marks the tip of the peninsula. Unlike many other structures on the Boliva Peninsula, it survived the onslaught of Hurricane Ike.

The Lost Pines

Buescher State Park to Bastrop State Park

24

General description: A paved 13-mile route through the Lost Pines of Texas.

Special attractions: Bastrop State Park, Buescher State Park, thick pine forest, hiking, camping, cycling.

Location: Central Texas. The drive starts near Smithville, about 40 miles southeast of Austin.

Drive route number: Park Road 1.

Travel season: All year. The drive is hot and humid in summer, making spring, fall, and sunny winter days the best driving times.

Camping: Both Bastrop and Buescher State Parks maintain campgrounds.

Services: Food, gas, and very limited lodging are available in Smithville; all services are available in Bastrop.

Nearby attractions: Monument Hill/Kreische Brewery State Historic Site, McKinney Falls State Park, State Capitol, parks, museums, shopping, and numerous other attractions in Austin.

For more information: Bastrop State Park, Box 518, Bastrop, TX 78602; (512) 321-2101; www.tpwd.state.tx.us/spdest/findadest/parks/bastrop. Buescher State Park, P.O. Box 75, Smithville, TX 78957; (512) 237-2241; www.tpwd.state.tx.us/spdest/findadest/parks/buescher. Bastrop Chamber of Commerce, 927 Main St., Bastrop, TX 78602; (512) 303-0558; www.bastropchamber.com. Smithville Area Chamber of Commerce, P.O. Box 716, Smithville, TX 78957; (512) 237-2313; www.smithvilletx.org.

The Drive

This short drive passes through a unique area in Central Texas heavily wooded with loblolly pines, far to the west of their normal range. Because of the isolated, seemingly misplaced pines, the hilly area near Bastrop and Smithville is known as the Lost Pines.

The drive starts at **Buescher State Park** headquarters at the entrance of the park. To get there, turn off of TX 71 at the Smithville/TX 95/FM 153 exit and go northeast on FM 153, following signs for Buescher State Park. After not much more than half a mile, turn left into the park and proceed to the park headquarters just ahead.

Buescher State Park lies at the eastern edge of the Lost Pines but is less well-known than its sister park, Bastrop. Scenic, hilly Park Road 1 connects the woodland parks. On busy weekends when Bastrop is packed, Buescher is often relatively peaceful.

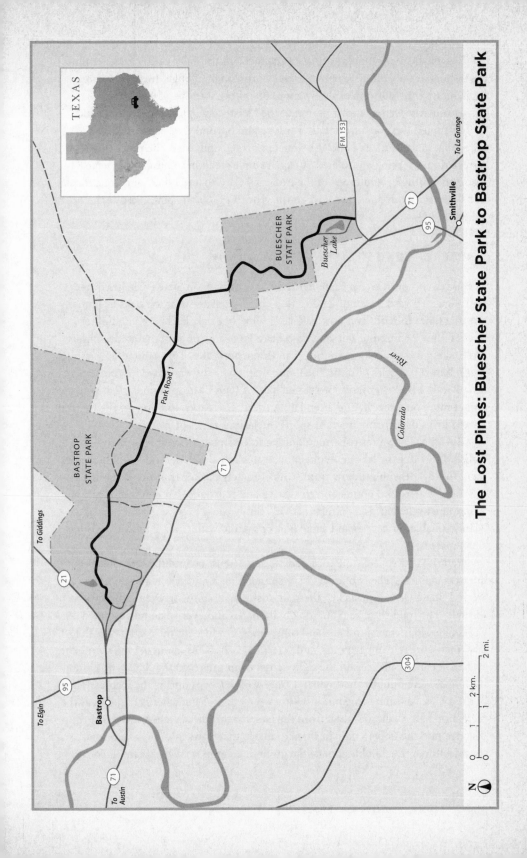

The Lost Pines: Buescher State Park to Bastrop State Park

The fresh scent of loblolly pines wafts through the air of both parks, reminding visitors of the East Texas pine forests. Surprisingly though, these pines are located on some hilly uplands only about 30 miles southeast of Austin.

During the wetter, cooler period of the Pleistocene, pine forests stretched uninterrupted westward from East Texas to and beyond the Bastrop area. As the ice age glaciers melted and the climate warmed and dried, the pines slowly retreated east, leaving an isolated 70-square-mile stand in Central Texas near Bastrop and Smithville. Outcrops of the iron-rich Carrizo and other sandstone formations create a sandy soil conducive to the growth of loblolly pines despite the drier climate.

Buescher Lake to Bastrop State Park

The north end of Buescher State Park, along with Bastrop State Park, lies in the Lost Pines. Toward the south end of Buescher State Park near the park headquarters, the pines thin out and post oak, cedar elm, live oak, hackberry, and other trees are more common. Buescher also has a large area of bottomland deciduous forest along drainages and around small **Buescher Lake.** This habitat helps attract more than 200 species of birds, including many types of waterfowl on the 25-acre lake. Because Buescher has more varied habitat than Bastrop State Park, it tends to attract more bird species and attendant birders. The parks' location on the Central Flyway helps draw many migrant species at various times of year.

Buescher Lake lures fishermen hoping to catch largemouth bass, crappie, and catfish. In winter the lake gets cold enough to allow the Parks and Wildlife Department to stock it with rainbow trout. Unfortunately the water is too warm in summer for a year-round population to survive and reproduce. In the heat of summer, swimming in the lake is a popular activity, but because of its small size the lake is only suitable for canoes and small boats powered with trolling motors or other small motors.

Park Road 1 splits into Park Road 1C and 1E just behind the Buescher headquarters building. The two forks are of similar length and rejoin after looping around Buescher Lake. I picked the right fork, 1E, because of several interesting features. The road climbs up and down drainages and over small hills wooded with oaks, cedar elms, junipers, and other trees. On the left, the road passes the lake, picnic areas, campgrounds, and screened shelters. At about 0.5 mile, note the attractive park residences on the right across from the recreation hall. These durable homes were built by the Civilian Conservation Corps during the Depression of the 1930s. An interesting but little-known feature of Buescher is found near the recreation hall. Walk southeast from the hall, toward the screened shelters, a short distance into the upper end of a small drainage that flows into the lake below. A warm sulfur spring bubbles out of the ground, creating a small stream lined with

The sun burns through mist rising from the small lake at Buescher State Park on a chilly morning.

odd greenish-white algae or mosses. The spring may be natural or it may have been the result of an old well drilled into an artesian aquifer.

At 0.8 mile the road passes the trailhead for the Buescher Hiking Trail. This 7.8-mile trail winds through dense stands of loblolly pine and deciduous forests of oak and cedar elm. In another 0.1 mile Park Roads 1C and 1E meet near the tent camping area at the north end of the lake. Turn right onto Park Road 1C, following the sign to Bastrop State Park. The road is in a creek bottom here and the trees, tall and lush, arch over the road. Pines begin to become common as you continue along the route.

Park Road 1C is narrow, with lots of sharp curves and short, steep hills. Because the highway is very scenic and traffic is light, it has become popular with cyclists. It's a beautiful bike ride but strenuous with the many hills. Be sure to keep an eye open for cyclists as you drive.

As the soil becomes sandier and redder, loblolly pines become more and more common, eventually dominating the forest canopy. There is a nice overlook of the

Canoes are a popular way to explore the small lake at Bastrop State Park.

Colorado River Valley on the left at 2.2 miles. A large part of Buescher State Park is occupied by the University of Texas M.D. Anderson Science Park. The entrance is on the right at 2.7 miles.

The road crosses a creek at 7.9 miles and enters **Bastrop State Park** at 8.5 miles. It then stops at the intersection with Park Road 1A at 11.6 miles. Park Road 1A makes a loop through part of Bastrop State Park; you can take either route. The left side of the loop leads to one of the campgrounds and to the two trailheads of the inviting Lost Pines Hiking Trail. I somewhat arbitrarily took the shorter right-hand fork.

At 12.2 miles the road passes a 10-acre lake tucked into the pines. On the far side of the lake, Park Road 1B turns off to the right and dead-ends at several park rental cabins. The rustic, solidly built cabins were constructed by the Civilian Conservation Corps during the Depression. They are extremely popular; if you wish to stay in them be sure to reserve them well in advance.

Park Road 1A meets with the other leg of the loop at a three-way junction at 12.8 miles in the heart of the recreational section of the park. On the left the CCC built a large, handsome recreation hall out of native wood and sandstone. Near it is the park swimming pool, popular during the summer months. To the right is the golf course, a rarity in the state park system. The popular 18-hole course winds through tall pines and crosses steep ravines, making it one of the most attractive courses in the state.

Bastrop

Going straight at the three-way junction will take you around the rest of the Park Road 1A loop. Going right will take you out of the park to TX 21 and the town of Bastrop. TX 21 is much busier than the drive between the two state parks, but it also is very scenic between Bastrop State Park and US 290 to the northeast.

The town of Bastrop, just to the west of Bastrop State Park on TX 21, lies in the Colorado River Valley, just outside of the Lost Pines. The town of Bastrop was founded in 1829, making it one of the oldest settlements in Texas. It was named after the Baron de Bastrop, who helped Moses Austin (father of Stephen F. Austin) obtain permission to settle American colonists in Texas. Originally lumbering, agriculture, and shipping were the principal economic bases. Today the town serves travelers on busy TX 71, a principal artery connecting Houston and Austin, and acts as a bedroom community for nearby Austin. A meal at one of the many restaurants in Bastrop makes a nice ending to the drive.

25

La Bahia Road

Burton to Washington-on-the-Brazos State Historic Site

General description: A 39-mile paved highway through pastoral countryside and historic sites important to the creation of the Republic of Texas.

Special attractions: Washington-on-the-Brazos State Historic Site, Old Baylor Park, wildflowers, Burton Cotton Gin and Museum.

Location: East-central Texas. The drive starts in Burton, a small town a short distance west of Brenham.

Drive route numbers: FM 390, TX 105, FM 912, FM 1155.

Travel season: All year. Temperatures are most pleasant in spring and fall. Wildflowers are best from late Mar through May.

Camping: There are no public campgrounds along the route. The closest campground is at Lake Somerville State Park.

Services: Gas and limited food can be found in Burton, Independence, and Wash-ington. All services are available in Brenham and Navasota.

Nearby attractions: Lake Somerville State Park, Fanthorp Inn State Historic Site, Blue Bell Creameries in Brenham.

For more information: Washington-on-the-Brazos State Historic Site, Box 305, Washington, TX 77880; (936) 878-2214; www.tpwd.state.tx.us/spdest/findadest /parks/washington_on_the_brazos. Lake Somerville State Park, 6280 FM 180, Ledbetter, TX 78946; (979) 289-2392; www .tpwd.state.tx.us/spdest/findadest/parks /lake_somerville. Burton Cotton Gin and Museum, 307 N. Main St., Burton, TX 77835; (979) 289-3378; www.cottongin museum.org. Brenham Chamber of Commerce, 314 South Austin, Brenham, TX 77833; (979) 836-3695; www.brenham texas.com. Navasota Grimes County Chamber of Commerce, 117 S. La Salle, Navasota, TX 77868; (936) 825-6600; www .navasotagrimeschamber.com.

The Drive

The drive passes through pastoral farm and ranch country important in the early days of the Republic of Texas. The area is particularly notable for spring wildflowers, such as bluebonnets, Indian paintbrush, and phlox. Most of the route follows FM 390, called La Bahia Road and designated as a scenic route by the Texas Department of Transportation. Unlike other Texas highway route markers, which are black and white, the FM 390 markers are brown and white to designate its scenic status. The signs still use the same shape, size, and symbols, however.

The drive starts in Burton, a small town a few miles west of Brenham on busy US 290, an important artery connecting Houston and Austin. Burton is an

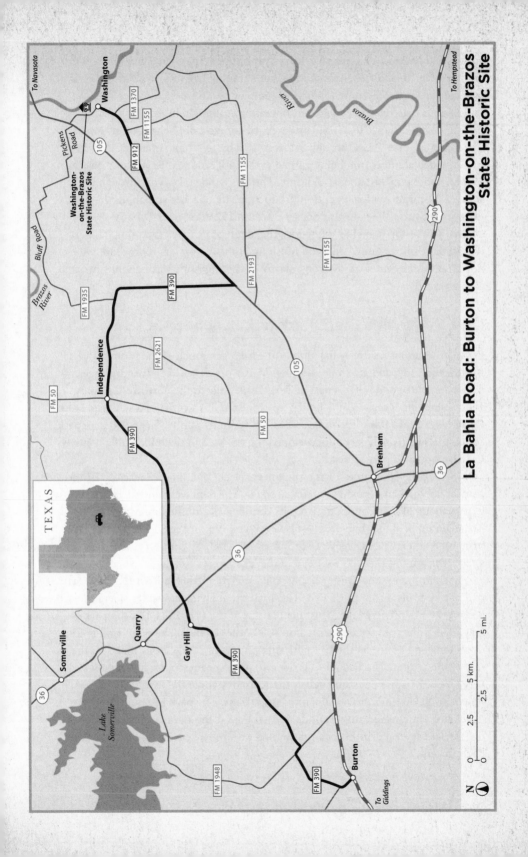

La Bahia Road: Burton to Washington-on-the-Brazos
State Historic Site

N

0   2.5   5 km.

0   2.5   5 mi.

TEXAS

To Navasota

Washington

FM 1370

FM 1155

Pickens Road

105

FM 912

Washington-
on-the-Brazos
State Historic Site

Bluff Road

Brazos River

FM 1935

FM 390

FM 2193

FM 1155

FM 1155

Brazos River

290

To Hempstead

Independence

FM 50

FM 2621

105

FM 50

FM 390

Brenham

36

Quarry

Somerville

36

Lake Somerville

Gay Hill

FM 390

FM 1948

36

290

FM 390

Burton

To Giddings

attractive town with a number of interesting old buildings. Particularly notewor-thy is the Burton Cotton Gin and Museum in the middle of town. The 1914-vintage cotton gin, tucked into a rambling complex of old wood and sheet-metal buildings, is believed to be the oldest operating cotton gin in America. Before driving a long distance to see the museum, be sure to call to check on its hours. The museum, open Tues through Sat from 10 a.m. to 4 p.m., offers exhibits and a short video about cotton being ginned at the mill. Tours, offered those days at 10 a.m. and 2 p.m. last about 1.5 hours. The tour guide takes you through the gin, shows a 20-minute video on cotton production, and teaches you about the production of cotton. The gin also houses a 16-ton 1925 Bessemer Type IV diesel oil engine. The restored engine still works, the oldest of its type remaining in operation in the United States. After you finish up at the cotton gin, follow FM 390 north out of the center of town on a narrow, winding route through mostly open, grassy pasture land.

Lake Somerville State Park to Independence

Overall the land is relatively flat with gentle hills, but much of the route between Burton and Independence follows a low ridge, a divide between two drainages. Views are quite good for this part of Texas, especially to the northwest. Nearby Lake Somerville is easily visible to the northwest and is worthy of a side trip. **Lake Somerville State Park** lies on its shores, split into two units. The 5,970-acre park contains a surprisingly large undeveloped tract of land in the middle of a relatively heavily populated part of Texas.

In 1962 the US Army Corps of Engineers began building Somerville Dam to control flooding and provide municipal water. The dam was constructed on Yegua Creek, about 20 miles upstream from its confluence with the Brazos River. The two main units of the state park, Nails Creek and Birch Creek, lie across the lake from each other. The extensive Lake Somerville Trailway connects the two units by looping around the wild west end of the lake.

Each unit contains campgrounds, boat ramps, picnic and swimming areas, and nature trails. From these two areas boaters, anglers, and water skiers can set out on the 11,460-acre lake. Most people stay at the two units, but the park's real jewel is the trail system, with almost 22 miles of trail. The main trail is 13 miles long and connects the two park units; spurs and side loops make up the rest of the system. The wide trail is open to hikers, equestrians, and mountain bikers. Because of small bridges that cannot handle the weight of a horse, one or two side trails are not open to equestrians. The park has built specially developed equestrian campgrounds in each unit at the start of the trail. Along the way are several primitive campgrounds with pit toilets for equestrians and backpackers.

The trail passes through a mix of two habitats, the blackland prairie and the post oak savannah. Lush meadows carpeted with wildflowers in the spring line some of the trail and offer broad views of the lake and surrounding country. Hillsides often contain a mix of yaupon, post oak, blackjack oak, and other plants. In creek bottoms a dense canopy of water oak, elm, hickory, and other trees shades the trail. Waterfowl and wading birds favor Flag Pond near the Nails Creek end of the trail. The large undeveloped area fosters abundant wildlife; raccoons, white-tailed deer, coyotes, rabbits, and many other creatures are commonly sighted.

After passing views of Lake Somerville, FM 390 continues along the ridge, passing horse ranches and a number of impressive homes, some old and some modern. At about 10 miles the highway enters the tiny village of Gay Hill. Be careful on the far side of the settlement where the road narrows to one lane to squeeze through a railroad underpass. After Gay Hill the highway crosses TX 36 and continues along the ridgeline, reaching **Independence** in about 20 miles.

Independence is a very small town but has been in existence since the earliest days of the Texas Republic. It was first settled in 1824 by John P. Coles, one of Stephen F. Austin's 300 original colonist families in Texas. Originally called Coles Settlement, the town name was changed in 1836 to commemorate Texas's independence from Mexico. The town was laid out to accommodate the Washington County courthouse, but Independence lost a hotly contested county seat election to Brenham by two votes.

Old Baylor Park along FM 390 on the west side of town was the birthplace of Baylor University, now in Waco, and Mary Hardin-Baylor College in Belton. Four tall stone columns mark the site of the original Baylor University, and John Coles' original home was relocated to the park and restored. Other interesting buildings in and around the park include Gilmartin's General Store and a dogtrot cabin. Shaded picnic tables make the park a pleasant stop along the drive.

The town cemetery, about a mile north of the park on McCrocklin Road, was started in 1823 and houses the remains of many notable citizens, including Sam Houston Jr., Moses Austin Bryan, and veterans of all US wars from the American Revolution through World War II. Old monuments and tilting gravestones dot the wooded grounds.

Independence Baptist Church stands at the junction of FM 390 and FM 50 in the center of town. This historic church was the first Baptist church founded in Texas, in 1839. The present building dates from 1872. The church and the adjoining Texas Baptist Historical Center house many pre–Civil War artifacts. Sam Houston was converted and baptized here in 1854; his wife, Margaret, and her mother, both longtime church members, are buried just across the street.

Washington-on-the-Brazos State Historic Site

After Independence FM 390 leaves the ridge and continues east until just past the intersection with FM 1935. It then turns south for a few miles and ends at TX 105 in about 30 miles. Turn left and follow TX 105 a little less than 5 miles to the junction with FM 912 on the right. Turn onto FM 912, marked by signs for Washington-on-the-Brazos State Historic Site, and follow it about 3 miles to where FM 1155 joins FM 912 from the right. Continue straight a short distance, on what is now FM 1155, through gently rolling woods and farms to the small village of Washington. The entrance to **Washington-on-the-Brazos State Historic Site** is on the right. The state park chronicles the important history of this small settlement.

Although Washington was never a big town, it looms large in Texas history. In 1821 Andrew Robinson and his family first settled the site when they joined Stephen F. Austin's colony. They farmed and raised livestock on the west bank of the Brazos River and operated a ferry at the La Bahia river crossing of the old Spanish road between Goliad and East Texas.

In 1835 Robinson's son-in-law John Hall purchased the property and with partners laid out the townsite of Washington. The lots were sold at a public auction on January 8, 1836, just in time for the Texas revolution. Even though the new town was rough and ragged, the provisional government of Texas designated it as the site of the convention to determine Texas's fate.

The delegates convened in Washington on March 1, 1836, in an unfinished frame building. As General Santa Ana's Mexican forces besieged the Alamo, the delegates declared Texas's independence from Mexico, wrote a constitution for the Republic of Texas, and organized a government. On March 17 the newly formed government and the citizens of Washington fled east ahead of the advancing Mexican army.

After the victorious Battle of San Jacinto on April 21, the residents of Washington returned home, finding the town little disturbed. Town citizens fought to retain the Texas capital but lost out to Houston and then Austin. In 1842, however, Mexican troops captured San Antonio, giving President Sam Houston an excuse to move the capital back to Washington. After a major fight with political enemies in Austin, Houston moved the capital to Washington in the fall of 1842, bringing new life to the town.

Although the accommodations had improved since 1836, they were still crowded and spartan. The Republic of Texas was in poor financial condition and subject to invasions by Mexican troops. To help shore up the Republic, the new government worked to gain recognition and diplomatic relations with the United States and other countries. Many Texans thought that the way to solve their problems with Mexico was to be annexed by the United States. After extended negotiations, annexation was approved by the US Congress and the people of Texas. On

The home of Anson Jones, the last president of the Republic of Texas, was moved to Washington-on-the-Brazos State Historic Site.

December 29, 1845, Texas officially joined the Union. The capital moved back to Austin, where it remains.

Washington prospered for a time after it lost the capital but was dealt a mortal blow in the mid-1850s when the railroad bypassed it. The Civil War sealed Washington's fate. At some point the town became known as Washington-on-the-Brazos.

Today the state park contains the old townsite and several museums. The building where the Texas Declaration of Independence was signed on March 2, 1836, has been reconstructed. Extensive exhibits chronicling Washington and Texas history are displayed in the interpretive center and the Star of the Republic Museum. The home of Anson Jones, the last president of the Republic of Texas, was moved from a nearby location to the park and restored. It is now surrounded by the recreated **Barrington Living History Farm,** with log buildings, farm animals, and costumed interpreters. Short walking trails and a pecan-shaded picnic area overlooking the Brazos River round out the day-use park.

The adjoining village of Washington is very small, with limited services. After getting your fill of wildflowers and history, consider driving back to Brenham on TX 105 to visit **Blue Bell Creameries.** The creamery was founded in 1911 and produced a mere two gallons of ice cream per day. Today the creamery dominates the Texas ice cream market and produces millions of gallons every year. *Time* magazine once called Blue Bell "the best ice cream in the world." Take the plant tour (Mon through Fri) and judge for yourself.

26

Sam Houston National Forest

Anderson to Huntsville State Park

General description: A 43-mile paved route from the eastern edge of the black-land prairie through the thick pine forests of Sam Houston National Forest to Huntsville State Park.

Special attractions: Sam Houston National Forest, Fanthorp Inn State Historic Site, Huntsville State Park, Lake Conroe, boating, camping, hiking, fishing, mountain biking.

Location: East Texas. The drive starts at Fanthorp Inn State Historic Site in Anderson, a small town southeast of Bryan.

Drive route numbers: FM 149, FM 1375, I-45, Park Road 40.

Travel season: All year. The drive is hot and humid in summer. Fall and spring are the best times.

Camping: Sam Houston National Forest, Huntsville State Park.

Services: Food and gas are available in Anderson and New Waverly. All services are available in Huntsville and Navasota.

Nearby attractions: Washington-on-the-Brazos State Historic Site, Lake Livingston State Park.

For more information: Fanthorp Inn State Historic Site, P.O. Box 296, Anderson, TX 77830; (936) 873-2633; www.tpwd.state.tx.us/spdest/findadest/parks/fanthorp_inn. Huntsville State Park, P.O. Box 508, Huntsville, TX 77342; (936) 295-5644; www.tpwd.state.tx.us/spdest/findadest/parks/huntsville. Sam Houston National Forest, 394 FM 1375 West, New Waverly, TX 77358; (936) 344-6205; www.fs.fed.us/r8/texas/recreation/sam_houston/sam houston_gen_info.shtml. Huntsville-Walker County Chamber of Commerce, P.O. Box 538, Huntsville, TX 77342; (936) 295-8113, www.chamber.huntsville.tx.us. Navasota Grimes County Chamber of Commerce, 117 S. La Salle, Navasota, TX 77868; (936) 825-6600; www.navasota grimeschamber.com.

The Drive

The drive starts at Fanthorp Inn State Historic Site on the south side of the tiny town of Anderson. Signs lead to the park from the main highway.

The Fanthorp Inn is a historic structure dating from the early days of Anglo settlement of Texas. It was restored by the Texas Parks and Wildlife Department and underwent further restoration in 2010. The inn is set on attractive, tree-shaded grounds with several picnic tables.

Travelers in the early days of the Texas Republic generally found accommodations rough or nonexistent. Usually they ended up staying in the tiny, primitive houses of settlers. As time passed, however, roadside inns developed to serve the

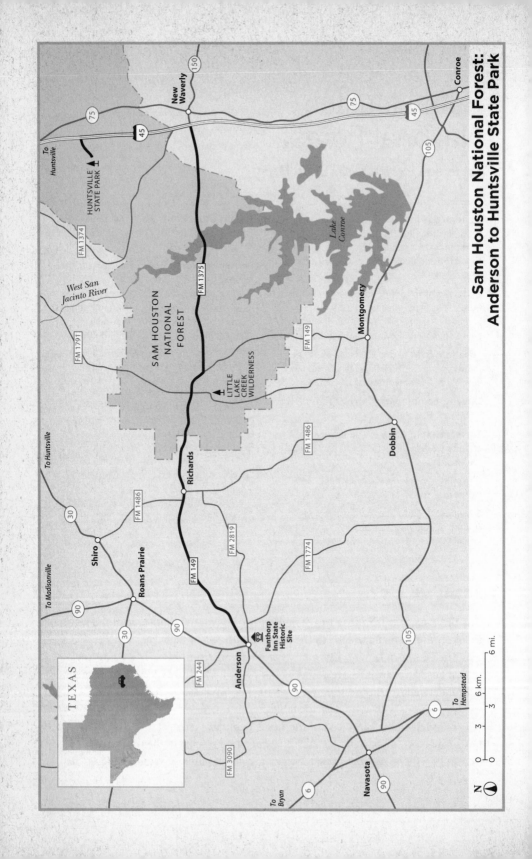

Sam Houston National Forest:
Anderson to Huntsville State Park

needs of travelers. Initially the Fanthorp Inn was little more than a small log house shared with travelers, but it later became a sizable, prosperous inn.

Henry Fanthorp, an Englishman, purchased land for the inn in 1832 from one of Stephen F. Austin's first colonists. Initially he built a corncrib and dealt in corn, buying when prices were low and selling when they were high. He soon built a 2-room dogtrot log home and married Rachel Kennard in 1834, having been widowed twice before. They had three children over the course of the following years.

The Fanthorps' home was well located on busy roads and became a popular stopping place for travelers. Several stage lines passed through, providing a steady flow of customers. Fanthorp charged one to two dollars per night for food and accommodations for one person and a horse. The food served was basic: beef, pork, corn bread, and sweet potatoes enlivened at times with chicken, turkey, and apple pie. One boarder described the coffee as "strong enough to bear up an iron wedge." Although the food received mixed reviews, it must have been better than alternatives because the inn grew in popularity.

To accommodate the increasing trade, Fanthorp steadily enlarged the inn. He built additions and a second story with an upstairs gallery, ultimately ending up with 18 rooms. To lessen the risk of fire and to keep the main building cooler, the kitchen was built as a separate structure in back. A barn boarded travelers' horses. Quite a few famous people, such as Sam Houston, Anson Jones, and Henderson Yoakum, stayed at the establishment over the years. Others rumored to have visited include Jefferson Davis, Robert E. Lee, Ulysses S. Grant, and Zachary Taylor. Kenneth Anderson, the last vice president of the Republic of Texas, died at the inn on July 3, 1845, and was buried in the Fanthorp family cemetery. The town developing around the inn was named Anderson in his honor.

The inn prospered during the Civil War, but Henry and Rachel Fanthorp died of yellow fever soon after in 1867. Their one surviving heir, daughter Mary Fanthorp Stone, closed the inn. She and her descendants used the hotel as a residence and kept it in the family until it was conveyed to the Texas Parks and Wildlife Department in 1977. The department has done a meticulous job of restoring the inn to its appearance during its heyday from 1850 to 1867. The inn is open all year for tours on weekends from 9 a.m. to 3:30 p.m. At other times the outside of the inn and the grounds can be viewed, plus there are tables for picnics.

Grimes County, within which the town of Anderson lies, was well established by the time of the Civil War. Cotton and food crops were raised on the surrounding blackland prairie. During the war it was a concentration point for troops and ordnance. An arms factory in Anderson produced cannons, guns, swords, and other related items. The courthouse, a stately Victorian structure built in 1891 of brick with stone trim and pressed metal ceilings inside, is the third courthouse built on the site. The 3-story building was constructed on a slight rise in the center of Anderson; it dominates the tiny town. The town was once much larger than it is today.

To start the drive travel north through town from the Fanthorp Inn to the courthouse. Continue north around and past the courthouse a short distance to FM 149, an east-west road that joins with TX 90 on the northwest side of Anderson. Turn right, or east, on FM 149 toward Richards, Montgomery, and New Waverly. Between Anderson and Richards the highway passes through rolling country, a mix of open pastureland and woods. As you approach Richards the vegetation slowly begins to change. The woods become more prevalent and the last vestiges of the blackland prairie, part of a large north-south belt through Central Texas, slowly disappear. A few scattered pines become evident near Richards.

Sam Houston National Forest

The highway zigzags through the hamlet of Richards. Beyond Richards the East Texas pine forests begin in earnest. FM 149 enters the **Sam Houston National Forest** about 15 miles from the Fanthorp Inn. The next 20 miles of the drive pass through the tall, lush pine woods of the national forest, along with occasional private inholdings.

Although the forest is attractive today, except in recently logged areas, it was once much different. In 1934, at the state's request, the federal government began buying land that no one else wanted. For the most part it was land that had been logged off or depleted by intensive farming. Some tracts had been seized for unpaid property taxes, other had been abandoned by their owners. Over the following 10 years, the Civilian Conservation Corps and the USDA Forest Service replanted the abused land with countless tree seedlings.

A short distance into the national forest, about 17 miles from Anderson, FM 1791 turns off to the left. To the right is poorly paved FR 211. To stretch your legs, consider a short detour on FR 211. Drive 2.1 miles—it turns into a good gravel surface after a bit—to a marked trailhead on the right side of the road. This is one of many trailheads for the 129-mile **Lone Star Trail,** by far the longest hiking trail in Texas. It winds all across the Sam Houston National Forest.

The trail crosses FR 211 and disappears into the woods on both sides of the road. I recommend the trail on the east side of the road. It and several side loops wind through the **Little Lake Creek Wilderness,** one of the wildest and most pristine areas along the trail. To avoid becoming lost, stay with the trail and be sure to note trail junctions and landmarks. If you want to hike far, you may want to stop in first at the Forest Service office farther along the drive near New Waverly. The 4,000-acre wilderness protects a small remnant of roadless area in highly developed East Texas.

A hiker enjoys the Lone Star Trail on a misty morning near Big Creek.

A short distance beyond the turnoff for the Lone Star Trail, at about 19 miles, turn left onto FM 1375. Continue east through rolling terrain thickly forested with pines on the upland areas and hardwoods such as oaks, black gums, and magnolias in the more moist bottomlands. At 23.8 miles a marked turnoff for the Stubblefield Lake campground is on the left, one of several recreation areas in the 160,000-acre national forest. The Lone Star Trail crosses the highway at a marked site at 25.3 miles. Soon thereafter the highway crosses the upper end of 21,000-acre **Lake Conroe** on a causeway. The lake, created by damming the West Fork of the San Jacinto River, is popular with boaters, water skiers, and swimmers. Fishermen pursue striped bass, catfish, crappie, and other fish in its sprawling waters.

A little past the lake, at 28.8 miles, there is a small interpretive site on the right about the endangered red-cockaded woodpecker. The woodpecker has very selective habitat requirements. Because it needs mature pines with rotted heartwood to create a nesting cavity, logging has greatly reduced its numbers. Most pines in East Texas are cut before they become old enough to be used by the woodpeckers.

Fog obscures Double Lake along the Lone Star Hiking Trail in the Sam Houston National Forest.

The main office of the Sam Houston National Forest lies on the left in about 31 miles. The office can supply maps and other information on the national forest. A few miles farther, at almost 34 miles, FM 1375 intersects busy I-45. The small town of New Waverly is a short distance down FM 1375 on the other side of I-45; the route turns north onto a boring but short stretch of I-45. Drive north on I-45 about 8 miles to exit 109 for Huntsville State Park. Exit and turn left under the freeway on Park Road 40. Tall hardwoods and pines arch over the quiet park road, a pleasant contrast to noisy, frenetic I-45. The state park headquarters is less than 2 miles down the road.

Huntsville State Park

Huntsville State Park is an excellent ending point for the drive. Not surprisingly, it is one of the most popular state parks in Texas. Loblolly and shortleaf pines tower over the shoreline of **Lake Raven,** a small impoundment that forms the heart of Huntsville State Park. As tall as the pines are, however, they are second-growth trees dating from the early 20th century. From 1880 to 1930 almost all harvestable trees were cut in the South, including East Texas. As in the surrounding Sam Houston National Forest, much of the land in the state park was devastated. With time and extensive replanting efforts, the forest has regrown, forming dense pine woodlands interspersed with hardwoods such as willow and water oak, American and cedar elm, black gum, black willow, and green ash. Understory trees in the pine forests include red maple, dogwood, and sassafras.

The thick forest supports abundant wildlife. White-tailed deer, fox squirrels, raccoons, opossums, and armadillos are commonly seen. Bobcats also roam the woods but are reclusive and rarely observed. Occasionally, alligators can be seen in the lake, floating motionless and almost completely submerged. Many species of birds flit through the forest canopy, especially during spring and fall migrations. Some birds make their presence obvious—crows squawking loudly over the lake, pileated woodpeckers hammering away at tree trunks.

The nearby town of Huntsville and the park were named because an early trader and settler from Huntsville, Alabama, believed that the area resembled his home. Sam Houston, commander in chief of Texas forces during the war for independence, first president of the Republic of Texas, and governor of the state of Texas, bought a plantation near Huntsville in 1844. Houston had grown up with neighboring Cherokees in Tennessee and later married a Cherokee woman. He named the plantation Raven Hill in reference to the name given him by the Cherokees. Raven is the translation of his Cherokee name "Colonneh." Lake Raven within the state park was named after Sam Houston, not the raucous crows that frequent the area.

The 2,083-acre park offers plenty of recreational opportunities, including a large number of campsites. Canoes, sailboats, paddleboats, and small, no-wake fishing boats float on the lake's three arms. Boats and fishing piers let anglers fish for largemouth bass, crappie, and flathead and channel catfish. Miles of trails challenge hikers and mountain bikers. Buoys mark off an unsupervised swimming area near the bathhouse. Like many other Texas state parks, some of Huntsville's facilities were built during the Depression by the Civilian Conservation Corps of durable native materials. Many of the CCC buildings are still used today by people seeking a quiet escape in the piney woods of East Texas.

27

Big Thicket National Preserve

General description: An 18-mile paved and gravel drive through the dense forests of the Big Thicket of southeastern Texas.

Special attractions: Big Thicket National Preserve, lush forest, primeval-looking cypress sloughs, carnivorous plants.

Location: Southeast Texas. The drive starts at the Big Thicket National Preserve visitor information station just east of US 69/287 on FM 420.

Drive route numbers: FM 420, US 69/287, CR 4859, CR 4850.

Travel season: All year. The drive is hot and humid from May through Sept. Fall and spring are generally much more pleasant.

Camping: There is no public camping along the route, although backcountry camping is allowed in parts of the preserve with a permit. Village Creek State Park, near Lumberton, has the closest public campground.

Services: All services are available in Kountze, Silsbee, Lumberton, and Beaumont.

Nearby attractions: Village Creek State Park, Martin Dies Jr. State Park, Sea Rim State Park, Angelina National Forest, B. A. Steinhagen Lake, Alabama-Coushatta Indian Reservation.

For more information: Big Thicket National Preserve, 6044 FM 420, Kountze, TX 77625; (409) 951-6700; www.nps.gov /bith.

The Drive

The Big Thicket of southeast Texas is a unique area with an incredible diversity of plant and animal species. In some areas the soil and conditions are so poor that plants have developed carnivorous traits to survive. Yet only a few dozen yards away, the soil can be rich enough to support a dense forest of loblolly pine, beech, and magnolia. Within the thicket only slight differences in soil type, elevation, slope, and available water can create very different habitats. This drive and some short walks on preserve trails introduce the Big Thicket.

Start the trip at the Big Thicket National Preserve visitor center. To find it drive about 8 miles north of Kountze (about 30 miles north of Beaumont) on US 69/287 to the junction of FM 420 on the right. The junction is marked with Big Thicket National Preserve signs. The new visitor center lies on the northeast corner of the intersection. It houses exhibits, a selection of books, and information on the Big Thicket. Park rangers can answer questions about the preserve.

Before settlers arrived, the Big Thicket covered a vast area, from Conroe in the west to the Sabine River, and from Jasper and Woodville in the north to

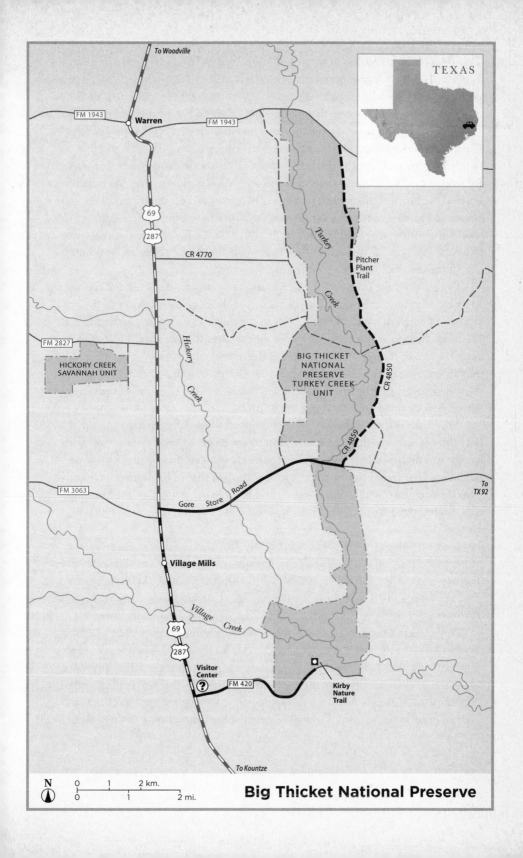

TEXAS

To Woodville

FM 1943   Warren   FM 1943

69
287

CR 4770

FM 2827

HICKORY CREEK
SAVANNAH UNIT

Hickory

Creek

Turkey

Creek

Pitcher
Plant
Trail

BIG THICKET
NATIONAL
PRESERVE
TURKEY CREEK
UNIT

CR 4850

CR 4859

FM 3063   Gore   Store   Road

To
TX 92

Village Mills

69
287

Village   Creek

Visitor
Center
?   FM 420

Kirby
Nature
Trail

To Kountze

N

0   1   2 km.
0   1   2 mi.

Big Thicket National Preserve

Beaumont. The thicket lies in an area of low-lying land that tilts gently from north to south. The surface geology consists of several different formations, leading to a variety of soil types. The area's high rainfall, 50 inches or more per year, combined with different soils and water-flow patterns, produces a great variety of habitats.

Before the Europeans arrived, humans had little impact on the Big Thicket. The Caddo and Atakapan Indians lived on its fringes. Early Spanish settlers avoided the area, calling the thicket "impenetrable woods." Americans first started arriving in the 1820s from Appalachia and the southern states. They too initially avoided the heart of the thicket, preferring to homestead on the fringes. The dense forests and murky swamps of the interior became a haven for fugitives and outlaws, but as unclaimed land became more scarce for new settlers in the 1830s and 1840s, people moved deeper into the thicket. Only enough lumbering was done to clear farmland, build a home, or produce firewood.

By the 1850s the forests of the Great Lakes region were depleted and timber companies began small lumbering operations in the Big Thicket. Most of the logs were floated down creeks and rivers to the mills. The railroads arrived in the 1870s, spelling doom for the great virgin forests. Branch lines spread from the main tracks like capillaries from a vein as the timber companies cut deeper into the thicket. Year after year the huge pines and hardwoods fell under the assault. In those days logging companies made little effort to replant after timber operations ceased, and a ruined landscape was left behind.

Towns developed in the Big Thicket centered around the sawmills. In the late 19th century, the thicket became famous for its bear hunts, even as the bear habitat was disappearing. The low-lying, densely wooded, frequently flooded terrain along Pine Island Bayou was the least disturbed part of the thicket. Naturally it was favored by the remaining wildlife and became the settlers' prime hunting area. Even today many people consider that area to be the true or traditional Big Thicket.

Uncontrolled lumbering was not the only problem faced by the Big Thicket. In 1901 the Spindletop well near Beaumont struck oil, igniting an oil boom. Other discoveries quickly followed at Batson, Sour Lake, and Saratoga. With no regulation, saltwater and oil spilled frequently, poisoning streams and killing vegetation. Towns swelled with people; roads and pipelines were cut through the forest.

As the years passed, oil companies became much more responsible, but much damage had already been done. Lumber companies began to replant logged land, although only with fast-growing pine plantations, not with the original mixed forests of the thicket. Bear, mountain lion, and ivory-billed woodpecker disappeared from the area. Virtually no virgin timber remains, although some areas have relatively mature second-growth forest. The original Big Thicket once covered some

Bald cypress trees thrive in sloughs along Village Creek.

3.5 million acres. Today less than 300,000 acres remain, of which about 107,000 receive protection in the 14 units of Big Thicket National Preserve.

The Kirby Trail

After stopping at the visitor center, follow FM 420 east a little less than 3 miles to the Kirby Trail and the old log cabin information station, the starting point of the drive. I highly recommend taking the Kirby Trail using the self-guided booklet available at the trailhead. The outer loop of the easy, mostly flat trail is 2.4 miles long; the inner loop is shorter. As with most areas in the Big Thicket, mosquito repellent is recommended, especially if the weather has been rainy and warm. The trail gives a quick introduction to some of the different habitats of the thicket.

The trail descends a gentle slope into the floodplain of Village Creek. A tall canopy of loblolly pines, magnolias, beeches, and other trees tower over the well-drained, relatively dry slope. This type of forest habitat favors slopes between the dry uplands and wet bottomlands and probably constitutes the climax forest for much of the Big Thicket. Unlike some of the other thicket habitats, the high dense canopy blocks the sun, preventing much underbrush from growing, not what the name "Big Thicket" would imply. Instead the forest floor is somewhat open and parklike.

Farther down the trail, boardwalks cross low, wet areas known as baygalls and acid bogs that have poor drainage and are fed by seeps and rainwater. The dark water and thick junglelike growth evokes the classic, mysterious Big Thicket image for most people. Tall bald cypresses and black gums thrive in the swampy terrain; smaller trees and shrubs grow in dense thickets at the water's edge. Rarely seen alligators lurk deep in the watery habitat, while water moccasins slide through dark-stained water pursuing prey.

Beyond the acid bogs and baygalls, the trail enters the floodplain of Village Creek. Village Creek and its many tributaries, including Turkey, Hickory, and Beech Creeks, drain a large area in the heart of the Big Thicket. Eventually it joins with the Neches River just north of Beaumont. A dense forest canopy of oaks, sweetgums, and other trees shades the floodplain. Sloughs and small oxbow lakes wind through the flat terrain, supporting bald cypresses and water tupelos in the shallow waters.

Beyond the cypress sloughs, the trail reaches the bank of Village Creek before looping back to the trailhead. The Turkey Creek Trail continues north from the Kirby Trail by crossing the creek on a footbridge. Except after floods, Village Creek flows with a clear, tea-colored water as it winds its way toward the Neches River. Although there is no white water along the low-lying creek, the broad waterway flows steadily, making it a popular canoeing destination. Occasional sandbars during low water periods and deadfalls create a few obstacles, but float

Biologists don't know if the knobby "knees" of cypresses help stabilize the trees in soft soil, help them breathe, or serve another purpose.

trips are relatively easy. A number of road crossings, especially near Kountze and Silsbee, allow easy access for put-in and take-out. Local outfitters offer canoe rentals and shuttles if needed.

The Turkey Creek Trail

After hiking the Kirby Trail, start the drive by retracing your route along FM 420 back to US 69/287. Turn right onto US 69/287 and drive north to Gore Store Road, a paved county road on the right marked with a brown sign for the Big Thicket **Turkey Creek Trail,** at 6.5 miles. Turn right and follow the road. It crosses Turkey Creek at 10.1 miles. The Turkey Creek Unit of the preserve is a long, narrow, north-south tract of land that follows Turkey Creek. A 15-mile hiking trail follows the creek from the Kirby Trail to FM 1943 on the north end. Several trailheads make possible hikes of shorter lengths. Two parking areas and trailheads for the Turkey Creek Trail are on both sides of the creek next to the county road. The remainder of this drive parallels the creek and trail to its north end on FM 1943.

Just past the creek, go left on a gravel county road, CR 4859, 10.5 miles from the information station. Except after heavy rains, the road is fine for most vehicles. If this road looks in poor condition, continue east less than a mile to another gravel county road on the left that is usually better maintained. The two gravel roads merge, becoming CR 4850 a short distance north.

Assuming that you take the first gravel road, the second road merges after 1.2 miles and the road improves. After 1.6 miles another gravel county road on the left crosses Turkey Creek and passes another trailhead for the Turkey Creek Trail. CR 4850 continues north through dense forest, occasionally passing through clearings with small farms and homes.

The Pitcher Plant Trail

About 5 miles from Gore Store Road (the paved county road), the road passes the marked **Pitcher Plant Trail** on the left. Be sure to stop and walk the short paved and boardwalk trail into a unique Big Thicket habitat, the pine savannah wetland. The flat terrain and clay soils hold standing water much of the year but can be very dry during dry spells. The soil also tends to be acidic and poor in nutrients. Fire once swept through these areas during dry periods, further limiting the types of plants that can live here. Generally only annuals and trees with extensive root systems, such as the long-leaf pine, can survive in these conditions.

Four types of carnivorous plants survive here, where many plants cannot, by supplementing photosynthesis with a diet of insects. The pitcher plant is the largest and most prominent of these plants on the trail. The plants grow into a 2-foot-tall, greenish-yellow, rain-shielded tube that emits a scent of nectar. Flies and other insects are drawn into the tube and trapped by fine, downward-pointing hairs. Slowly, inexorably, the hapless insects slide down into a small pool of digestive fluid at the base of the plant.

The Pitcher Plant Trail extends beyond the boardwalk to connect to the Turkey Creek Trail, creating another possible trailhead for the longer trail. A few picnic tables allow a pleasant lunch by the parking area. From the Pitcher Plant Trail, the county road continues north through the forest, ending at FM 1943 in about 2 miles. Several other units of the national preserve lie in the area and are worthy of exploration. The closest is the Hickory Creek Savannah Unit, notable in part for the sundew, another carnivorous plant.

28

Indian Mounds & Old Spanish Missions

Alto to Kennard

General description: A 24-mile paved route through the lush pine forests of Davy Crockett National Forest to Indian mounds, a Spanish mission, and a small forest lake.

Special attractions: Davy Crockett National Forest, Mission Tejas State Park, Caddo Mounds State Historic Site, Neches Bluff Overlook, Ratcliff Lake, Four C Trail, Big Slough Wilderness, hiking, fishing, canoeing, camping, scenic views.

Location: East Texas. The drive starts in the small town of Alto about 25 miles west of Nacogdoches.

Drive route numbers: TX 21, FM 227, TX 7.

Travel season: All year. The drive is hot and humid in summer, but you can swim in Ratcliff Lake to cool off. The most pleasant times of year are spring and fall; spring is more likely to have rain. Be wary of deer hunters in late fall in the national forest.

Camping: There are public campgrounds at Mission Tejas State Park and Ratcliff Lake in Davy Crockett National Forest.

Services: Food and gas are available in Alto and Kennard. Gas and snacks can be purchased at the junction of TX 7 and FM 227. Lodging is available in nearby Nacogdoches, Rusk, Lufkin, and Crockett.

Nearby attractions: Texas State Railroad, Rusk/Palestine State Park, Jim Hogg Historic Site.

For more information: Mission Tejas State Park, 120 State Park Rd. 44, Grapeland, TX 75844; (936) 687-2394; www.tpwd.state.tx .us/spdest/findadest/parks/mission_tejas. Caddo Mounds State Historic Site, 1649 TX 21 West, Alto, TX 75925; (936) 858-3218; www.visitcaddomounds.com. Davy Crockett National Forest, Route 1, Box 55FS, Kennard, TX 75847; (936) 655-2299; www.fs .fed.us/r8/texas/recreation/davy_crockett /davycrockett_gen_info.shtml.

The Drive

This drive traverses a section of the lush pine forests of East Texas within the boundaries of Davy Crockett National Forest. Along the way it passes two sites important in Texas history, the locations of a former Caddo Indian village and an early Spanish mission. Recreational opportunities also abound, including a small forest lake for fishing, canoeing, and swimming; a wilderness area; and one of the longest hiking trails in Texas.

The drive starts in the small town of Alto, named after the Spanish word for "high" because it was the highest point on the Old San Antonio Road between the Neches and Angelina Rivers. Much of TX 21, which passes through Alto, follows

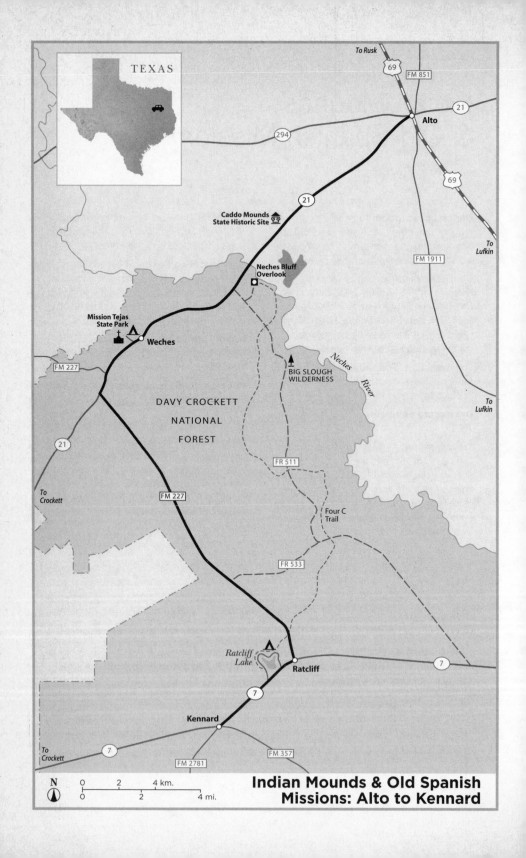

TEXAS

To Rusk

69   FM 851

Alto

294

21

21

Caddo Mounds
State Historic Site

FM 1911

Neches Bluff
Overlook

To
Lufkin

Mission Tejas
State Park

Weches

BIG SLOUGH
WILDERNESS

Neches River

To
Lufkin

FM 227

DAVY CROCKETT

NATIONAL

FOREST

FR 511

21

To
Crockett

FM 227

Four C
Trail

FR 533

Ratcliff
Lake

Ratcliff

7

7

Kennard

To
Crockett

7

FM 2781

FM 357

N

0   2   4 km.
0   2   4 mi.

**Indian Mounds & Old Spanish
Missions: Alto to Kennard**

the route of the Old San Antonio Road, also known as El Camino Real or the King's Highway. The Spaniards used this route to supply missions and establish dominion over East Texas in the face of incursions by the French and others.

Caddo Mounds State Historic Site

From Alto go west on TX 21 toward Weches and Crockett. For the first few miles, the road passes through rural country with a mix of farms, fields, and woods and slowly drops down into the broad Neches River Valley. After about 6 miles be sure to stop at Caddo Mounds State Historic Site on the right, marked by a visitor center and several odd earthen mounds in a field.

The history of the site stretches far back in time. For more than 2,500 years, from about 1000 BC to AD 1500, the Mound Builder culture spread across the woodlands of eastern North America. In AD 800 the Early Caddos, the westernmost group of Mound Builders, selected a site above the Neches River for a village and ceremonial center. The site was a frontier location for the Early Caddos, whose culture was centered farther east in the area around the Great Bend of the Red River in southwestern Arkansas. The village at Caddo Mounds State Historic Site proved to be the southwesternmost outpost of the Mound Builders.

The site was probably selected because it had good soil for agriculture, was level, had water in the nearby Neches River, and had abundant natural food sources in the mix of bottomland hardwoods and upland pine forests. Using wooden frames and bundles of cane for thatch, these people built round, conical homes in the village area around the earthen mounds.

Archaeologists believe that the mounds were built for temple sites, burials of members of the ruling class, and religious ceremonies. Through careful excavation of the mounds and village, archaeologists have learned much about the Early Caddos. They appeared to have had an elite ruling class that lived in and around the temple mounds and had greater power and material wealth than average villagers. The common people lived in outer areas of the village and in outlying farming settlements.

Excavations of the burial mound yielded remains of an estimated 90 individuals. Group burials suggest that servants and/or family members were sacrificed upon the death of an important member of the ruling class.

The Early Caddos achieved the most highly developed prehistoric culture known in Texas when it peaked at about AD 1000. Their trade network extended from Central Texas to beyond the Mississippi River; artifacts found include Gulf Coast seashells and copper from the Great Lakes region. The culture was prosperous enough and had a strong enough social organization to devote massive amounts of labor to building the large earthen mounds.

The Caddo Indians built sizable earthen mounds in the Neches River Valley long before Europeans arrived.

The Caddos abruptly abandoned the village in the 13th century, probably after the ruling class lost its influence and power. War does not appear to have played a role in the abandonment. The Late Caddo culture remained in the area until Europeans arrived, but it never reached the same level of material wealth and sophistication as its forbears.

The park museum offers exhibits and an audio-visual program describing the early history of the site. An easy interpretive trail loops through the mounds and village site. The park is open Tues through Sun; call ahead to verify days and times.

Davy Crockett National Forest

From Caddo Mounds continue driving southwest on TX 21. The highway soon drops down into the Neches River floodplain and crosses the river after 1.5 miles. After crossing the river the road enters **Davy Crockett National Forest,** one of

Texas's four national forests. The four forests came into being in the 1930s when the federal government began buying "land that nobody wanted" in East Texas. During the preceding years the land had been devastated by logging with no replanting effort and by intensive farming until the soil was depleted. Some of the land had been abandoned by owners, while other tracts had been taken back by local governments for delinquent taxes. Because of the way the national forests were acquired, there are still many private inholdings. During the following years the forests were replanted, in large part with the assistance of the Civilian Conservation Corps. The CCC was established during the Depression to provide employment for young men. Today, lush forests grow where once the land was abused and depleted. Extensive logging still continues today but is more controlled than in earlier times.

About a mile past the Neches River, gravel FR 511-3 turns off to the left, leading toward the **Neches Bluff Overlook** and Big Slough Wilderness. Both sites are worth a side trip. Neches Bluff is about a mile down the road and overlooks the Neches River Valley. At one time the bluff provided a good view of the valley below, but the trees have grown up and partly block the view. The bluff is also the northern terminus of the **Four C Trail,** a popular hiking trail that winds through 20 miles of the national forest before ending at Ratcliff Lake near the end of this drive.

The Four C Trail was named for the Central Coal and Coke Company, which logged much of the area's virgin timber early in the 20th century. Because almost no virgin forest remains in the Davy Crockett National Forest or anywhere in Texas, the trail passes mostly through second- and third-growth forest. The well-maintained trail is very easy to follow and is marked by white plastic rectangles nailed to trees. The trail is crossed by numerous forest roads, making car shuttles and much shorter hikes possible.

Much of the Four C Trail follows abandoned railroad grades or tramways used during bygone lumbering operations. Probably the most interesting part of the trail is in the **Big Slough Wilderness,** one of several small wildernesses found in the East Texas national forests. To get there follow FR 511-3 and 511 several miles south. A Davy Crockett National Forest map would be helpful for navigating the forest roads and the Four C Trail.

Big Slough Wilderness is a swampy, primeval backwater area adjoining the Neches River. Not only does the Four C Trail and a side loop cross the wilderness, but a marked canoe trail also winds through the area. To span some of the broad, boggy creeks, several bridges and boardwalks have been built, one at least 500 feet long. Because much of the wilderness is very wet and swampy and difficult to travel through, some trees escaped the loggers' saws. Some huge pines and hardwoods still stand today in this part of the forest. If you do hike the Four C Trail, try to avoid deer hunting season during late fall.

Mission Tejas State Park

From the turnoff to Neches Bluff, TX 21 continues southwest through wooded hills, arriving in the small settlement of Weches in a few miles. On the right in Weches is **Mission Tejas State Historic Site.** Today picnickers and campers relax under the tall pines of the park where 300 years ago Spanish priests and Indians once toiled.

In the 1600s the Spaniards laid claim to vast areas of land northeast of Mexico, including Texas, but made little effort to colonize them. In 1685 a Frenchman, Robert Cavalier, Sieur de La Salle, established a small settlement on what is today Matagorda Bay. The Spaniards, worried about losing territory, began an effort to secure the claimed area. By the time an expedition led by Alonso de Leon found the French settlement in 1689, La Salle had died and only two members of his command were found.

The following year de Leon set out from Monclova, Mexico, with a large expedition to establish a mission in East Texas. In May the expedition met a group of Caddoan-speaking Indians, the Nabadache. The Spaniards used tejas, the Caddoan word for friends, as the name for the Caddos and their land. Later, tejas became Texas. The Nabadache invited the Spaniards to their homeland on the Neches River. In their villages of conical, thatched huts, the Nabadache raised crops of corn, beans, melons, and squash and hunted in the surrounding country. The Franciscan priests accompanying the expedition built a cluster of rough wood buildings for a mission and dedicated it on June 1, 1690, as San Francisco de los Tejas.

The missionaries settled in to learn the Caddo language, improve the Indian's agricultural methods, and foster Christianity. Initially all went well and a second mission was established a few miles away. But the following winter brought a smallpox epidemic that killed several thousand people in the missions and surrounding villages. The Nabadache believed that the Spaniards' Holy Water of Baptism was causing the disease. Fray Casanas worsened the situation by ridiculing the Indians' religious practices and their leaders. The summer of 1691 brought drought and increasing enmity. Spanish reinforcements and supplies arrived in August, but a second drought in 1692 worsened the missionaries' plight. Ironically, in the spring of 1693, floods washed away the second mission. Disease and attempts to change Nabadache religious practices led to the Indians' disenchantment, and hostilities increased. That fall Father Massanet received word of an impending attack, so the missionaries loaded supplies, burned the mission, and fled to Mexico under the cover of night.

Domingo Ramon returned with an expedition to reestablish the mission in 1716, but poor success, plus conflict between the French and Indians, led to its abandonment only 3 years later. The Spaniards tried once again in 1721, but food and supplies continued in short supply, and few Indians joined the mission and converted to Christianity. Finally the mission was moved temporarily to a site to

The Civilian Conservation Corps built a chapel at Mission Tejas to commemorate the mission built by the Spaniards in the late 1600s.

the west on the Colorado River in 1730. The next year it was moved to the San Antonio River and named San Francisco de la Espada; it thrived there for many years.

By modern times nothing remained of the original mission buildings. During the Depression the Civilian Conservation Corps built a wooden chapel to commemorate the original Spanish mission, plus constructed roads, trails, a pond, and picnic area. In 1974 the Rice family home was moved to the park from its original site 16 miles to the southwest. It was built between 1828 and 1838 and is one of the oldest structures in the area.

Today the park showcases the two historic buildings plus offers a quiet retreat in the tall pines of the uplands above the Neches River. Campers, picnickers, hikers, and anglers enjoy the shady woods where the Spaniards once tried to colonize East Texas.

From Mission Tejas continue southwest on TX 21 about 2 miles and turn left onto FM 227. The highway travels southeast for about 12 miles to Ratcliff through gentle, pine-forested hills with little development. Observant travelers may notice where the Four C Trail crosses the highway a little before Ratcliff.

In Ratcliff, a small settlement with gas and a convenience store, turn right onto TX 7 toward Kennard. Look for the entrance to Ratcliff Lake Recreation Area on the right in about 1 mile. The CCC established a camp here in 1933–1934 and worked to restore the surrounding forest land. The Corps planted about three million trees and constructed roads and fire towers. The CCC men built a small lake on Lee Creek and recreational facilities out of an old sawmill pond. The lake was named Ratcliff after J. H. Ratcliff, who had a sawmill here in the 1880s.

Only small boats without gas engines are allowed on Ratcliff Lake, making it a quiet woodland retreat. Canoes and paddleboats can be rented at a small concession. The south end of the Four C Trail is here, offering plenty of hiking opportunities. Fishing, camping, swimming, and picnicking round out possible activities at Ratcliff Lake. From the recreation area the drive continues a short distance farther through the national forest on TX 7 to the small town of Kennard.

29

Cypresses & Steamboats

Daingerfield State Park to Caddo Lake

General description: A 54-mile paved road through two of Texas's most interesting state parks, with beautiful lakes and the historic inland port town of Jefferson.

Special attractions: Caddo Lake State Park, Daingerfield State Park, Lake O' the Pines, Jefferson, hiking, camping, fishing, boating, waterskiing, fall colors.

Location: Northeast Texas. The drive starts at Daingerfield State Park about 40 miles north of Longview.

Drive route numbers: Park Road 17, TX 49, FM 250, US 259, FM 729, FM 134, FM 2198.

Travel season: All year. The drive is hot and humid in summer, but you can swim in the lakes to cool off. Spring and fall are most pleasant for travel; some years there is good fall color on the route, especially at the state parks.

Camping: Caddo Lake State Park, Daingerfield State Park, and Lake O' the Pines have large campgrounds.

Services: All services are available in Jefferson and Daingerfield. Gas and food are available in Lone Star and Karnack.

Nearby attractions: Lake Bob Sandlin State Park, Atlanta State Park, Starr Family Home State Historic Site.

For more information: Caddo Lake State Park, 245 Park Road 2, Karnack, TX 75661; (903) 679-3351; www.tpwd.state .tx.us/spdest/findadest/parks/caddo_lake. Daingerfield State Park, 455 Park Road 17, Daingerfield, TX 75638; (903) 645-2921; www.tpwd.state.tx.us/spdest/findadest /parks/daingerfield. Marion County Chamber of Commerce, 101 N. Polk St., Jefferson, TX 75657; (903) 665-2672; www .jefferson-texas.com.

The Drive

This drive starts at Daingerfield State Park, a popular site with good fall color. From there it passes through Lone Star, a large steel-making center along the shores of Lake O' the Pines, one of the most attractive lakes in East Texas, and into the historic port town of Jefferson. The drive ends at mysterious Caddo Lake, where cypress-dotted waters sometimes appear to be more swamp than lake.

Start the drive at **Daingerfield State Park,** hidden in the dense mixed-pine and hardwood forests of northeast Texas. In spring, masses of dogwoods adorn the woods with their white blooms like a late-season snowstorm. The forests resume their lush green appearance for the long days of summer, but as temperatures drop and days shorten in fall, sweetgums and maples dot the park with splotches of orange and scarlet, an uncommon sight in most of Texas.

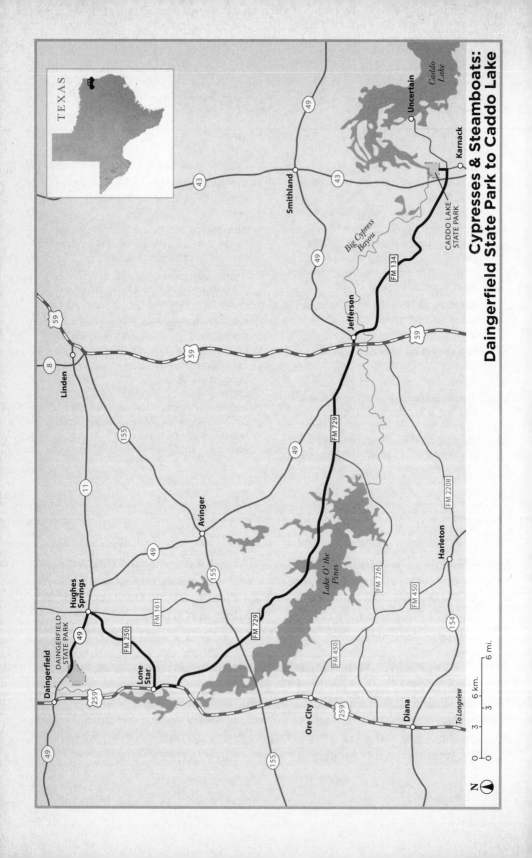

**Cypresses & Steamboats:
Daingerfield State Park to Caddo Lake**

This 507-acre park was established in the 1930s and has been carefully protected since then. The forest is mature, with towering loblolly pines, oaks, sweetgums, and other trees. The Civilian Conservation Corps built many of the park facilities with their usual meticulous craftsmanship. Most of their buildings, including the cabins, lodge, and bathhouse, are still in use today. The most obvious CCC project is the small lake around which the park is centered. The corps built an earthen dam to impound the spring-fed 80-acre reservoir.

Most park activities involve the small, no-wake lake, especially in summer. In warm weather people swim in its cool waters or lounge on the grassy banks. Canoes and small sailboats glide silently across the lake, while paddleboats churn through the water. Anglers pursue largemouth bass, crappie, chain pickerel, and blue and channel catfish from the fishing pier, the shore, or from small boats. Winter weather cools the water enough so that even rainbow trout are stocked periodically.

A 2.5-mile hiking trail circles the reservoir. One segment of the trail on the west side of the lake climbs to the top of a hill, a respectable height for East Texas. Although the view to the southwest from the top is somewhat obscured by trees, it is quite expansive. Notice the reddish rock and soil on parts of the hike; iron has stained it. Nearby, as will be seen on a later part of the drive, iron ore is rich enough to be mined and smelted for steel production.

If possible, take the hike on a quiet fall weekday. Autumn color dots the lakeshore beneath a deep blue sky. The cool, crisp air carries the astringent smell of decaying foliage. Fallen leaves pile up on the trail, crunching noisily underfoot. Visitors may feel they have landed in New England.

The park is very popular on weekends during the warm part of the year; camping reservations are recommended then. There are also three cabins and a larger lodge available for overnight stays. If swimming isn't enough lake activity for you, the park also has a seasonal canoe and paddleboat rental. The park started major construction projects in 2010, so in 2011 call ahead to verify that the amenities you want to use have reopened.

From park headquarters begin the drive by following Park Road 17 out of the park to TX 49 and go right, toward Hughes Springs. Drive 3.5 miles to the junction of FM 250 in the center of the small town of Hughes Springs. Those short on time should continue along TX 49 to Jefferson; otherwise, I recommend the longer route described here. Turn right onto FM 250 toward Lone Star. The next few miles are not especially scenic, but they are historically and industrially interesting.

People do not think of Texas as a steel-producing state, but some of the sedimentary rocks, particularly in East Texas, contain substantial amounts of iron ore. Here and there mining and smelting efforts developed during Texas's history. Some of the steel towns were even named after big iron centers in Britain and Alabama, including Newcastle and New Birmingham. Most iron-production efforts ended long ago in Texas, but the Lone Star mills still operate.

Approaching Lone Star on FM 250, notice the many industrial plants along the highway. After about 5 miles the road passes an old abandoned mill on the left across from a small lake on the right. The road then passes through a few hills and drops into the outskirts of the small town of Lone Star. Turn left at the junction with US 259 and follow it 1.5 miles to the junction with FM 729 on the left. The junction is across from the entrance to the massive Lone Star Steel mill. The sprawling plant seems out of place in the small towns of the area; Ohio or Pennsylvania would be more likely locations for such a mill. Although the mill is not scenic, it is an impressive example of the industrial infrastructure of the United States. The mill was started by the federal government during World War II and sold to the private sector afterwards.

Lone Star to Jefferson

Leave Lone Star by taking FM 729 toward **Lake O' the Pines.** The road rolls along through thickly wooded hills of pines and hardwoods just north of the lake. The lake is close but not visible through the forest until the highway crosses a bridge over an arm of the lake about 12 miles from Lone Star. Two more lake bridges follow within the next few miles. The lake is very pretty, with tall pines marching right down to the shoreline. The 18,700-acre reservoir was created by damming Big Cypress Creek, the same waterway that feeds Caddo Lake downstream.

The drive along FM 729 is dotted with signs for US Army Corps of Engineers parks along the lakeshore. To enjoy the lake more fully, consider taking some of the short side roads to the parks. The lake is great for swimming, boating, water-skiing, and fishing. To see the dam or access the south shore, take FM 726 on the right a few miles after the third lake bridge.

FM 729 ends when it intersects TX 49, about 23 miles from Lone Star. The shorter route from Daingerfield State Park to **Jefferson** stays on TX 49 the entire way. In less than 4 miles, TX 49 takes you into Jefferson. Cross US 59 and stay on TX 49 into the center of the older part of town, which is graced by old Victorian homes and buildings. Turn right onto FM 134 toward Karnack and stop in the restored central business district only a few blocks down the road.

Today the small downtown area is filled with shops, restaurants, and museums, making it hard to believe that Jefferson, more than 200 miles inland, was once the second busiest port in Texas, surpassed only by Galveston. Jefferson was first settled sometime between 1836 and 1840, and the town was laid out on the banks of Big Cypress Creek in 1842. Starting around 1800, a huge logjam of debris blocked the Red River, of which the creek was a tributary, in nearby Louisiana. The jam backed up large amounts of water, creating Caddo Lake and making Big Cypress Creek navigable to shipping. Steamboats followed the Mississippi and Red River upstream from New Orleans to Jefferson to unload manufactured goods and to load up area products, including iron, cotton, and lumber. The port boomed; by 1870 as many as 15 steamboats at a time were tied up at the docks while scores of wagon trains rumbled through the streets. The population peaked at 30,000, making Jefferson the sixth-largest city in Texas. Jefferson was the first city in Texas to use gas for a street-lighting system and had one of the state's first breweries. The town also had the first ammonia-refrigerant ice plant. Palatial homes and a large downtown grew, fed by the massive amount of money flowing through the town.

In 1874 the town suffered a mortal blow when the US Army Corps of Engineers blasted away the massive jam on the Red River. The water level fell in Caddo Lake and Big Cypress Creek, preventing steamboats from making the trip upriver to Jefferson. The population plummeted to 3,000.

The Texas and Pacific Railroad might have saved Jefferson, but the town fathers, confident in the steamboat trade, refused to contribute land to the railroad as other towns had done. Angry railroad magnate Jay Gould predicted the town would die and laid his tracks through Marshall. He was almost right; once steamboat traffic ended, the town went into a long sleep and nearly died.

Although the loss of steamboat traffic and the railroad were massive blows to Jefferson's economy, they were a boon to modern-day historians. Unlike other cities that continued to grow, Jefferson's historic buildings were not replaced and overwhelmed by modern structures of concrete and steel and no suburbs sprawled out across the hills. Instead, the town appears much as it did during the steamboat era, with dozens of old houses and buildings still standing, most of which have been restored. Many of the homes are now bed-and-breakfasts, and the downtown buildings hold shops, restaurants, hotels, and museums. A number of homes and buildings are open for tours; some of the more notable include the House of the Seasons and the Excelsior House Hotel. In a final irony, Jay Gould's luxurious private railroad car has been restored and parked downtown for viewing.

Caddo Lake State Park

To continue the drive take FM 134 south from downtown across Big Cypress Creek, or Bayou. Stay left on FM 134 at a junction across the bridge from the town. After about 13 miles FM 134 crosses TX 43 and becomes FM 2198. Signs mark FM 2198 as the route to **Caddo Lake State Park.** Follow FM 2198 for 0.5 mile to the state park entrance on the left. Park headquarters is just down the road from the massive stone entrance gate.

After checking in at headquarters, drive down to **Saw Mill Pond,** an offshoot of the Big Cypress Bayou and the lake. Towering bald cypresses trailing long, gray-green streamers of Spanish moss dot its waters. Shadowy side channels branch off, leading to mysterious sloughs and ponds. The occasional splash of a fish jumping

and the squawking of birds break the silence of the primeval-seeming lake. The peaceful scene belies the turbulent history of **Caddo Lake,** the second-largest natural lake in the South.

According to legend, a great Caddo Indian chief had a vision of impending disaster. He quickly moved his tribe to higher ground. The earth trembled and shook, the ground sank, and floods filled the tribe's former homeland. Caddo Lake was born. Although people now believe that Caddo Lake was created by the Red River logjam, the Indian legend may have been influenced by the great New Madrid earthquake of 1811 that shook the United States from Texas to Illinois.

Researchers believe that the enormous logjam was created sometime around 1800 by masses of timber washing downstream. At one time the jam stretched more than 100 miles, from Natchitoches, Louisiana, to north of Shreveport. The jam, known as the Great Raft, filled the river from bank to bank. The intermittent jam, with pools of dead water in between, was a solid mass of tree trunks 25 feet high cemented together with roots, silt, moss, and even growing trees. Some water was able to flow through the Raft but most was forced to bypass the dam on the Texas side, forming swamps and lakes. Caddo Lake formed when Big Cypress Bayou was blocked as the Raft grew upstream.

After the Louisiana Purchase of 1803, Spain and the United States disputed their mutual boundary in the Caddo Lake area. In 1806 the two countries agreed to declare the area "Neutral Ground." No settlers were to be allowed into the region, but of course they came anyway. Renegades, outlaws, rustlers, swindlers, and pirates flocked to the area, out of reach of either government's jurisdiction.

The Neutral Ground, often called the Texas Badlands or No Man's Land, remained lawless and in dispute after Mexico gained its independence from Spain. So many outlaws came to the area that a common mode of address was "What was your name before you came to Texas?"

Peace didn't come to the Caddo region with Texas independence. From 1840 to 1844 a virtual civil war raged between two factions known as the Regulators and the Moderators. Pitched battles were fought with as many as one hundred men. No man could remain neutral; all had to join one side or the other.

Texas historian Henderson Yoakum wrote that the Badlands were one area of Texas where the "law was only a passive onlooker." Finally, an impassioned plea made in person by Sam Houston put an end to the war. Both sides disbanded, although some personal feuds lasted for a number of years.

In the 1830s Henry Shreve cleared the logjam as far north as Shreve's Landing. Steamboat captains soon found a way to continue upstream through Caddo Lake and Big Cypress Bayou to Jefferson. Since the town was the terminus of

Spanish moss–draped cypress trees give much of Caddo Lake an eerie, primeval feel.

Cypresses thrive in the shallow waters of Sawmill Pond in Caddo Lake State Park.

the waterway, it became Texas's second most important port, with trade arteries branching out all over northeast Texas.

Surprisingly, steamboats as long as 200 feet plied the shallow, hazardous waters of Caddo Lake, carrying as many as 4,500 bales of cotton downstream on a single load. After the Corps of Engineers blasted loose the logjam, some say at the behest of Henry Shreve, steamboat traffic in Caddo Lake ended, and Shreveport became the premier port on the Red River. In 1914 the Corps built a dam near Mooringsport, Louisiana, to maintain the lower water level.

Steamboat whistles no longer echo across the water, but people still come to enjoy the lake's natural beauty. The lake's shallow waters provide ideal habitat for the bald cypress. The trees cover much of the lake, singly and in dense stands. Although there are large areas of open water, much of the lake is a series of sloughs and bayous.

The 30,000-acre maze of waterways and ponds that make up the lake straddles the Texas-Louisiana border. Water plants such as duckweed, lotus, water lilies, and water hyacinths cover much of the surface, adding to Caddo Lake's eerie swamplike charm. The lake is the most diverse fishery in Texas, so be sure to bring a fishing pole. The Texas Parks and Wildlife Department has identified 71 species of fish in the lake, including crappie, warmouth, largemouth bass, and channel catfish. Particularly interesting is the alligator gar, a prehistoric looking fish that can grow as long as 8 feet.

Because the intersecting, twisting channels of the lake can be confusing to boaters, the Parks and Wildlife Department marked a series of boat trails in the 1960s. Lake maps show colorful names such as Whangdoodle Pass, Pig Pen, Devil's Elbow, and Buzzard Bay. Don't let a scenic slough entice you off the main routes late in the day or you may get to spend a night in the "Caddo Motel," dreaming of Regulators and Moderators. It is easy to get lost; even local guides have to be careful, especially at night.

Caddo Lake State Park is a great place to start a visit to Caddo Lake. The Civilian Conservation Corps developed the park in the early 1930s on the shores of Big Cypress Bayou on the upper end of the lake. The stone entrance gates and solidly built cabins are sure signs of the CCC's lasting craftsmanship. In the 1960s the park structures underwent a major renovation and improved campsites were built. The entrance headquarters and visitor center offer an introduction to the history and biology of Caddo Lake.

At Saw Mill Pond you can rent a canoe and wend your way through the tall cypresses. The pond, beautiful as it is, is only a warm-up to the rest of the lake. If you plan to venture far out onto the lake, be sure to pick up a lake map beforehand at any of the stores and marinas surrounding Caddo. Until you are familiar with the lake, stick to the established boat trails, even though numerous mysterious sloughs will beckon. Several people offer guide services for the lake.

The unique lake is the main attraction of the park, but there are other reasons to visit. On dry land, well maintained hiking trails pass through ravines densely wooded with loblolly pines, magnolias, oaks, and other hardwoods. An old CCC pavilion is hidden away in the woods on one of the hiking trails. In fall, the bald cypress needles turn burnt orange, providing an excellent display of fall foliage. History and nature meet in the area of Caddo Lake.

Scenic Views
& Steam Trains

Love's Lookout to Rusk

General description: A 32-mile paved drive from one of the best viewpoints in East Texas to the steam trains and historic sites of Rusk.

Special attractions: Love's Lookout, Texas State Railroad, Lake Jacksonville, Jim Hogg Historic Site, Rusk/Palestine State Park, fishing, boating, hiking, camping, scenic views.

Location: East Texas. The drive starts at Love's Lookout, a rest area and scenic viewpoint along US 69 about 5 miles north of Jacksonville (22 miles south of Tyler).

Drive route numbers: US 69, US 79, FM 747, CR 3111, CR 3108, FM 2138, FM 1910, FM 347, US 84, Park Road 50.

Travel season: All year. The drive is hot and humid in summer, making fall and spring the most pleasant times.

Camping: Rusk Park maintains a campground.

Services: All services are available in Jacksonville and Rusk.

Nearby attractions: Tyler State Park, Caddo Mounds State Historic Site, Mission Tejas State Park, Davy Crockett National Forest.

For more information: Texas State Railroad, including Rusk and Palestine Parks, P.O. Box 166, Rusk, TX 75785; (903) 683-2561 or (888) 987-2461; www.texasstaterr.com. Jim Hogg Historic Site, Route 5, Box 80, Rusk, TX 75785; (903) 683-4850; www.tpwd.state.tx.us/spdest/findadest/parks/jim_hogg. Jacksonville Chamber of Commerce, 526 E. Commerce, Jacksonville, TX 75766; (903) 586-2217; www.jacksonvilletexas.com. Rusk Chamber of Commerce, 184 S. Main, Rusk, TX 75785; (903) 683-4242; www.ruskchamber.com.

The Drive

The drive starts at Love's Lookout, one of the best viewpoints in East Texas. It passes through thick mixed-pine and hardwood forest, past the shores of Lake Jacksonville, to an historic steam railroad that carries passengers on excursions through the woods. The drive ends nearby at Jim Hogg Historic Site, the tranquil birthplace of Texas's first native-born governor.

This is a very intricate drive on many different roads, some of which do not appear on many standard highway maps. Be sure to follow this guide's map and the directions carefully.

Start the drive at Love's Lookout, a highway rest area and scenic overlook along US 69 about 5 miles north of Jacksonville. The lookout lies on a long ridge

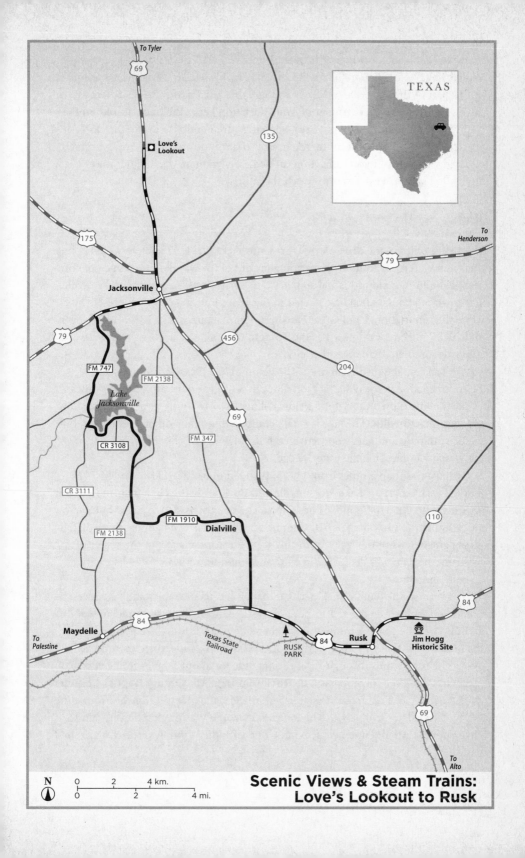

TEXAS

To Tyler

69

Love's
Lookout

135

175

To
Henderson

79

Jacksonville

79

456

204

FM 747

FM 2138

Lake
Jacksonville

69

CR 3108

FM 347

CR 3111

110

FM 2138

FM 1910

Dialville

84

Maydelle

To
Palestine

84

Texas State
Railroad

RUSK
PARK

84

Rusk

Jim Hogg
Historic Site

84

69

To
Alto

N

0   2   4 km.

0   2   4 mi.

Scenic Views & Steam Trains:
Love's Lookout to Rusk

that stands considerably higher than most hills in East Texas. It was owned by Wesley Love before being donated to the state by his widow. Broad views are rare in this part of the state due to lack of topographic relief and the thick forest. At Love's Lookout, the Department of Transportation keeps the trees cleared on the slope of the ridge below the rest area, allowing a tremendous view to the east. An abandoned fire tower next to the rest area also once took advantage of the ridge's elevated viewpoint. If you can get out of bed early enough, the lookout may well be the best spot in East Texas to watch the sunrise.

Jacksonville to Dialville

The first 5 miles of the drive along US 69 into Jacksonville are not very scenic, but there is no alternate route without going far out of the way. After a parade of commercial buildings and industrial shops, US 69 arrives in the center of Jacksonville. The town of about 14,000 first started in the 1840s but moved to the present site when the International and Great Northern Railroad arrived in 1872. In the 1930s and 1940s, the city was known as the Tomato Capital, when more tomatoes were shipped from here than any other city.

In Jacksonville turn right onto US 79 and follow it east 2.5 miles to FM 747 on the left. After leaving Jacksonville, attractive rural terrain returns—thick woods, rolling hills, and pastoral fields. Follow FM 747 south along the west shore of **Lake Jacksonville.** The lake is small, compared to many other Texas lakes, but scenic with pine and hardwood-covered hills hugging the shoreline. Not surprisingly, many homes line the water's edge.

In just less than 3 miles from US 79, turn left onto CR 3111 from FM 747, marked with a sign for Lake Jacksonville and Buckner Dam. Go left again in about 0.5 mile onto CR 3108/South Shore Drive. The county roads are paved but narrow and winding, so use care. CR 3108 climbs onto Buckner Dam almost immediately, giving great views of the lake. According to the historic marker at the center of the dam, the dam was dedicated in 1957 and impounds a 1,352-acre lake with a 25-mile shoreline.

Just across the dam a small park on the left has picnic tables and lake access. The road winds along the south shore of the lake through a lush tunnel of woods arching over the road. A number of smaller side roads lead to lake homes. At the junction with FM 2138, turn right. After less than a mile, turn left onto FM 1910. The road winds through rural countryside for about 5 miles to the village of Dialville. Along the way it passes the **Rocky Springs Missionary Baptist Church** and cemetery. The church was established in 1848; the oldest legible headstone in the cemetery dates from 1849. The Reverend George Washington Slover, said to have built the Atlanta hotel depicted in Gone with the Wind, was the church's first pastor.

Dialville to Rusk

FM 1910 ends in **Dialville** at the junction with FM 347. A historic marker on FM 347 just to the left of the junction tells a little of the small town's history. At one time the railroad ran through the small community, but today, like many small towns, its tiny business district is closed up, the tracks are gone, and only a scattering of homes make up Dialville.

Go right onto FM 347. FM 347 ends in a few miles at the junction with US 84 in the village of Oakland. Turn left onto US 84 toward **Rusk.** In less than 2 miles, be sure to stop in at the **Texas State Railroad** on the right.

Deep in the piney woods the past still lives where the steam trains of the Texas State Railroad carry passengers between Rusk and Palestine. Construction of the railroad was begun in 1896 by the state prison system in an effort to make the prisons self-supporting. Using penitentiary money, bonds, and legislative appropriations, the railroad was built between Palestine and Rusk. A foundry was built at the Rusk prison to make pig iron and pipe for the state. The railroad was used to haul hardwood from Palestine to make coke for the iron plant.

In 1913 the iron plant in Rusk was closed, and the penitentiary was converted into a mental hospital 4 years later. After that the railroad was used only intermittently. In 1921 the railroad was taken from the Prison Commission's jurisdiction and placed under a separate board of managers. The state ceased regular railroad service and leased the line to the Texas & New Orleans, part of the Southern Pacific.

In the early 1960s the railroad lease was transferred to the Texas Southeastern Railroad. At the end of 1969, the company terminated freight operations and removed its rolling stock. In 1972 most of the railroad was transferred to the Texas Parks and Wildlife Department to preserve a part of the age of steam locomotives and railroading in Texas. A 3.7-mile stretch of track is still used commercially by the Missouri Pacific Railroad to serve a meat-packing plant near Palestine.

Today passengers board the train at depots in either Rusk or Palestine at each end of the line. The stations are not original but were built to resemble railroad architecture at the turn of the 20th century. Food, drinks, and gifts are available at both depots; the one at Rusk also has a small theater with film presentations of the railroad's history and other topics.

For each run, steam locomotives, dating from 1901 to 1927, chug out of both stations pulling a string of passenger cars. The route passes through 25 miles of thick forest, crossing 30 bridges. The longest bridge, over the Neches River, is 1,100 feet long. Near the halfway point the east- and westbound trains pass each other on a siding.

At the stations each train pauses long enough for passengers to eat lunch and stretch legs before making the return trip to the originating station. The trains run on weekends from about the middle of March through November; in June and

A locomotive of the Texas State Railroad steams through the forest between Palestine and Rusk.

July they also run on Thursday and Friday. Call ahead for reservations and current dates, times, and ticket prices. Even if you do not have time to ride the train, it is worth a stop to see the old steam engines chugging into and out of the station.

Rusk & Palestine Parks

The railroad depots in Rusk and Palestine adjoin the **Rusk and Palestine Park,** formerly operated by the Texas Parks and Wildlife Department as state parks but now managed by American Heritage Railways. The two parks were designed to serve the passengers of the railroad plus provide additional recreational activities. Both park units lie in the thick mixed-pine and hardwood forests of East Texas.

The area was settled in the early part of the 19th century. Palestine started life as Fort Houston in 1835, and Rusk was born soon after. Rusk was named after Thomas Jefferson Rusk, a signer of the Texas Declaration of Independence and inspector general of the Texas revolutionary army. The town is probably best known as the birthplace of Texas's first two native-born governors, James Stephen Hogg and Thomas Mitchell Campbell.

Although the terrain in the two parks and surrounding area consists of gentle, unassuming hills with few rocks or minerals visible, the area is important geologically. Underlying the area are thick beds of sedimentary rock containing enormous reserves of oil and gas. Some of the oil fields are found near salt domes, a number of which lie near Palestine. Near Rusk shallow layers of iron-bearing rock were once mined and smelted for iron.

Rusk Park contains a 15-acre lake with rental paddleboats, a campground, and a picnic area. The 136-acre park makes an ideal spot to spend the night before or after a ride on the railroad.

Jim Hogg Historic Site

After visiting the railroad continue into Rusk on US 84. Follow the signs for US 84 past the courthouse square in the center of town. Cross US 69 and continue east on US 84 another 1.7 miles to Fire Tower Road on the right and the entrance of **Jim Hogg Historic Site.** This quiet park is not as busy as the railroad and adjoining Rusk Park. Although the birthplace of Jim Hogg is the park's main emphasis, there are also many other recreational opportunities.

James Stephen Hogg was the first native Texan to hold the state office of governor. His father, Joseph Lewis Hogg, moved with his wife to Texas in 1838 and carved out a plantation in the tall woods of the park site near Rusk in 1846. His son Jim was born here at Mountain Home. Joseph Hogg was a respected lawyer, planter, and military leader.

Sadly, Jim learned compassion firsthand through a series of tragedies that struck his family. His father died of dysentery near the battlefield of Shiloh in 1862 when Jim was only 11 years old. His younger brother, Richard, died of illness only a year later, followed shortly thereafter by his mother, Lucanda.

Jim Hogg supported himself and paid for a law degree by taking on a succession of jobs with newspapers and working as a sharecropper. In the late 1860s he moved to Quitman, where he met and married Sallie Ann Stinson. Eventually he became state attorney general and then governor from 1891 to 1895. During his political life he helped regulate industry and pushed for antitrust laws during the difficult transition from an agricultural to industrial society. He also supported strong law enforcement, perhaps influenced by an episode in Quitman when he was shot in the back by an outlaw. His major achievement was the establishment of the Railroad Commission to regulate railroads' trade practices and their monopoly power. Years later the commission became the powerful regulator of the Texas oil industry.

A large oak tree frames the view from Love's Lookout in Cherokee County.

After Hogg left the governor's office, he returned to his law practice and participated in oil ventures. He was a partner in the formation of what became Texaco. He died in 1906 and was buried at his request without a headstone in Austin's Oakwood Cemetery. Instead he requested that a pecan be planted at his head and a walnut at his feet and that their nuts be distributed to the people of Texas for planting throughout the state.

The city park, at the site of Mountain Home, has a scale replica of the governor's birthplace furnished with period furniture and artifacts. It also contains exhibits on the Hogg family, including a printing press and other items from Hogg's newspaper days. The family cemetery lies on the park grounds next to the birthplace. There are also two picnic areas, a reservable pavilion, a campground, an observation tower, and five relocated historic cabins. Several trails wind through a lush forest of pines, oaks, dogwoods, and other trees past a historic iron-mining site, springs, and an old dam built by slaves before the Civil War. The peaceful park makes an excellent ending for this busy drive.

31

Laguna Atascosa National Wildlife Refuge

General description: A 17-mile paved and gravel road through one of the few large tracts of wild land remaining in the Rio Grande Valley.

Special attractions: Endangered and threatened species such as the ocelot, the Aplomado falcon, and the piping plover; many birds found only in the Rio Grande Valley and Mexico; hiking; mountain biking; views; wildflowers.

Location: South Texas. The drive starts at the headquarters of Laguna Atascosa National Wildlife Refuge, about 25 miles east of Harlingen or about 17 miles northwest of Port Isabel.

Drive route names: Bayside Drive and Lakeside Drive.

Travel season: Nov through mid-Apr is the most pleasant time. The long summers can be very hot and humid.

Camping: There are no campgrounds along the drive within the refuge. The pleasant Adolph Thomae Jr. County Park lies at the north side of the refuge at the east end of FM 2925.

Services: All services are available in Harlingen, Brownsville, and Port Isabel.

Nearby attractions: Port Isabel Lighthouse State Historic Site, Palo Alto Battlefield National Historic Site, South Padre Island, Santa Ana National Wildlife Refuge, Sabal Palm Audubon Center.

For more information: Laguna Atascosa National Wildlife Refuge, 22817 Ocelot Rd., Los Fresnos, TX 78566; (956) 748-3607; www.fws.gov/southwest/refuges/texas/STRC/laguna/Index_Laguna.html. Harlingen Chamber of Commerce, 311 East Tyler, Harlingen, TX 78550; (956) 423-5440; www.harlingen.com.

The Drive

The 45,187-acre Laguna Atascosa National Wildlife Refuge is known worldwide for its large variety of birds and other wildlife. Its mix of subtropical, coastal, and desert ecosystems harbors a broad range of species in the largest tract of natural habitat remaining in the Lower Rio Grande Valley. The vast majority of the valley's natural habitat was cleared for agriculture over the last century. Today much of the farmland is being paved over for development because of a growing regional population. The federal, state, and local governments, along with groups such as the Nature Conservancy, Audubon Society, and Valley Land Fund, are making a huge effort to protect the few remaining patches of habitat, and to even restore some farmland to its natural state.

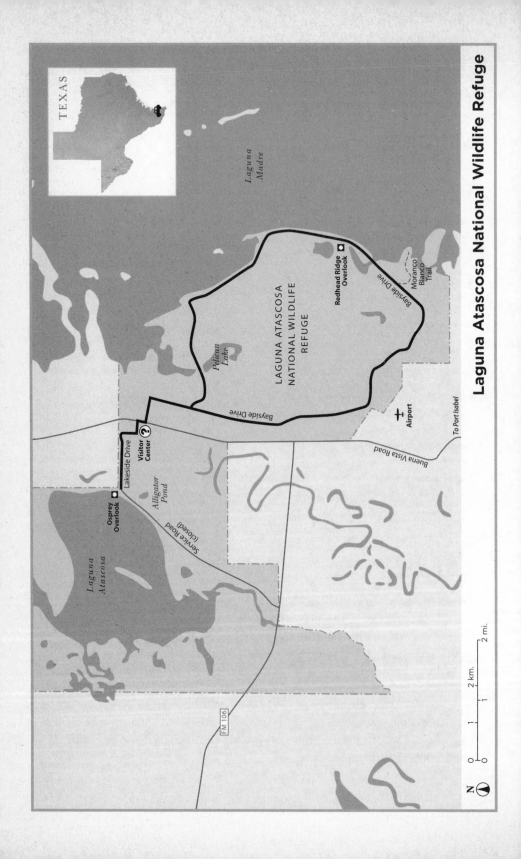

Laguna Atascosa National Wildlife Refuge

Birders visit the refuge and other valley sites in droves in large part because of the subtropical location adjoining Mexico. Many species, such as the chachalaca, green jay, Altamira oriole, white-tipped dove, and ringed kingfisher, aren't found anywhere else in the United States. Endangered and threatened species such as the Aplomado falcon, piping plover, and reclusive ocelot live at the refuge.

Start the drive at the visitor center, which lies in a low-growing forest of heat-tolerant trees and shrubs, many with thorns. Although the area gets moderate amounts of rain, the high heat and evaporation rates don't allow tall, lush trees to grow. The visitor center offers exhibits, restrooms, and information, plus two short, easy trails that lead through the thorn forest past small ponds and an observation blind. The paths provide a good introduction to the refuge's habitat and birds. Be sure to bring insect repellent on hikes. Mosquitoes, ticks, and chiggers share the refuge habitat with the rest of the wildlife. Depending on the time of year, rainfall, temperature, and other factors, the bothersome insects can be virtually nonexistent or a major nuisance. Come prepared.

Bayside Drive

Dawn is a great time to do this drive. The visitor center won't be open yet, so retrace south on the main road 0.1 mile to the entrance to the **Bayside Drive** on the left (east) side of the road. The Bayside gate opens at sunrise. This 15-mile loop makes up the bulk of this scenic drive. The narrow road begins by winding through dense thorn forest hiding all manner of creatures. The first part of the loop has two-way traffic, so drive carefully at blind corners. You'll soon pass the parking area for the 1-mile **Paisano Trail** on the left. If it's sunrise, skip the trail for the time being. Otherwise, park and stroll along the paved trail. It follows an old paved road from a World War II gunnery range that predated the refuge. It's a good mud-free trail to take on a rainy day. On this trail and all refuge trails, carry binoculars and walk quietly to see the birds and other wildlife. Mountain bikes can be used on some of the refuge trails and service road. Check at the visitor center for more information.

The woods begin to open up and the road soon hits a fork, the beginning of the one-way section. Take the left fork, as required, and head east toward the bay. Soon you will pass **Pelican Lake,** a great spot to look for waterfowl and wading birds. From there, continue on to the edge of **Laguna Madre,** the broad shallow bay that separates the mainland from South Padre Island. If you arrived as soon as the gate opened, you'll be able to watch the sun rising over the water. The edge of the bay is lined with some low ridges, former dunes that are now vegetated by grasses, shrubs, and yuccas. The tall yuccas are beautiful when crowned with creamy white blossoms in February.

The road follows the edge of the bay south for several miles. Watch for many wading and seabirds as you go. A small pavilion at Redhead Ridge allows you to

The sun peeks over the horizon at Laguna Madre at Laguna Atascosa National Wildlife Refuge.

get out of the sun while you observe the view across the bay. Far across the water to the southeast rise the tall hotels and condos of South Padre Island. Shortly after Redhead Ridge the road heads inland past coastal prairie and shallow, marshy ponds.

The **Moranco Blanco Trail** on the left offers an opportunity for a good 3-mile hike or mountain-bike ride across the prairie with more yuccas and views of the bay.

The road slowly curves north and passes another part of Pelican Lake before reaching the end of the one-way loop. After doing the Bayside Drive, return to the visitor center. If you haven't already stopped at the center, be sure to do so. You'll need to pay your entrance fee and will want to walk the short trails around the center.

Lakeside Drive to Laguna Atascosa

After stopping at the visitor center, go left onto Lakeside Drive, which starts paved and turns into a gravel road. Look closely for birds and alligators where the road crosses a broad, shallow channel, the Resaca de los Cuates. The road ends in 1.5 miles at **Osprey Overlook,** a small bluff with a shelter on the shore of the refuge's namesake, **Laguna Atascosa.** The name means "muddy lake" in Spanish. Sure enough, on windy days the large but shallow lake gets muddy. Two telescopes in the shelter will help you search for wildlife. From the parking lot, the Lakeside Trail heads north along the lakeshore for 1.5 miles and gives good views of both the lake and the thorn forest. Bank erosion has caused part of the hiking trail to be rerouted onto a gravel refuge road. In spring, wildflowers sometimes abound on this route.

Just back along the road from the Osprey Overlook parking lot is a refuge service road heading south along the lakeshore. It can be followed on foot or bicycle for miles. However, be sure to at least walk the 0.3 mile to **Alligator Pond.** It's the best spot in the refuge to spot an alligator. Take binoculars and scan the banks for sunning reptiles. Be sure to keep small children close to you.

On any of the drives and walks, you should see plenty of birds, very likely whitetail deer, and maybe a snake. You may also see coyotes or javelinas, the large piglike animals that often roam in groups. If you are extremely fortunate at dusk or dawn, you might catch a fleeting glimpse of a small spotted cat, the ocelot, as it darts out of sight. Probably not many more than one hundred ocelots remain in all of South Texas. Laguna Atascosa, a crown jewel of the national wildlife refuge system, is their best remaining habitat.

32

The River Road

Big Bend National Park

General description: A 51-mile rough dirt and gravel road through the wild Big Bend backcountry along the Rio Grande, past old mines, ranch sites, and rugged desert.

Special attractions: Big Bend National Park, Rio Grande, Mariscal Mine, Mariscal Canyon, historic ranch sites, hiking, camping, river trips, scenic views.

Location: West Texas. The drive starts about 15 miles southeast of park headquarters at Panther Junction along the main park road to Rio Grande Village.

Drive route name: River Road.

Travel season: Oct through Mar. The rest of the year can be very hot, with temperatures sometimes reaching 110 degrees in midsummer.

Camping: The park maintains the pleasant Rio Grande Village Campground about 5 miles east of the start of this drive. About a dozen primitive car campsites lie along or just off of this drive.

Services: Within the park, snacks and limited groceries are available at Rio Grande Village. Gas can be purchased at both Rio Grande Village and Panther Junction. Food and limited lodging are available in the Basin. All services can be found in Terlingua and Study Butte just outside the park's west entrance.

Nearby attractions: Other Big Bend National Park sites such as the Chisos Mountains, Santa Elena Canyon, and Boquillas Canyon; Big Bend Ranch State Park; ghost town of Terlingua.

For more information: Superintendent, P.O. Box 129, Big Bend National Park, TX 79834; (432) 477-2251; www.nps.gov /bibe.

The Drive

This drive crosses a large swath of remote and empty but beautiful desert on the south side of the park. Here and there the drive passes signs of human activities—an old mine complex, abandoned ranches, cemeteries—but overall, there are few signs of humanity along the drive. Although the route is called the River Road and roughly parallels the Rio Grande, most of the time it lies well back from the river. A number of short spur roads provide access to the Rio Grande in many locations.

Unlike the other drives in this book, this route follows dirt roads along its entire length. A high-clearance vehicle is necessary and sometimes, especially during and after a rain, four-wheel drive is required. If the road has been recently graded, it can be quite easy. Be sure to check on its condition at one of the park visitor centers before starting. In general, the western half of the drive is rougher. If the road is in poor condition or beyond the abilities of your driving skills or

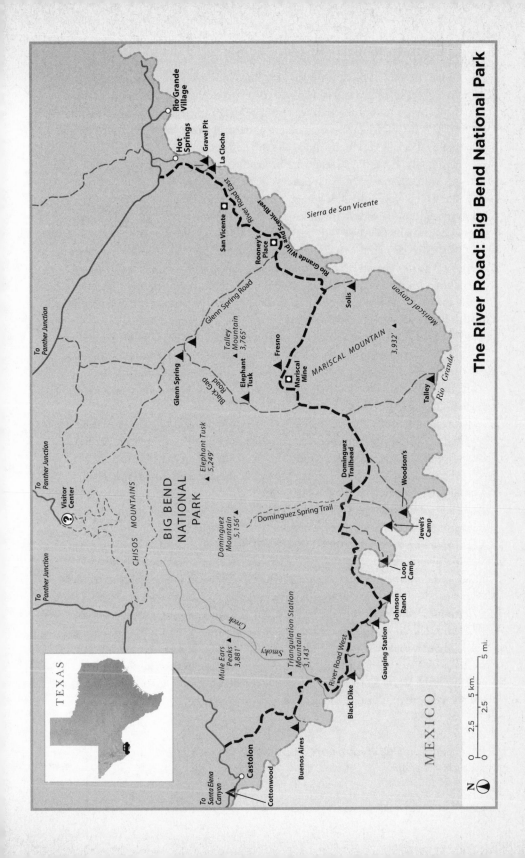

The River Road: Big Bend National Park

TEXAS

MEXICO

Rio Grande Village

Hot Springs

Gravel Pit

La Clocha

River Road East

San Vicente

Rio Grande Wild and Scenic River

Rooney's Place

Sierra de San Vicente

Glenn Spring Road

Talley Mountain
3,765'

Elephant Tusk

Glenn Spring

Black Gap Road

Solis

Fresno

Mariscal Mine

MARISCAL MOUNTAIN

Mariscal Canyon

3,932'

Talley

Rio Grande

BIG BEND
NATIONAL
PARK

CHISOS MOUNTAINS

To
Panther Junction

To
Panther Junction

To
Panther Junction

To
Panther Junction

Visitor
Center

Elephant Tusk
5,249'

Dominguez
Mountain
5,156'

Dominguez Spring Trail

Dominguez
Trailhead

Woodson's

Jewel's Camp

Loop
Camp

Mule Ears
Peaks
3,881'

Triangulation Station
Mountain
3,143'

Smoky Creek

River Road West

Johnson
Ranch

Gauging Station

Black Dike

Buenos Aires

Castolon

Cottonwood

To
Santa Elena
Canyon

N

0   2.5   5 km.
0   2.5   5 mi.

vehicle, return via the eastern half of the drive rather than continuing on the western section. Be sure to fill up with gas. Take lots of water for both you and the vehicle, a good spare tire and jack, food, and extra clothing. If you break down, it's usually better to wait for another visitor or park ranger to come by rather than try to hike out. Tell friends where you are going and check in with them when you return. Be especially careful if you do the drive in summer.

If you park along the river to hike or explore, be sure to lock your vehicle and take any valuables with you. Leave as few items as possible in the vehicle. Bring only things that you need with you on the drive, rather than leaving tempting items in sight in the vehicle if you leave it. The park has occasional problems with Mexicans crossing the river and breaking into vehicles parked nearby.

Be sure to stay on the road; don't tear up the fragile desert by driving cross-country. The designated car campsites along the way are an excellent way to enjoy the desert with no neighbors. There are no tables, bathrooms, or other facilities at the campsites. If you want to camp at one of them, be sure to obtain a permit from a park visitor center before the drive.

From the Rio Grande Village highway, the River Road heads south across the desert. The spiny green rosettes of lechuguilla plant, aromatic creosote bush, prickly pear cacti, and tall, spindly stalks of ocotillo dominate the Chihuahuan Desert along the drive. In a little less than 2 miles you'll pass the Gravel Pit road spur on the left. It's the first river access point on the drive and a primitive campsite. In less than another mile, the La Clocha spur forks left and goes to the Rio Grande and another primitive campsite. As mentioned in other drives in this guide, due to overuse and drought, the Rio Grande is a shrunken version of its former self.

The next few miles pass through the site of San Vicente, Texas. The small farming and ranching village was abandoned upon formation of the park. Old stone and adobe ruins and the lonely cemetery remain, although you have to hike around and look for them. The still-inhabited sister village of San Vicente, Mexico, can be seen across the river. The old road that goes off to the closed San Vicente River Crossing forks off to the left after the site of the old village. After the closed fork, the road has a clay surface that can become impossible to traverse after a good rain, so keep an eye on the weather.

About 7-plus miles into the drive, you'll pass the turnoff on the left to Casa de Piedra. The short, rough side road leads to the ruins of a rock house above the river. About a mile past the Casa de Piedra turnoff lies another left fork, this time to Rooney's Place, another tumbled-down stone house. Across the river from Rooney's, the Sierra San Vicente rise above the desert flats. The Rio Grande has cut a small canyon through the north end of the range here.

Over many thousands of years, the Rio Grande has cut deep Mariscal Canyon through Mariscal Mountain.

Soon after the Rooney's turnoff is the junction with the Glenn Spring Road on the right. The Glenn Spring Road climbs up into the Chisos Mountains foothills to the site of the old Glenn Spring settlement. The namesake spring fed a ranch, a wax factory (it produced wax from the desert candelilla plant), a small village, and a military encampment. The road to Glenn Spring is long and best done as a separate trip another day.

Solis, Mariscal Mine & Talley

About 4 miles past the Glenn Spring junction, you'll reach the turnoff to **Solis,** site of a farm that existed before the park and a primitive campsite. Solis is one of the side roads probably worth visiting. Mariscal Mountain towers above the river, and remnants of the farming operation can be explored. When the river is high enough, most boaters use Solis as the take-out point for Mariscal Canyon trips. Experienced hikers in cool weather can attempt the Cross Canyon Trail that climbs up onto Mariscal Mountain. It's long and poorly marked, so be prepared. The trail rewards strong hikers with great views and river access in the heart of Mariscal Canyon.

After Solis the road leaves the river behind as it turns northwest to get around Mariscal Mountain. In about 5 miles the road reaches the **Mariscal Mine** and the Fresno primitive campsite. Martin Solis found mercury ore here in 1900, but Ed Lindsey filed a claim and actually began mining operations. In 1916 W. K. Ellis built the furnace and refining facilities visible on the hill above the parking lot. Other stone ruins, mostly workers' homes, dot the flats at the base of the hill. The mine was worked somewhat erratically until it closed in 1923. It reopened for a short time during World War II but has been inactive since. Unlike the mercury mines in Terlingua, the Mariscal Mine was never highly productive. When exploring the site, be sure not to enter the old, unstable mine workings. Also, don't remove artifacts. Not only does removal prevent future visitors from enjoying them, but also many items here are contaminated with mercury.

As the road rounds the north end of Mariscal Mountain, it gets a bit rough. About 2 miles from the mine, the Black Gap Road forks off to the right. The very rough road joins the Glenn Spring Road about 8 miles north in the Chisos Mountains foothills. It's not maintained and should be attempted only by experienced drivers with good four-wheel-drive vehicles.

About 2 miles past the Black Gap junction lies the **Talley** turnoff on the left. The Talley road follows the west flank of Mariscal Mountain south about 6 miles to an old ranch on the river at the mouth of Mariscal Canyon. Boaters use it to begin Mariscal Canyon trips when water levels allow. The road is a worthwhile side trip, especially for seasoned hikers. The trailhead for the Mariscal Canyon Rim Trail lies near the end of the Talley road. The steep, rugged trail climbs 1,200

A stone ruin overlooks the lonely country along the Rio Grande at Solis.

feet in 3.3 miles to the rim of Mariscal Canyon. The first half of the hike is easy; you pay on the second half when the trail climbs in earnest. The vertigo-inducing view at the rim is spectacular because the canyon wall drops sheer all the way to the river far below. Be sure to have lots of water, sunscreen, a map, and a trail guide for the hike. There's no shade, so don't even think about trying it in hot weather. Talley is one of the spots along the river most prone to vehicle burglaries, so leave as little as possible in your vehicle when you hike.

Talley to Smoky Creek

From the Talley turnoff, the River Road continues southwest across desert flats. Although it's hard to imagine, in wet years the desert can be blanketed with Big Bend bluebonnets, desert marigolds, bladderpods, and many other wildflowers in spring. In about 2 miles the road reaches another left fork leading to the river and a primitive campsite at Woodson's. In another mile the road passes the

Because the Rio Grande makes a large loop here, the Chisos Mountains appear to be on the other side of the river when they are not.

Dominguez Spring trailhead and campsite. The 7-mile trail leads north to an old ranch and some springs tucked into a canyon leading deep into the Punta de la Sierra, the dramatic southern ramparts of the Chisos Mountains.

Soon after the Dominguez Spring trailhead, the road passes left forks for Jewel's Camp and **Loop Camp,** two more primitive campsites on the river. Loop Camp is interesting because when you look north at the Chisos Mountains, you are looking across the Rio Grande even though you are still in Texas. The river has carved almost a complete circle here, meaning that it is flowing west at the campsite. It eventually loops back around and resumes its path eastward.

After the Loop Camp turnoff, the road moves closer to the river again. Giant reeds and tamarisk, a pesky exotic species, line the riverbanks, creating a green ribbon in the dry country. A short turnoff on the left leads to the site of the Johnson Ranch and a campsite. The ranch supported goats in the desert uplands and raised cotton on the river floodplain until the 1940s. Ruins and a cemetery mark the once-bustling site.

Another mile or so up the road lies the **Gauging Station** on the left. It is another campsite and a measurement station that has taken river flow readings since 1936. The terrain gets more rugged after the Gauging Station. The high cliff to the north 1.2 miles past the Gauging Station is Red Dike, which formed when lava forced itself into a large vertical crack in softer rock and hardened. Over millions of years, the softer rock eroded away, leaving the dike.

Smoky Creek to Ross Maxwell Scenic Drive

About a mile past Red Dike, another side road leads left to a house ruin above the river called Sierra Chino. In another mile is the Black Dike primitive campsite spur road on the left. It is named after another dike that crosses the river. Not far past Black Dike, the road leaves the river, enters the **Smoky Creek** drainage, and turns northeast. Smoky Creek is dry except after a flood and may not appear particularly impressive, but it drains almost 100 square miles, including much of the southwestern flank of the Chisos Mountains. The road follows the creek's path through the hills called the Sierra de Chino. After cutting through the hills, the road leaves Smoky Creek and turns back northwest. A primitive trail that starts at the road follows Smoky Creek upstream for miles to the Mule Ears, Dodson, and other Chisos Mountains trails. The path is lightly used and difficult to follow, so it should be taken only by experienced hikers.

After Smoky Creek the road winds its way through some hills, providing good views. At 3.5 miles past Smoky Creek lies the last primitive campsite, Buenos Aires, on the left. Like other spots along the river, it was once a small farming settlement. Finally, after at least 4 miles, the drive ends at the paved **Ross Maxwell Scenic Drive** (Drive 6). Go left to get to Castolon and Santa Elena Canyon; go right to return to other parts of the park. Enjoy the smooth, quiet ride of pavement.

33

Two Forts & Two Rivers

South Llano River State Park to Fort McKavett State Historic Site

---

General description: A 60-mile paved highway through the western Hill Country from the spring-fed South Llano River past an old Spanish fort to the 19th-century frontier outpost of Fort McKavett.

Special attractions: Fort McKavett State Historic Site, Presidio de San Saba, South Llano River State Park, hiking, kayaking, swimming, tubing.

Location: Central Texas. The drive starts at South Llano River State Park on US 377, a few miles south of Junction, a small Hill Country town on I-10.

Drive route numbers: US 377, US 83, US 190, RM 864.

Travel season: All year. The drive is hot in summer, but swimming or boating at South Llano River State Park relieves the heat. The rest of the year is usually more pleasant, with fall and spring most ideal.

Camping: South Llano River State Park has a developed campground.

Services: All services are available in Junction and Menard.

Nearby attractions: Caverns of Sonora, San Angelo State Park, Lost Maples State Natural Area, Fort Concho.

For more information: Fort McKavett State Historic Site, 7066 RM 864, Fort McKavett, TX 76841; (325) 396-2358; www.visitfortmckavett.com. South Llano River State Park, 1927 Park Road 73, Junction, TX 76849; (325) 446-3994, www.tpwd.state.tx.us/spdest/findadest /parks/south_llano_river. Kimble County Chamber of Commerce, 402 Main, Junction, TX 76849; (325) 446-3190; www .junctiontx.net. Menard County Chamber of Commerce, 100 E. San Saba Ave., Menard, TX 76859; (325) 396-2365, http://site .menardchamber.com.

The Drive

The drive starts at **South Llano River State Park,** a beautiful area of wooded bottomland lining about 1.5 miles of the crystal-clear South Llano River. The South Llano River winds through its broad valley at the state park a few miles upstream from its confluence with the North Llano River in the town of Junction. Most of the 524-acre park lies in the floodplain, a lush, shady area thickly wooded with large, majestic pecan trees and lesser numbers of cedar elms, live oaks, American elms, and chinkapin oaks.

The pecan bottomland of the park and adjoining properties is one of the largest and oldest winter roosting sites of the Rio Grande turkey in Texas. Although the wild turkeys frequent the park all year, in winter as many as five hundred turkeys gather in the floodplain. Because of the roost's importance, most of the bottomland is closed to visitors from October through March to prevent disturbance

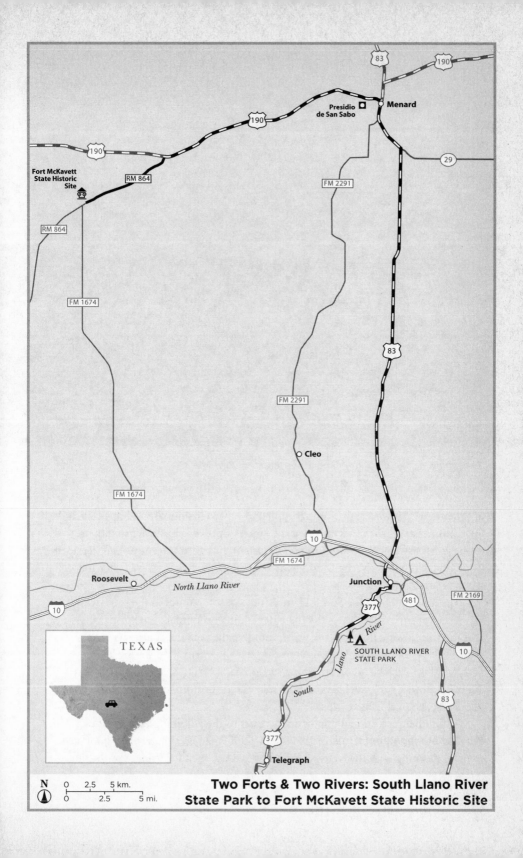

N
| 0 | 2.5 | 5 km. |

| 0 | 2.5 | 5 mi. |

Two Forts & Two Rivers: South Llano River
State Park to Fort McKavett State Historic Site

TEXAS

Fort McKavett
State Historic
Site

RM 864

RM 864

FM 1674

FM 1674

FM 1674

Roosevelt

North Llano River

190

190

190

83

190

Presidio
de San Sabo

Menard

29

FM 2291

FM 2291

Cleo

83

10

Junction

377

481

FM 2169

10

10

83

South Llano River

South Llano River
STATE PARK

377

Telegraph

The calm waters of the South Llano River reflect a sunrise sky.

of the turkeys. However, the campground and other facilities are still open, including a blind that allows observation of the large, impressive birds. During the rest of the year, easy trails allow hikers and mountain bikers to travel through the open woodland, along the riverbank and by two small oxbow lakes where fishermen can try their luck.

The headwaters of the South Llano River rise some miles to the southwest in Edwards County. Water levels fluctuate depending on rainfall, but springs insure that the river always flows. In the warm months, the cool water attracts canoeists, kayakers, and tubers. Various access points allow trips of differing lengths, both within the park and on adjoining sections of river. In shallow areas, where the water flows over gravel bars, canoes may scrape bottom, but overall, the river offers easy, enjoyable float trips.

Additional recreational opportunities exist in the adjoining **Walter Buck Wildlife Management Area.** In 1977, the wildlife management area was donated to the state along with the state park land by Walter Buck for wildlife protection and enjoyment by the public. The 2100-acre wildlife management area begins at the south side of the state park, at the edge of the valley bottom. Unlike the broad, relatively flat bottomland of the state park, it consists of rugged, hilly terrain typical of the Texas Hill Country. Along with a blanket of grasses, stunted Ashe junipers and live oaks dot the hills. The small ravines and canyons are more lushly vegetated with larger trees and thicker grasses. Wildlife such as white-tailed deer, turkeys, rabbits, and armadillos are common. The rare black-capped vireo can sometimes be seen.

Several miles of old ranch roads provide access to the wildlife management area for mountain bike riders and hikers. One short, steep hike leads to a scenic overlook that gives tremendous views of the park and river valley.

Presidio de San Saba

Once you've seen the turkeys and hiked and boated your fill at South Llano River State Park, head north from the park entrance on US 377 for 4.3 miles to the intersection with TX Loop 481 in Junction. Go left and follow combined US 377/ TX Loop 481 north across I-10. If your stomach is growling, consider Lum's along the route on the left 0.9 mile after the intersection or Cooper's on the left just after crossing I-10 for some good Hill Country barbeque. About 0.9 mile north of I-10, stay left on US 83 where it splits with US 377.

Continue north from the fork for about 29 miles through gently rolling hills to **Menard,** a sleepy Hill Country town on the banks of the San Saba River. Although the town is quiet today, it was the scene of a major battle between the Spaniards and the Indians in 1758. In 1757 the Spaniards built a *presidio,* or fort, to guard the northern frontier of Spanish lands from the French and Indians, protect the nearby Mission Santa Cruz de San Saba, and to investigate rumors of nearby silver deposits. The mission was built to Christianize area Apache Indians and to establish a Spanish presence. However, by creating good relations with the Apache, the Spaniards unknowingly alienated the Apaches' enemies, the Comanche, Caddo, and Wichita. These Indian groups controlled a large area of the Southern Plains and East Texas.

On March 16, 1758, a large group of 2,000 of these Indians attacked the mission, killing a number of the residents and burning much of it. To the missionaries' surprise, the Indians were armed with guns obtained from the French. Soldiers at the presidio 4 miles away heard the battle and saw smoke, but with only 30 men present on that day, they didn't have enough soldiers to come to the mission's rescue. Two-thirds of the presidio's soldiers were away from the fort on various expeditions. The presidio was itself soon surrounded by hostile Indians, but was able to defend itself. At the mission, the surviving Spaniards and their Indian allies took refuge in the church, holding off the attacking tribes until nightfall. That night, while the attacking Indian groups celebrated their victory, the missionaries slipped away and joined the soldiers at the presidio. Fortunately, the next day the presidio's troops returned from the field, reinforcing those holed up there and saving the fort from being overcome by the hostile tribes.

The mission, burned and destroyed less than a year after its founding, was not rebuilt and the surviving missionaries retreated south after the battle. The Spanish maintained the presidio for another 14 years, hoping for eventual silver discoveries to justify the effort. However, no significant deposits were ever found and the last troops marched out in 1772. The stone ruins of the presidio were substantial and durable and remained a local landmark for years. The mission, however, was poorly constructed and largely destroyed in the raid. By 1900, its location was lost. Finally, after archaeologists began searching for it in the 1960s, its site was conclusively found in 1993.

The presidio was partially and reasonably faithfully reconstructed in 1936 and 1937 through a Depression-era WPA grant. However, the reconstructed fort was not maintained and also fell into ruins, just like the original. Today the interesting stone ruins lie at Menard's municipal golf course and can be easily visited. From the center of Menard, drive north across the San Saba River on US 83. Right after the bridge, turn left onto US 190 toward Fort McKavett. In 0.8 mile, turn left, following the signs for the golf course and **Presidio San Saba.** Drive a half mile through the golf course, staying on the paved road, to the presidio ruins. An interpretive sign tells about the presidio and the historic events that happened there.

Fort McKavett

After you've toured the ruins of the old Spanish presidio, head west on US 190 from Menard toward **Fort McKavett** and Eldorado. The highway follows the San Saba River valley upstream. The country is very lightly populated, with only the occasional ranch or farm along the way. After about 16 miles, turn left onto RM 864. The road continues up the river valley, passing occasional pecan groves and fields. It crosses the clear-running river 4.8 miles from the junction and then climbs up a hill into the tiny settlement of Fort McKavett. The hamlet was named after the substantial frontier fort located here. The fort is larger than the village surrounding it. The only commercial establishments are a small store and the little post office. Turn right into the fort entrance 1.4 miles after crossing the river.

In 1852, the federal government established Fort McKavett to protect settlers on the western frontier and travelers on their way west. A Comanche war trail passed near the fort and both Comanches and Lipan Apaches were common in the area. The fort was built on a hill above the San Saba River and was initially named Camp San Saba. In the following year, it was renamed in honor of Captain Henry McKavett, a hero of the battle of Monterrey in the Mexican-American War.

The porch of the restored post headquarters frames other buildings and ruins of Fort McKavett.

The fort was built of native limestone, oak, and pecan, along with finished lumber freighted in from San Antonio.

The fort was abandoned in 1859 when problems with the Indians moved farther north and west. Settlers moved into the buildings during the following years. By the end of the Civil War, when the government lost effective control of western frontier lands, Indian raids had become more frequent again, so the post was reactivated in 1868. The facilities had fallen into ruin and were rebuilt under the leadership of Colonel Ranald S. Mackenzie. Much of the work was done by black buffalo soldiers stationed at the fort. Construction was frequently interrupted by military actions and scouting expeditions. Official inspectors and civilian visitors alike were impressed with Fort McKavett. It was "the prettiest post in Texas," said General William Tecumseh Sherman after an inspection in 1871.

Peace returned to the surrounding area as the years passed and the need for Fort McKavett declined. The main body of troops was reassigned in the fall of 1882, and by June 30, 1883, the remaining soldiers had completed their official duties. The flag was taken down and Company D of the 16th Infantry marched away for the last time.

Local settlers again moved into some of the post's buildings and the military installation became the town of Fort McKavett. In 1968, the fort was acquired by the state and is now managed as a historic site. Today visitors see a mix of 19 restored fort buildings and a number of ruins managed by the Texas Historical Commission. The visitor center, located in the former post hospital, contains displays and exhibits detailing the fort's history. Reenactments, with men and women dressed in authentic clothing, periodically bring Fort McKavett to life again as a busy post on the western frontier.

In addition to touring the fort buildings, consider taking the quarter-mile nature trail. The trail leads to the rock quarry and lime kiln used by the soldiers for building material and to Government Springs, a shady retreat that supplied the fort with water long ago. The water bubbling to the surface in a hidden canyon under a shady canopy of large pecan trees is a surprisingly lush oasis in the dry country.

Once you finish your tour of Fort McKavett, consider taking RM 1674 south from the fort for an alternative and shorter return route to Junction. The road goes south through quiet Hill Country terrain before arriving at I-10 in about 25 miles. Go left, or east, on I-10 for about 15 miles to return to Junction.

34

Creeks & Hills

Cibolo Nature Center toTarpley

General description: A 44-mile paved and gravel route from a great nature center on Cibolo Creek in Boerne through the tourist-oriented town of Bandera and Hill Country State Natural Area.

Special attractions: Cibolo Nature Center, Polly's Chapel, Hill Country State Natural Area, Medina River, hiking, mountain biking, horseback riding, kayaking, swimming, tubing.

Location: Central Texas. The drive starts at the Cibolo Nature Center on City Park Road, which turns south off TX 46 0.9 mile east of the junction between TX 46 and Business US 87/Main Street in the center of Boerne.

Drive route number: City Park Road, TX 46, TX 16, TX 173, RM 1077, CR 131, FM 462.

Travel season: All year. The drive is hot in summer, but swimming or boating in the Medina River will help relieve the heat. The rest of the year is usually more pleasant, with fall and spring most ideal.

Camping: Hill Country State Natural Area has a developed campground, although without potable water. Be sure to bring drinking water.

Services: All services are available in Boerne and Bandera.

Nearby attractions: Cave Without a Name, Guadalupe River State Park, Lost Maples State Natural Area, Garner State Park.

For more information: Cibolo Nature Center, 140 City Park Rd., Boerne, TX 78006; (830) 249-4616; www.cibolo.org. Hill Country State Natural Area, 10600 Bandera Creek Rd., Bandera, TX 78003; (830) 796-4413; www.tpwd.state.tx.us /spdest/findadest/parks/hill_country/. Greater Boerne Chamber of Commerce, 126 Rosewood Ave., Boerne, TX 78006; (830) 249-8000; www.boerne.org. Bandera County Chamber of Commerce, 331 Main St., Bandera, TX 78003; (830) 796-3280; www.banderatex.com.

The Drive

The drive starts at the Cibolo Nature Center. To find it, take TX 46 east from Business US 87/Main Street for 0.9 miles. Turn right on City Park Road and go about a half mile past the Agricultural Heritage Museum and the ball fields to the nature center on the right. The nature center was begun in 1988 when Carolyn Chipman Evans approached the city of Boerne about restoring marshes and building nature trails in 100 unused acres of the Boerne City Park. Two years later the center opened and now includes a visitor center with exhibits, a learning center, and a network of trails through marshes and along beautiful cypress-lined Cibolo Creek.

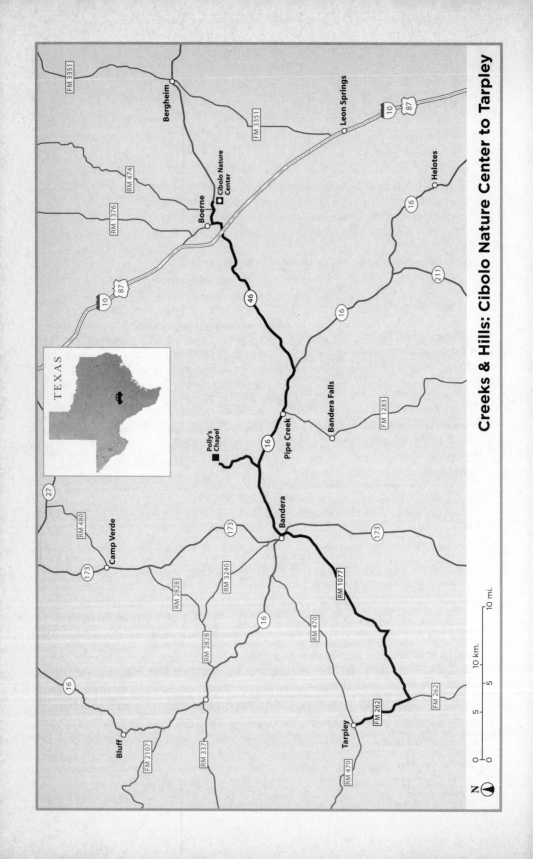

Creeks & Hills: Cibolo Nature Center to Tarpley

The center lies in what was once part of the 10,000-acre Herff Farm. The ranch was started in 1852, but much of it has been subdivided and developed, especially in recent years. The nature center recently acquired the original farm homestead with its historic buildings and 62 acres. Before you get in the car and proceed with the drive, be sure to walk the boardwalks in the marsh and along the banks of shady Cibolo Creek.

From the junction of City Park Road and TX 46, go left into the heart of Boerne. In 0.9 mile, go left onto TX 46/Business US 87/Main Street. In 0.6 mile, go right, staying with TX 46. The road soon crosses I-10 and heads west out of town toward Bandera. The commercial development quickly drops away and the land gets more hilly, but new, expensive subdivisions are common for the first few miles. TX 46 ends at its junction with TX 16 about 10 miles from Boerne. Go right on TX 16 toward Bandera. Development increases again, basically an extension of suburban San Antonio.

Polly's Chapel & Bandera

In 6.7 miles, consider a short side trip on the right to **Polly's Chapel.** Turn right on Privilege Creek Road and carefully follow the small lead-in signs at two road forks for about 3 miles to the small stone chapel. The pavement turns to gravel after a bit. Drive carefully on the last short segment of gravel road from near the cemetery to the chapel. The lonely, peaceful church is lost by itself in the oak and juniper wooded hills. It was built in 1882 of native limestone by José Policarpio "Polly" Rodriguez. He was a Texas Ranger and army scout who settled in the area in 1858. He converted to the Methodist faith and built the chapel with his own hands. Today the beautiful chapel is used periodically for weddings and other events, but doesn't have regular services.

Once back on TX 16, continue west to **Bandera.** The small town lies on a bluff above the Medina River and calls itself the "Cowboy Capital of the World." The many area guest ranches helped to foster the nickname. Western-themed clothing and gift shops centered in the old buildings of downtown take advantage of the town's reputation. Before you head on down the road, consider a meal at one of the town's restaurants. There isn't much in the way of eating establishments on the rest of the drive.

At the stoplight in downtown, go left on TX 173. The road immediately crosses a bridge over the Medina River. If you have time, consider a stop in the large park on the riverbank on the right side of the bridge. Tall bald cypresses line its crystal-clear waters and deep pools invite swimming in warm weather.

Hill Country State Natural Area

Just a short distance past the bridge, turn right on RM 1077, marked with a sign for **Hill Country State Natural Area.** Urban development quickly disappears as the land gets more and more hilly. RM 1107 ends in about 8 miles and the road becomes a narrower county road. In another 1.5 miles, the pavement ends and the road enters the state natural area. Continue into the park, crossing West Verde Creek, for about a mile to park headquarters.

Although the park has some of the best hiking and mountain biking in the Hill Country, it's best known by the equestrian community. Horse lovers have discovered its 40 miles of dirt roads and primitive trails that wind up grassy valleys, cross spring-fed streams, and climb steep limestone hills.

The ranch that became the natural area was originally part of a Spanish land grant. It was registered during the republic period in 1840, but the State of Texas first deeded the land to William Davenport in 1877. He and his family worked the Bar O Ranch until 1925, when it was sold to the first of a succession of owners. In 1945, the land was purchased by S.E. Lindsey, who conveyed the property to his daughter, Louise Lindsey Merrick, the following year. She and her husband operated the ranch for the next 29 years. During its years of operation, the ranch was known as a productive operation.

After Merrick's husband died, she decided to donate her 4,753-acre property to the state. She was an avid horsewoman and enjoyed riding across her property. She wanted Texans to have a public place where they could ride their horses across a large tract of undeveloped land. Her deed stated that the ranch was "to be kept far removed and untouched by modern civilization, where everything is preserved intact, yet put to a useful purpose." The state took over full ownership in 1982, purchased an adjoining tract of land, and opened the site as a 5,370-acre state natural area.

True to Merrick's wishes, the Texas Parks and Wildlife Department has left the ranch undeveloped. Visitors need to bring their own drinking water and carry their trash out with them when they leave. Roads are good, but gravel-surfaced.

The natural area lies on the **Edwards Plateau,** a large uplifted area of land in central Texas. Over the course of millennia, erosion has carved steep hills and broad valleys out of the limestone plateau. A mix of grasslands and scrubby woods of live oak, Ashe juniper, and red oak cover the hills. Along West Verde Creek and other watercourses, large sycamores, cedar elms, and oaks arch over clear pools.

An extensive complex of old dirt roads and trails creates miles of paths for equestrians, hikers, and mountain bikes. Novice riders, hikers, and cyclists may want to stay on the easier, main routes in the valley bottoms. Several backcountry camp areas offer primitive campsites to backpackers and equestrians. Two trails offer particularly good views from two of the highest hills–the Twin Peaks Trail and the Boyles Loop (4b) on the Cougar Canyon Trail.

A hiker enjoys the view from the Twin Peaks Trail at Hill Country State Natural Area.

Hill Country State Natural Area is a quiet, undeveloped site with few amenities in one of the most rugged parts of the Hill Country. The rapidly expanding urban center of San Antonio still seems far away. Get out and do a hike or ride through the hilly country before driving on to **Tarpley.**

Continue through the park on the main dirt road, CR 131. The road leaves the park about 2 miles from headquarters. Stay with the gravel road through empty hills for another 3 miles to FM 462. Turn right and follow FM 462 northwest up the Hondo Creek Valley. Big hills line the undeveloped valley, with its large live oaks, permanent creek, and grassy meadows. In 4.3 miles, FM 462 and this drive end at the junction with FM 470 in the small village of Tarpley. For a quicker return to Bandera, go right on FM 470, rather than taking the route back through Hill Country State Natural Area. Or continue west on FM 470 to Leakey, Utopia, and Vanderpool in the most scenic, hilliest part of the Hill Country.

SUGGESTED READING

Crow, Melinda. *Rockhounding Texas.* Guilford, Conn.: Globe Pequot Press, 1998.

Cummings, Joe. *Texas Handbook,* fifth ed. Emeryville, Calif.: Moon Handbooks/ Avalon Travel Publishing, 2004.

Hess, Christopher. *Mountain Biking Texas.* Guilford, Conn.: Globe Pequot Press, 2002.

Kelso, John. *Texas Curiosities.* Guilford, Conn.: Globe Pequot Press, 2003.

Metz, Leon C. *Roadside History of Texas.* Missoula, Mont.: Mountain Press, 1994.

Miller, George Oxford. *Texas Parks and Campgrounds,* fifth ed. Lanham, Md.: Taylor Trade Publishing, 2003.

Naylor, June. *Texas Off the Beaten Path,* eighth ed. Guilford, Conn.: Globe Pequot Press, 2008.

Parent, Laurence. *Hiking Texas,* second ed. Guilford, Conn.: Globe Pequot Press, 2009.

Spearing, Darwin. *Roadside Geology of Texas.* Missoula, Mont.: Mountain Press, 1991.

Texas Atlas & Gazetteer, sixth ed. Yarmouth, Maine: DeLorme, 2005.

The Roads of Texas. Fredericksburg, Tex.: Mapsco, Inc., 2008.

White, Mel. *Exploring the Great Texas Coastal Birding Trail.* Guilford, Conn.: Globe Pequot Press, 2003.

INDEX